Medical Humanity and Inhumanity in the German-Speaking World

FRINGE

Series Editors
Alena Ledeneva and Peter Zusi, School of Slavonic and East European Studies, UCL

The FRINGE series explores the roles that complexity, ambivalence and immeasurability play in social and cultural phenomena. A cross-disciplinary initiative bringing together researchers from the humanities, social sciences and area studies, the series examines how seemingly opposed notions such as centrality and marginality, clarity and ambiguity, can shift and converge when embedded in everyday practices.

Alena Ledeneva is Professor of Politics and Society at the School of Slavonic and East European Studies of UCL.

Peter Zusi is Associate Professor of Czech and Comparative Literature at the School of Slavonic and East European Studies of UCL.

FRINGE

Medical Humanity and Inhumanity in the German-Speaking World

Edited by Mererid Puw Davies and Sonu Shamdasani

UCLPRESS

First published in 2020 by
UCL Press
University College London
Gower Street
London WC1E 6BT

Available to download free: www.uclpress.co.uk

A CIP catalogue record for this book is available from The British Library.

ISBN: 978-1-78735-773-0 (Hbk.)
ISBN: 978-1-78735-772-3 (Pbk.)
ISBN: 978-1-78735-771-6 (PDF)
ISBN: 978-1-78735-774-7 (epub)
ISBN: 978-1-78735-775-4 (mobi)
DOI: https://doi.org/10.14324/111.9781787357716

Contents

List of figures

Notes on contributors

Sebastian Coxon is Reader in German at UCL. He joined the Department of German in 2000, having studied in Oxford and Cologne. His principal field of research is in medieval German literature. His main research interests include laughter and comedy, pre-modern narrative technique and beards.

Mererid Puw Davies is Associate Professor in German at UCL. She has published widely on modern German-language literature, film, cultural and comparative studies. Publications include *The Tale of Bluebeard in German Literature from the Eighteenth Century to the Present* (Oxford University Press, 2001), *Writing and the West German Protest Movements: The Textual Revolution* (imlr books, 2016) and, as co-editor with Beth Linklater and Gisela Shaw, *Autobiography by Women in German* (Peter Lang, 2001).

Mark Hewitson is Professor of German History and Politics at UCL. His publications include *Germany and the Modern World, 1880–1914* (Cambridge University Press, 2018), *Absolute War: Violence and Mass Warfare in the German Lands, 1792–1820* (Oxford University Press, 2017) and *The People's Wars: Histories of Violence in the German Lands, 1820–1888* (Oxford University Press, 2017). He is the co-editor with Timothy Baycroft of *What is a Nation? Europe, 1789–1914* (Oxford University Press, 2006), and with Matthew D'Auria of *Europe in Crisis: Intellectuals and the European Idea, 1917–1957* (Berghahn, 2012).

Martin Liebscher is Principal Research Fellow at the German Department, and Honorary Senior Lecturer at the Centre for the History of Psychological Disciplines at UCL. His research interests lie in nineteenth-century German philosophy, especially Friedrich Nietzsche and Arthur Schopenhauer, in the conceptual history of the unconscious, and in the historical and philosophical foundations of Jungian psychology. His publications include *Thinking the Unconscious: Nineteenth-Century*

German Thought (Cambridge University Press, 2010), *Libido und Wille zur Macht: C.G. Jungs Auseinandersetzung mit Nietzsche* (Schwabe, 2011) and *Analytical Psychology in Exile: The Correspondence between C.G. Jung and Erich Neumann* (Princeton University Press, 2015).

Annie Ring is Lecturer in German at UCL. Her research focuses on topics of surveillance and subjectivity in modern German and comparative culture, and she teaches modern German and comparative literature, film and thought. Annie Ring is a member of the Uncertain Archives international research collective, co-investigator of the UK-based German Screen Studies Network, and co-convenor of the Picturing Austrian Cinema Symposium. She is the author of the monograph, *After the Stasi: Collaboration and the Struggle for Sovereign Subjectivity in the Writing of German Unification* (Bloomsbury, 2015 and in paperback, 2017) and co-editor with Henriette Steiner and Kristin Veel of the volume *Architecture and Control* (Brill, 2018) and of a glossary of terms relevant to the study of big data and cultural theory, *Uncertain Archives* (MIT, forthcoming). Other publications include articles on critical data studies, Harun Farocki's use of film archives, surveillance and complicity in German workplace documentaries, Kafka and pleasure, the critical spectatorship of pornography and theories of the archive.

Ernest Schonfield is Lecturer in German at the University of Glasgow. His research interests focus on German literature from around 1800 to the present day, especially literature of the *Vormärz* (Heinrich Heine, Georg Büchner) and modern German novels. His most recent publications are *Georg Büchner: Contemporary Perspectives*, co-edited with Robert Gillett and Daniel Steuer (Brill, 2017), and *Business Rhetoric in German Novels: From Buddenbrooks to the Global Corporation* (Rochester, NY: Camden House, 2018). Ernest Schonfield also edits a website: www.germanlit.org.

Sonu Shamdasani is Professor in German at the School of European Languages, Cultures and Society (SELCS) at UCL, and Co-Director of the UCL Health Humanities Centre. He works on the history of the psychological disciplines, with a particular focus on Jung's work and on the history of psychotherapies. He is the author and editor of numerous volumes, which have been translated into many languages.

Thomas Wilks works on modern and contemporary literature in German, French and English, on translatabilities and the autobiographical. He currently researches modes of distraction in these languages, and the European character of London. Publications include the monograph *Experimentation and the Search for Autobiographical Identity in the Projects of Michel Leiris and Hubert Fichte* (Edwin Mellen Press, 2006), three further articles on Leiris, and, in the context of theatre translation, the first of several planned thematic analyses of Wilhelm Genazino's writing. Lecturer in German at Queen Mary University of London since 2019, Thomas Wilks has taught widely on language, literature and culture at Aberystwyth, UCL, Southampton, York, Reading, Braunschweig, Mainz, Würzburg and Royal Holloway.

Preface

The UCL Press FRINGE series presents work related to the themes of the UCL FRINGE Centre for the Study of Social and Cultural Complexity.

The FRINGE series is a platform for cross-disciplinary analysis and the development of 'area studies without borders'. 'FRINGE' is an acronym standing for Fluidity, Resistance, Invisibility, Neutrality, Grey zones and Elusiveness – categories fundamental to the themes that the Centre supports. The oxymoron in the notion of a 'FRINGE CENTRE' expresses our interest in (1) the tensions between 'area studies' and more traditional academic disciplines; and (2) social, political and cultural trajectories from 'centres to fringes' and inversely from 'fringes to centres'.

The series pursues an innovative understanding of the significance of fringes: rather than taking 'fringe areas' to designate the world's peripheries or non-mainstream subject matters (as in 'fringe politics' or 'fringe theatre'), we are committed to exploring the patterns of social and cultural complexity characteristic of fringes and emerging from the areas we research. We aim to develop forms of analysis of those elements of complexity that are resistant to articulation, visualisation or measurement.

The present volume challenges our natural impulse to associate 'medicine' with notions of understanding and aiding humanity. The essays collected here explore the grey areas where discourses and practices of medicine designate and create both the human and the inhuman, both the humane and the inhumane. Bringing to bear perspectives from the fields of literary studies, cultural studies, history, and the history of medicine and psychiatry, this is the first collection dedicated to the exploration of this interface in the German-speaking lands, offering in the process novel, critical perspectives on the burgeoning field of medical and health humanities.

Alena Ledeneva and Peter Zusi,
School of Slavonic and East European Studies, UCL

1

Medical In/Humanities: The Human and the Humane in the German-Speaking World. An Introduction

Mererid Puw Davies and Sonu Shamdasani

We are living in an era of biomedical humanism in which it is not possible to study definitions of the human, as well as of humane and inhumane conduct, without considering the signal role of medicine.[1] The discipline and practice of medicine have played a critical role in defining what constitutes the human and distinguishes it from the inhuman, and with it, ethical standards of humane and inhumane conduct.[2] Therefore, biomedicine occupies an exalted status in contemporary societies, such that its ontological claims are taken to form the basis of legally binding imperatives that go to make up a just and humane society. If medicine is the discipline where the body became a site for positive, scientific knowledge, it is also, by extension, the interface where science touches us, and affects us most directly. This is true not just with regard to our ailments, but with our very self-understanding and self-definition. As Nikolas Rose has noted, 'medicine makes us what we are by reshaping the relations of meaning through which we experience our worlds.'[3] Medicine thus plays a critical role in contemporary ways of 'world-making', to use Nelson Goodman's expression.[4] Similar perspectives are offered by medical anthropology. As Byron Good has argued, diseases are not simply discrete entities, but explanatory models that operate in the shared worlds of meaning and experience inhabited by both patients and practitioners.[5]

Within this context, developments in the German-speaking world have played pivotal roles. For example, one may consider the role of such luminaries as Rudolf Virchow and Robert Koch in the making of modern medicine; the work of Samuel Hahnemann, the founder of homeopathy, in alternative medicine; or the provision and definition of the very terms 'Psychiatrie' by Johann Christian Reil in 1808 and 'Psychoanalyse' by Sigmund Freud in 1896. Indeed, the very field of medical history is of German lineage.[6] Yet at the same time, this particular strand in the history of medicine is fraught, for it includes too, for example, experiences of many wars, and the atrocities of the Nazi years. Those events themselves flowed into later understandings of medicine and ethics, as in the case of the post-war Doctors' Trial (1946–7) at Nuremberg, which had a major impact on subsequent international stipulations for experimentation on human subjects.[7] It is unsurprising therefore that the German-speaking world has produced a particular wealth of writing of many kinds (and not only in German) on medicine and health, which invites ongoing exploration. In that realm, historical and life-writing exist alongside and in relation to long and distinguished traditions of philosophy and literature, by physicians and others, which reflect on medicine.

In response, this volume tracks the designation and making through medicine of the human/inhuman, and simultaneously the humane/inhumane, in the German-speaking world. In this focus, it examines a central field in the development of medical history and of thinking about medicine in multiple forms. Thus, the essays that follow undertake multidisciplinary, critical explorations into some of the ways in which practices and theories of medicine have come to define the human in that world, and in so doing, have consolidated, or undermined, notions of humane behaviour, sometimes even simultaneously. On the one hand, this collection traces selected aspects and representations of the history of medicine and related fields – often those that begin with a critical relationship to conventional medicine – and the ways in which these disciplines have conceptualised humanity. But on the other hand, as the volume's double-edged title suggests too, it considers the ways in which medicine has been intimately linked in various ways with power, abuse and dehumanisation. These studies consider, too, how such ideas are reflected and refracted in important textual and cultural forms. They bring to bear perspectives from the fields of literary studies, cultural studies, history, and the history of medicine and psychiatry, in the first collection dedicated to the exploration of this interface. Thus, the study is historical in the most expansive sense, for it debates what historical accounts, life-writing and literary texts, and their analysis, all bring to our understanding of this powerful discipline.

The works discussed represent medical treatments in a wide variety of ways, or imagine the experience of practising or being subject to it. Such writing can expose medicine to critical analysis by highly varied formal means, from *inter alia* apparently factual, clinical description, to profoundly personal writings such as diaries and correspondences, and to humour, polemic and Modernist play with narrative technique.

Yet all these texts explore the symbolic potential of medicine as a trope. Thus, among other things, the chapters that follow consider and theorise what role literature and life-writing play in illuminating the world of medicine, and furthermore, ways in which that world can be figured in writing, in terms of form as well as theme.[8] A further, striking feature in many of the contributions to this volume is their emphasis on conditions and treatments affecting the mind, suggesting that this realm is particularly compelling in the cultures of modernity.[9] It is perhaps here that the identity effects of medicine are most marked, and the contested knowledges of psychology and psychiatry, and incertitudes of their therapies, offer themselves up as particularly rich sites of interface with interested societal stakeholders, including actual and potential patients. Equally eloquent is the fact that many of the texts in question seek to challenge the societal status of medicine and to comment critically on its practices and effects.

While the topics in question here are not intended to be comprehensive or fully representative, they are nonetheless illustrative of some of the key intersections between medicine, humanity and inhumanity. They highlight, too, selected modes of reading that help illuminate those intersections, as is shown by the comparative example that now follows in this Introduction.

Historical studies have shown that the claims and imperatives of medicine are by no means constants, and that the rise of modern scientific medicine is bound up by a progressive enlargement of its moral purview.[10] For instance, in the immediate aftermath of the Second World War, contemporary with the Doctors' Trial, canonical debate on humanism took place between the philosophers Jean-Paul Sartre and Martin Heidegger. Interestingly, neither the former's *Existentialism Is a Humanism* (1946), nor the latter's rejoinder 'Letter on "Humanism"' (1947) makes use of the term that at that historical juncture was coming to play such a prominent role in the reformulation of humanism, namely, medicine.[11] Yet at the very same time, when discussions were held that led to the formation of the United Nations, one of the first priorities was the establishment of a global health organisation.[12] Thus, in 1946, the constitution of the World Health Organization (WHO) was drawn up, as a specialised agency under the charter of the United Nations (UN). The key provisions of its Charter were as follows:

> Health is a state of complete physical, mental and social well-being and not merely the absence of disease or infirmity.
>
> The enjoyment of the highest attainable standard of health is one of the fundamental rights of every human being without distinction of race, religion, political belief, economic or social condition.
>
> The health of all peoples is fundamental to the attainment of peace and security and is dependent upon the fullest co-operation of individuals and States.
>
> The achievement of any State in the promotion and protection of health is of value to all.
>
> Unequal development in different countries in the promotion of health and control of disease, especially communicable disease, is a common danger.
>
> Healthy development of the child is of basic importance; the ability to live harmoniously in a changing total environment is essential to such development.
>
> The extension to all peoples of the benefits of medical, psychological and related knowledge is essential to the fullest attainment of health.
>
> Informed opinion and active co-operation on the part of the public are of the utmost importance in the improvement of the health of the people.
>
> Governments have a responsibility for the health of their peoples which can be fulfilled only by the provision of adequate health and social measures.[13]

The positing of health as a fundamental right links this document with the first part of Article 25 of the Universal Declaration of Human Rights (UDHR) of 1948:

> Everyone has the right to a standard of living adequate for the health and well-being of himself and of his family, including food, clothing, housing and medical care and necessary social services, and the right to security in the event of unemployment, sickness, disability, widowhood, old age or other lack of livelihood in circumstances beyond his control.[14]

These statements can be read at face value as lists of crucial societal aims, and there is no shortage of empirical studies concerning their differential implementation in various countries.[15] These documents inscribe the intrinsic right to health, well-being, access to medical care and so on, within the very definition of the human. The tight coupling of health and humanity in documents such as the WHO Charter and the UDHR indicate that henceforth, discussions of humanism must take medicine and health into account. This reformulation does not only have ontological implications, but ethical ones as well, for as medicine has come to define the human, medical therapies have come to define humane conduct, such that the withholding of medical therapies, for example, is taken as a marker of the inhumane.

The WHO Charter and the UDHR therefore direct the terms of humanism as discussed by Sartre and Heidegger significantly towards the inclusion of health and medicine. Indeed, these documents suggest that in the aftermath of the horrors of the mid-twentieth century, the Platonic quest in search of the nature of the 'good life' changed rapidly, and increasingly became one of determining the means to health. The WHO Charter and the UDHR present their statements as axiomatic, and this kind of expression is an important part of their power. But to recall their original context, and the shifts they represent in longer philosophical traditions, represented in this argument by Sartre and Heidegger, is also a reminder that they can be read as historical texts that emanate from very specific circumstances. As such, the WHO Charter and the UDHR become more evidently open to critical contextualisations and readings. It is in part in offering such accounts that work in the humanities becomes a productive vantage point on the twin themes of medicine and humanity, and how they have increasingly become inseparable. Such work offers tools also to address the insight that in this field, simple distinctions between fact and value cannot necessarily easily be made.[16]

The present volume takes a particular interest in literary criticism. A close reading using methods of such criticism can be applied of course to apparently straightforward texts such as the WHO Charter and the UDHR. Likewise, the juxtaposition of those writings with more evidently literary works can provoke thought. A case in point is offered by an exemplary comparison with the novella *Die Verweigerungen der Johanna Glauflügel / Johanna Glauflügel's Refusals* (1977), by the (West) German author Birgit Pausch, who was born in 1942 in Wrocław (Breslau) and grew up in Düsseldorf. This work intersects with some of the texts examined by some of the contributors in his volume, and rewards study partly because it was published in West Germany three decades after the WHO Charter and the UDHR were written, and so is rooted in the same broad historical moment; yet it offers distance to reflect upon it.

Die Verweigerungen der Johanna Glauflügel can be read as an eloquently emblematic work of post-war (West) German literature, in part because it is conscious of its origins in the turmoil of the past. This novella is characteristically modern, too, in its interest in urban and workplace experience, alienated states of mind and uses of a subtly distanciating Modernist style to express them. It narrates a period in the life of its eponymous protagonist in an unnamed city on the Rhine in 1973 and after, alongside flashbacks to her childhood and youth, presumably in the Federal Republic of the 1950s or earlier 1960s.[17] Glauflügel (the narrative voice refers to the protagonist by her surname throughout, forming part of the novella's unexpected stylistic effects) is a hospital nurse; this characterisation is not incidental, for the figure of the nurse traditionally represents the interface between biomedicine, therapeutics and humanity.

Glauflügel is troubled by news of the contemporary putsch in Chile and a growing preoccupation with social injustice. However, initially at least, she lacks language and conceptual resources to frame that preoccupation, let alone possible solutions for it, and is stranded in a sense of anxiety and unease. Her concern is prompted, among other things, by her relationship with a left-wing artist, Dortrecht, and seeing her working-class women patients made ill by the circumstances of their lives and disregarded by the medical hierarchy. Glauflügel is disturbed too by her witnessing and experience of latently and manifestly violent everyday sexism, and by a fearful, hostile public mood in the wake of left-wing terrorism and the state's responses to it. Finally, she is mindful of the virulent legacy of the Nazi past in the present day.

At the outset, Glauflügel's life seems to be modelled on the happy ending to the classic plot of that popular genre of romantic fiction, the *Arztroman* [novel set in a medical milieu], for she is married to a successful doctor named Ronnen. However, the couple become increasingly estranged, and Glauflügel leaves Ronnen after a fraught Christmas celebration with her extended family, because it seems to her that some of society's ills are deeply inscribed into her marriage and family life. Thus, the plot traces Glauflügel's increasing alienation from her work, which goes hand in hand with alienation in her marriage. This process culminates in her abandonment of both, in search of more dignified ways of working, living and caring for the sick and dying in that classic locus of escape for the German literary subject, Italy, where she joins Dortrecht in Florence. However, the end of the novella is ambiguous, and there is no certainty that Glauflügel has found a way forward.

Very different as these texts seem at first sight, a number of parallels link *Die Verweigerungen der Johanna Glauflügel* and the WHO Charter and the UDHR. These works all emerge, albeit in varying ways, from the mid-century, identify health issues as central to individual and social well-being, and consequently place a high value on medical care as a key index of society's humanity. In addition, they have in common a sense that health is a far wider and greater matter than the mere 'absence of disease or infirmity', for Pausch's text registers the ways in which mental, emotional and social well-being are of a piece with the treatment of illness. The novella, like the WHO Charter, recognises the responsibility of society and the state in the generation and protection of well-being and health, for Glauflügel's condemnation of all that is wrong with her experience of healthcare is inseparable from her broader social and political critique. Likewise, in line with the WHO Charter's affirmation of the importance of patients' 'informed opinion' and 'active co-operation', she is in search of more democratic ways of administering care.

All these texts express, too, a sense that the creation of well-being is a transnational issue. The WHO Charter notes that achievements in health in any state are 'of value to all', and conversely, that '[u]nequal development in different countries ... is a common danger'. Analogously, Glauflügel's knowledge of events in Chile prevents her from taking a complacent view of the apparently more peaceful and democratic West Germany; her quest for more humane medicine is as pressing to her in Italy as it is in the Federal Republic. The WHO Charter draws attention to the special status of children and their needs, and Glauflügel's turning point on Christmas Eve is triggered by observing her extended family's influence on children. In particular, she is shocked by a story told by her mother in 'Ekstase' / 'ecstasy' (42) about proudly watching a Nazi parade and extreme street violence towards a 'Rotfrontkämpfer' / 'Red Front fighter' during the so-called Third Reich (43). This anecdote is told in front of young grandchildren (the protagonist's niece and nephew), and the granddaughter starts excitedly repeating its words. This scene brings home to Glauflügel the ways in which the family hands down its narratives and emotions about the past uncritically to its children, who, it is implied, may thus be at risk of repeating it. It is no coincidence that she herself does not wish to become pregnant, despite Ronnen's pressure on her to discontinue her contraception just before this episode takes place.

Yet at the same time, the novella moves in different directions from the earlier texts. The WHO Charter and the UDHR stress their applicability to all, regardless of 'race, religion, political belief, economic or social condition'. While Glauflügel would no doubt subscribe to that view, *Die Verweigerungen der Johanna Glauflügel*, by contrast, points up the depth of the social divisions, such as class and gender, which must be overcome to make such ideals realistic. It focuses on the deep social divisions that affect patients' experiences even in prosperous, European societies such as the Federal Republic or Italy, for instance the types of health insurance that are available to them, and the ensuing differences in treatment. Glauflügel notes ailments that arise from social divisions, such as those that are the product of damaging labour for the working class. She observes, too, socially determined addictions that drive poor women factory personnel into early infirmity and undignified death in a medical system that sees them as second class. The novella is, in addition, conscious of the gendered nature of medicine. Glauflügel is steered by a teacher into her ancillary role as a nurse due to her perceived feminine qualities of 'Fleiß' / 'diligence' and 'Bescheidenheit' / 'modesty' (29). She notes that while (women) hospital patients are at the very bottom of an inflexible hierarchy, she too as a (woman) nurse is patronised and stereotyped by her superior, the (man) doctor who dismisses her thoughts. That hierarchy is all-encompassing and apparently immutable, for the doctor considers it to be underwritten by divine power and instructs the non-religious Glauflügel to speak about God to a poor woman patient undergoing a difficult death, and so to accept her fate: 'Sie solle ihr sagen, daß der *Herr* Widerspruch nicht liebt. Der Arzt lächelte' / 'she should tell her that the *Lord* doesn't like contradiction. The doctor smiled' (9).

Die Verweigerungen der Johanna Glauflügel stresses the apparent lack of remedy for such problems, even in a society as rich in resources as the Federal Republic. Pausch's work is moreover interested in the power of the ideologies that uphold social divisions, and the ways in which they are discursively reinforced by diverse means, which range from supposedly religious precepts, such as those presented by the doctor quoted above, to the power of the popular romance that her marriage seems at first sight to evoke. This work points, therefore, to the linked, deep-seated attitudes and assumptions of different subjects around healthcare, for example the very different expectations inculcated in men and women, including indeed around reading, as *Die Verweigerungen der Johanna Glauflügel* makes clear. Read in tandem with the WHO Charter, then, the novella might suggest that such a document, which endorses humanist ideals around healthcare and well-being, yet decouples them from their broader social, political, economic and psychological contexts, leaves critical issues open for further inquiry. It is to some of these interfaces that this volume is dedicated.

Die Verweigerungen der Johanna Glauflügel indicates the possibility that competing notions of health, defined as a 'complete state of well-being', may exist. Glauflügel herself, at the start of the text, could be considered to be in just such a state of well-being. She seemingly has her health, and control of her reproductive prospects, widely considered to be a key to women's welfare in the modern period, and achieves the aspirational goals taught to women of her class and generation. She has an appropriate profession, marriage to a high-status professional man and material stability. Yet she herself increasingly disputes such a concept of well-being, although she initially lacks a vocabulary to do so. In another example, the doctor quoted above remarks of his patient, who is dying of cirrhosis of the liver, 'Ein Leben mit mehr Verstand geführt, führe auch zu einem angenehmeren Ende' / 'leading a life with more sense leads also to a more pleasant end' (11). Yet he has no feeling for the hard circumstances that drive the woman to drink. With such examples, the novella shows how complex identifying a 'complete state of well-being' can be, and raises the question of who, if anyone, can adjudicate on it, on what grounds and with what words. Likewise, if according to the WHO Charter, governments are responsible for 'provision of adequate health and social measures', a reading of *Die Verweigerungen der Johanna Glauflügel* very evidently opens up the question of what the contestable term 'adequate' might mean.

According to the WHO Charter, 'informed opinion' and 'active co-operation' on the part of the public are valorised and to be cultivated. Yet *Die Verweigerungen der Johanna Glauflügel* problematises such questions, not only since poor women, such as those for whom Glauflügel cares, are less likely to have the resources to obtain and evaluate information, but also because, in any case, the doctor refuses to believe that they can understand and address questions about their own care. The dying woman described here comes to a different view from her doctor on the suitability of her demeaning end-of-life care and is not minded to cooperate with what he wants. In that case, a dilemma becomes evident for which the Charter offers no answer, namely on how to proceed where a patient and healthcare professional are in fundamental disagreement. Additionally, the novella thematises some of the difficulty and ambiguity involved in the making of patients' informed opinion. While Glauflügel takes a contraceptive pill, it is hinted that she is exposed to conflicting messages about it. In such circumstances, it may be difficult even for a trained professional such as herself to pick out a straightforward argument that is not biased by personal or political interest.

Such differences between the two non-fiction documents cited here and *Die Verweigerungen der Johanna Glauflügel* carry over into matters of style. The WHO Charter and the UDHR speak and derive authority from the language of universality and timelessness. By contrast, Pausch inserts history and difference into her debate on medicine and well-being, and adopts for this purpose a very different mode of expression. The diction of the Charter and the UDHR is predicated on the linked assumptions of stable subjects of enunciation and reception, and of mutually comprehensible language. But the narrative techniques of the novella subtly undermine such qualities, and thus propose the possibility that, while politically powerful, their solidity is questionable.

At the same time, *Die Verweigerungen der Johanna Glauflügel* sets out to explore different, less totalising modes of communication. For example, it contains two important instances of ekphrasis and interpretation of visual art. The first is a passage early on of some four pages outlining Dortrecht's thoughts on Diego Velázquez's large painting *Las Meninas* (c.1656–66). The second is shorter and consists of Glauflügel's own reflections, close to the end of the novella, on Donatello's sculpture *Penitent Magdalene* (c.1453–5). In turn, she links this work to her recent viewing of a film entitled *Il tumulto dei Ciompi / The Wool Workers' Rebellion*, about the Florentine revolts of 1378–82, with which she sympathises. These passages of interpretation cannot deliver a factual or definitive account of what the works in question mean, let alone of their historical subject matter. Instead, they highlight the value of suggestive media, which communicate in different, more enigmatic ways. As such, they offer an alternative to the language of the hospital, which seeks to be transparent and omnipotent, but that Glauflügel feels fails her.

These passages on art in *Die Verweigerungen der Johanna Glauflügel* appear to address very different issues from healthcare and well-being. However, their significance in the present argument is to illustrate the importance of alternative modes of expression and signification. Such modes, like fantasy and body language, which are also important in the novella, and indeed Pausch's own distinctive prose, go beyond the clinical idiom of healthcare, or the serene diction of documents such as the WHO Charter. Such expressive modes may be able to convey something of the complexities that other, more monological language cannot. In some ways, then, *Die Verweigerungen der Johanna Glauflügel* offers a more fissured, ambiguous, but also a more complex, critical, historically sensitive and multifaceted account of issues around healthcare, well-being and philosophy in the post-war era than texts that set out more ostentatiously and authoritatively to do so. That said, the novella shares an ethical impetus with the WHO Charter and UDHR. These texts all convey an urgent commitment to the humane treatment of individuals in modern society, centred on appropriate medical treatment and approaches to health and well-being. Hence, the present discussion, rooted as it is in the medical and health humanities, may suggest that in the consideration of what makes for a more humane life, such very different writings may be productively read in counterpoint or tension with one another.

The post-Second World War developments referenced here should not be taken as indicating that the conjunctions of medicine and the human are a uniquely recent affair. Rather, they serve to highlight linkages that, as several of the chapters that follow show, are present in earlier historical periods too. This continuum is made visible by the arrangement of the contributions, broadly speaking according to the chronological order of the material they discuss, as well as the prefaces of the individual chapters, which reflect in various ways on their relationships with the volume as a whole. These principles allow both for the tracing of some multi-stranded histories and the circulation and exchange between different genres of texts, and for the creation of thought-provoking juxtapositions between ideas in apparently very different fields.

This volume has arisen through a departmental research project in the Department of German in the School of European Languages, Cultures and Society at UCL on 'Medical In/Humanities'. In addition to the contributors to this volume, we would like to thank the UCL Grand Challenges programme for funding an early stage of our project, the Editorial Board of UCL Press's FRINGE series, all colleagues at UCL Press, and the many participants in several years of seminars for their engagement, which helped to shape the direction this inquiry has taken.

Notes

1. See Cooter and Stein, *Writing History in the Age of Biomedicine*. On wider issues regarding how the human has come to be historically defined, see Smith, *Being Human*. On the history of the differential definition of the human and the animal, see Bourke, *What It Means to Be Human*.
2. See Maehle and Geyer-Kordesch, *Historical and Philosophical Perspectives on Biomedical Ethics*.
3. Rose, 'Beyond Medicalisation', 701. On this question, see Panese and Barras, 'Médicalisation de la "vie"'.
4. Goodman, *Ways of Worldmaking*.
5. Good, *Medicine, Rationality, and Experience*.
6. See Stein, 'Divining and Knowing'.
7. See Schmidt, *Justice at Nuremberg*; Weindling, *Nazi Medicine*.
8. The collection adds to the insights of such works as Behrens and Zelle, *Der ärztliche Fallbericht*; Klocke, *Inscription and Rebellion*; Pethes and Richter, *Medizinische Schreibweisen*; and Rigoli, *Lire le délire*.
9. See Micale, *The Mind of Modernism*.
10. See Cooter and Pickstone, *Medicine in the Twentieth Century*.
11. Sartre, *L'existentialisme est un humanisme*; Heidegger, *Platons Lehre von der Wahrheit*.
12. See, for example, Charles, 'Origins, History, and Achievements of the World Health Organization'.
13. WHO, 'Constitution'.
14. UN, 'Universal Declaration of Human Rights'. On the role of human rights within the formation of the UN, see Mazower, 'Strange Triumph of Human Rights' and Mazower, *No Enchanted Palace*.
15. See, for example, CSDH, *Closing the Gap in a Generation*.
16. Compare Putnam, *Collapse of the Fact/Value Dichotomy*.
17. Pausch, *Die Verweigerungen der Johanna Glauflügel*. Further references follow in the text.

Bibliography

Behrens, Rudolf and Carsten Zelle, eds. *Der ärztliche Fallbericht: Epistemische Grundlagen und textuelle Strukturen dargestellter Beobachtung*. Wiesbaden: Harrassowitz, 2012.

Bourke, Joanna. *What It Means to Be Human: Reflections from 1791 to the Present*. London: Virago, 2011.

Charles, John. 'Origins, History, and Achievements of the World Health Organization', *British Medical Journal* 2 (1968): 293–96.

Cooter, Roger and John Pickstone, eds. *Medicine in the Twentieth Century*. Amsterdam: Harwood Academic, 2000.

Cooter, Roger and Claudia Stein. *Writing History in the Age of Biomedicine*. New Haven: Yale University Press, 2013.

CSDH (Commission on Social Determinants of Health). *Closing the Gap in a Generation: Health Equity through Action on the Social Determinants of Health: Final Report of the Commission on Social Determinants of Health*. Geneva: World Health Organization, 2008.

Good, Byron J. *Medicine, Rationality, and Experience: An Anthropological Perspective*. Cambridge: Cambridge University Press, 1994.

Goodman, Nelson. *Ways of Worldmaking*. Hassocks: Harvester Press, 1978.

Heidegger, Martin. *Platons Lehre von der Wahrheit: Mit einem Brief über den "Humanismus"*. Bern: Francke, 1947.

Klocke, Sonja E. *Inscription and Rebellion: Illness and the Symptomatic Body in East German Literature*. Rochester, NY: Camden House, 2015.

Maehle, Andreas-Holger and Johanna Geyer-Kordesch, eds. *Historical and Philosophical Perspectives on Biomedical Ethics: From Paternalism to Autonomy?* Aldershot: Ashgate, 2002.

Mazower, Mark. 'The Strange Triumph of Human Rights, 1933–1950', *The Historical Journal* 47, no. 2 (2004): 379–98.

Mazower, Mark. *No Enchanted Palace: The End of Empire and the Ideological Origins of the United Nations*. Princeton: Princeton University Press, 2009.

Micale, Mark S., ed. *The Mind of Modernism: Medicine, Psychology, and the Cultural Arts in Europe and America, 1880–1940*. Stanford: Stanford University Press, 2004.

Panese, Francesco and Vincent Barras. 'Médicalisation de la "vie" et reconfigurations médicales', *Revue des Sciences Sociales* 39 (2008): 20–29.

Pausch, Birgit. *Die Verweigerungen der Johanna Glauflügel*. Berlin: Rotbuch Verlag, 1977.

Pethes, Nicolas and Sandra Richter, eds. *Medizinische Schreibweisen: Ausdifferenzierung und Transfer zwischen Medizin und Literatur (1600–1900)*. Tübingen: Niemeyer, 2008.

Putnam, Hilary. *The Collapse of the Fact/Value Dichotomy and Other Essays*. Cambridge, MA: Harvard University Press, 2004.

Rigoli, Juan. *Lire le délire: Aliénisme, rhétorique et littérature en France au XIXe siècle*. Paris: Fayard, 2001.

Rose, Nikolas. 'Beyond Medicalisation', *The Lancet* 369, no. 9562 (2007): 700–2.

Sartre, Jean-Paul. *L'existentialisme est un humanisme*. Paris: Nagel, 1946.

Schmidt, Ulf. *Justice at Nuremberg: Leo Alexander and the Nazi Doctors' Trial*. Basingstoke: Palgrave Macmillan, 2004.

Smith, Roger. *Being Human: Historical Knowledge and the Creation of Human Nature*. Manchester: Manchester University Press, 2007.

Stein, Claudia. 'Divining and Knowing: Karl Sudhoff's Historical Method', *Bulletin of the History of Medicine* 87 (2013): 198–224.

UN (United Nations). 'Universal Declaration of Human Rights'. Accessed 21 September 2019. www.un.org/en/universal-declaration-human-rights.

Weindling, Paul Julian. *Nazi Medicine and the Nuremberg Trials: From Medical War Crimes to Informed Consent*. Basingstoke: Palgrave Macmillan, 2004.

WHO (World Health Organization). 'Constitution'. Accessed 21 September 2019. www.who.int/about/mission/en/.

2

Pain and Laughter: Dental Treatment as a Comic Motif in Medieval and Early Modern Literature

Sebastian Coxon

Preface

Given that this chapter provides a close reading of comedic texts from the twelfth to the sixteenth centuries, it promises to cast the central themes of this volume – the (in)human and (in)humanity in medical contexts – in a historical light. For the medical 'field' of dentistry, it ought to be acknowledged, the Middle Ages and the Early Modern period were not times of great development in terms of knowledge and practice: forcible tooth extraction (without anaesthetic) remained the treatment of last resort for centuries. However, what this particular corpus of literary material does make clear is that for a long time comedic scenarios involving the (painful) pulling of teeth were very popular and appear to have depended for their success on the interplay of effects that, from our perspective today at least, relate to ideas of humanity and inhumanity.

In one way or another, all of the texts discussed here recognise that pain relief, while most desirable(!), represents something of a challenge to reason when the necessary treatment involved is itself excruciatingly painful. The fact that such scenes are portrayed in lurid detail and, apparently, with a certain amount of glee in order to entertain listeners and readers alike, is relevant also. Two opposing drives seem to be at work in the process of reception of pre-modern comedy surrounding toothache. On the one hand, identification appears grounded in a sense of common humanity or the shared experience of bodily frailty; on the other hand, an attitude of estrangement and distance enables recipients to take delight in the imagined suffering of (certain) others, a licence for vicarious inhumanity as it were.

The narratives and plays in question are all about the 'drama' of dental treatment in the age before anaesthetic. To that extent, they reflect an experience of medicine that has been entirely superseded, as is made only too clear by comparing them with a modern novel about dentistry, such as *örtlich betäubt / Local Anaesthetic* (1969) by Günter Grass, discussed below in Mererid Puw Davies's contribution to this volume. Grass's interweaving of complex and sustained levels of symbolism throughout his narrative is not something we should expect to find in these pre-modern texts either. Here, toothache and tooth extraction are not metaphors for anything else; however, their various literary 'enactments' alert listeners and readers to themes of greater consequence, such as folly and the limitations of human understanding.

Introduction

> Virgo martyr egregia / pro nobis Appollonia/ funde preces ad dominum / ne reatu criminum vexemur morbo dentium. / Ora pro nobis sancta/ Appollonia /
>
> Excellent virgin and martyr, Apollonia, for our sakes pour out your prayers to the Lord so that we may not be afflicted by toothache on account of our sins. Pray for us, Saint Apollonia
>
> (prayer, c.1470)[1]

Toothache is and always has been perceived to be a particularly nasty affliction. Not only that, but for a very long time bad teeth also presented a medical problem whose treatment was potentially even more painful.[2] This double bind might explain why none other than St Apollonia, an elderly virgin of Alexandria (d.249), was so widely venerated by sufferers of toothache across medieval Europe, for St Apollonia, so the legends went, knew only too well the agonies of forcible tooth extraction: 'Thus she offered her devout soul to God and handed over her most chaste body to the persecutors to be tortured. The executioners, cruelly wreaking their wrath upon her, first beat out all her teeth ...' (Jacobus de Voragine, *The Golden Legend*, [chapter] 66).[3] Late medieval devotional images of St Apollonia tended to portray her holding a fearsome set of pincers or blacksmith's tongs in which one of her own teeth is still clasped, the exaggerated size of the implement reflecting not only the extent of the saint's imagined torment but also the supplicant's horror of what lay in store for them, should their prayers fail to have the desired effect.[4]

In these same images, St Apollonia's beautiful face rarely betrays any sign of pain; the ideal of her sublime state as martyr-saint in heaven prohibits this. For visual representation of such torment we have to look elsewhere, at the iconographic motifs used to decorate the 'margins' of otherwise majestic buildings,[5] for instance, such as the grimacing toothache-heads or mouth-pullers that adorn the interiors of cathedrals.[6] Within the grand scheme of things, caricatures of toothache (in a much more mundane sense) acted as a reminder to all of the ugliness and frailty of the human body, a subject for all onlookers, rich and poor alike, to laugh at or identify with, or indeed both.

In general, we might say that nothing ruins the ideal of beauty in women and heroic fortitude in men as quickly and completely as the affliction of bad teeth and the indignity and pain of their treatment by extraction. As far as the Middle Ages is concerned, this rule of thumb applies to literature no less than to art, where references to bodily infirmity and deficiency, everyday aches and pains, however excruciating, are the preserve of certain text types and literary traditions.[7] The idealised portrayal of the courtly ladies and knights of Arthurian romance, for instance, does not allow them to suffer from bad breath and tooth decay; nor do their teeth ever have to be pulled as a remedy for such ailments.[8] The stories that do contain detail of this kind tend to be overtly comic and designed primarily to entertain their recipients by deflating ideals and delighting in bodily matters (sexuality and violence; pleasure and pain).[9] To describe the significance and functions of toothache and dental treatment in medieval literature is thus to engage with pre-modern literary comedy.[10]

As the following readings will show, dental treatment at its most extreme – that is to say, the brutal extraction of teeth – is a particularly resonant comic motif from the twelfth to the sixteenth centuries. Such longevity is perhaps not so surprising given that this treatment of last resort remained standard practice throughout the Middle Ages and well into the modern period.[11] However (and this almost goes without saying), so many other things did change during this time, including the processes of literary production and reception, that one wonders what scope for variation there was when it came to burlesque scenes of teeth-pulling, as opposed to the altogether more serious business of depicting a saint's martyrdom. Poets over the centuries were faced with the same fundamental challenges of maintaining comic effect and stimulating audience laughter. Exactly what kind(s) of comic effect did this work entail and what kind(s) of laughter? The success of much (but by no means all) of the following material as comic entertainment seems to have been predicated upon an unsympathetic attitude on the part of recipients that we could perhaps characterise, in Henri Bergson's terms, as 'une anesthésie momentanée du coeur' / 'a momentary anaesthesia of the heart'.[12] But what are the literary strategies that were required to bring about this state in the first place? And if the content of these texts is cruel, to what extent is this cruelty mitigated or compounded by the ostensibly medical frame of reference?

This article aims to answer these questions with a close reading of a number of selected texts that epitomise three different types of comedy in the context of torturous dental treatment: comedy of spite, festive comedy, comedy of miscommunication. This list is in no way meant to be exhaustive. There will doubtless be other medieval texts that could, or indeed should, have been taken into account here, and quite possibly other types of comedy too. However, there is enough material here to help us get a sense of just how much (comic) portrayals of tooth extraction change and/ or remain the same in the course of medieval literary tradition.

Unnecessary Treatment, or the Comedy of Spite

From the twelfth to the fifteenth centuries the comic theme of dental treatment most commonly occurs in bawdy stories of adultery and deception, where the scheming wife and her lover seek their own sexual gratification at the expense of the former's inadequate husband. Tooth extraction in this context is entirely gratuitous, a test that the lover demands of the wife in order to prove her fidelity(!) to him, but one that is calculated to inflict pain and humiliation on the husband. In order for the cuckold to accept that such treatment is necessary, he must first be persuaded that he requires it; hence stories of this kind also devote considerable attention to the symptoms of bad teeth, albeit as an elaborate fiction.

The first outstanding example of this plot type is a twelfth-century comedy (or *comedia*) in Latin verse entitled *Lidia*, concerning a certain duchess of the same name who, at the behest of the man she wishes to be her lover, Pirrus, conspires against her husband, Decius, with the help of her maidservant, Lusca.[13] The text encourages its recipients to be amused by the pain the husband suffers, no less than by the illicit pleasures enjoyed by the lovers. Licence to do so is effectively granted by Decius's utter stupidity, which reduces him to the status of a puppet in our eyes, laughably easy to manipulate and mutilate, and hence fully deserving of his fate.

The forcible tooth extraction is in fact the third of three tests of fidelity that Lidia must pass. Having first killed Decius's favourite hunting bird in front of his own eyes (298–310) – an attack on her husband's prestige – and then having plucked five hairs from his beard (313–28) – an attack on her husband's masculinity – the pulling of one of Decius's teeth represents the climax to this particular sequence of action (345–422), in that it constitutes irreversible physical injury.[14] Moreover, to those recipients of this text with knowledge of St Apollonia's martyrdom (gleaned, say, from Eusebius's *History of the Church* [VI. 41]), the status of this third test is enhanced by the apparently outrageous coincidence that Lidia's husband has for a namesake the same emperor, Decius, who was said to have encouraged the persecution of Christians in Alexandria and elsewhere.[15]

The elaborate set-up alone contains a wealth of detail concerning dental ailments and oral hygiene. Thus, in order to persuade Decius that he suffers from the most atrocious bad breath (that can only be the result of a hideously rotten tooth), Lidia secretly instructs two young squires to avert their faces as they serve the duke's wine so as not to inflict the stench of their own bad breath on their lord and master. Anxious not to be held solely responsible for any offensive smell, the squires check each other's mouths before attending at table, falsely diagnosing such ailments as 'feda palato' / 'bad gums' (367), a 'male lingua tumet' / 'swollen tongue' (368) and a 'dens niger' / 'black tooth' (370). When Lidia then reveals to her husband that the squires' bizarre behaviour is a reaction to the bad smell coming from his mouth, Decius reluctantly consents to whatever treatment she deems suitable, and she immediately proposes the most drastic measure: 'Si tibi dens noceat, uellatur' / 'If a tooth is causing you problems, then it must be pulled' (405).

The delight taken in the spurious diagnosis of dental ailments that do not exist is matched only by the gleeful cruelty of the ensuing 'operation' on Decius's mouth as executed by the conspirators. Lidia has already set about tormenting Decius by pulling at one of his teeth (413–4) when Lusca and Pirrus enter the bedchamber and join in: 'En, quantus dolor hunc urget, quantus labor illam! / Dux gemit et, forsan teste cruore, dolet' / 'How great was his pain, how heavy the burden of her labour! The duke groaned and suffered grievously, as his blood made only too clear' (417–8). The focus here is on the painful injury done to Decius, and by emphasising just how arduous a process it is to extract one of his teeth, the poet renders the agonising experience of the 'patient' all the more palpable.[16] Given that the brutal dentistry is quite unnecessary, the comic effects of this scene are extremely aggressive in tone, expressive of a considerable degree of *Schadenfreude* at the inadequate husband's expense.[17] Indeed, such a response to Decius's suffering forms part of the story itself when Pirrus removes himself from the scene for fear of bursting out in laughter (423). Nor does Decius's subsequent behaviour do anything to diminish the pleasure we are meant to take in his pain. The fact that he allows himself to be comforted by the hope that another tooth will grow in the extracted one's place (477–84) clearly demonstrates that he is still as absurdly gullible as he was before. It seems only right therefore that a man without even the most rudimentary 'medical' knowledge, should be punished and abused in the way that he is.

Lidia's triumph over Decius is typical of the topsy-turvy world of much pre-modern comedy, in which traditional power relations and gender roles, not least those of husband and wife, are turned on their head. Yet although the plot of *Lidia* depends on cynical, anti-feminist notions of female guile and sexuality,[18] the entertainment offered by this text is largely unencumbered by explicit moralising on the part of the author-narrator. Other versions of the story deal with the didactic implications of this material differently, and this in turn has a bearing on how the husband's torturous dental treatment is portrayed.

In Boccaccio's *Decameron* (completed by 1353), for instance, the story (VII, 9) is altered in such a way as to emphasise Lidia's superiority to her husband, now called Nicostrato, and her ability to hoodwink and hurt him without the aid of her lover, Pirro. Thus, here we have a new scene in which Lidia actually pretends to examine her husband's mouth before offering her expert diagnosis.[19] And the terrible pain Nicostrato subsequently endures during the extraction is rendered all the more hilarious by Lidia's explanation as to why she wishes to 'help' him herself rather than employ a professional (619):

> E d'altra parte questi maestri son sì crudele a far questi servigi, che il cuore nol mi patirebbe per niuna maniera di vederti o di sentirti tralle mani a niuno; e per ciò del tutto io voglio fare io medesima, ché almeno, se egli ti dorrà troppo, ti lascerò io incontanente: quello che il maestro non farebbe.

> … these surgeons are quite barbaric when it comes to extracting people's teeth, and I couldn't possibly bear to see you suffering under the hands of any one of them. No, I absolutely insist on doing it myself, and then at least, if you're in too much pain, I shall stop at once, whereas a surgeon would take no notice.

In the broader narrative context of the *Decameron* this Lidia's victory is a perfect illustration of the chosen theme for Day VII: '… the tricks which, either in the cause of love or for motives of self-preservation, women have played upon their husbands, irrespective of whether or not they were found out' (521).[20] That Nicostrato deserves to be abused in this way is furthermore suggested by his advanced years and his inability to provide his wife 'with the one thing that gives young women their greatest pleasure' (569).[21] The primacy of love is evidently a most appealing idea to the *brigada* (the seven ladies and three gentlemen who have retreated from plague-stricken Florence and tell each other the hundred tales of the *Decameron*). Boccaccio's ironic detachment towards conventional morality is clearly signalled at the outset when Panfilo, whose story this particular one is, advises the ladies in the company not to follow Lidia's example, not because what she does is wrong but because 'Fortune is not always so kindly disposed' and 'men are not equally gullible' (569).[22]

Other versions of the story, both before and after Boccaccio, pursue a far more traditional didactic agenda, using the wife's assault on the husband's person to warn against the deceitful nature of (many) women. This 'moral' remit brings with it the tendency to strip away much of the detail of the story as we know it, reducing the action to a bare minimum. Thus, in an exemplum – *Sermones vulgares* [no.] 248 – commonly attributed to the Dominican preacher Jacques de Vitry (d.1240), famous for the amusing anecdotes and fables he used in his sermons, an (unnamed) lover will only believe an (unnamed) married woman's profession of love for him if she hands him the 'best tooth' ('meliorem dentem', 104) from her (unnamed) husband's mouth.[23] Having been persuaded that there is only one remedy for his chronic bad breath, the gullible husband complies with his wife's demands – 'Et ita ad hortationem uxoris fecit extrahi bonum et sanum dentem' / 'And thus, urged on by his wife, he had a good, healthy tooth removed' (104–5) – only for her to present the tooth to her paramour. Notably, almost all of the moments that might encourage a thirteenth-century listener to laugh at the husband are elided, not least the process of torturous extraction itself and the pleasure this affords the wife and her lover. The husband's suffering may be implied, but the emphasis is on the concluding lesson, which is as obvious as it is succinct: 'Non est facile credenda uxori nec consiliis adultere acquiescendi' / 'Seldom trust a wife or follow the advice of adulterers' (105).

Elsewhere, in a late fourteenth-century(?) German verse narrative now known as *Der Zahn / The Tooth*, a number of alternative strategies are deployed to make essentially the same point.[24] On the one hand, the bare-bones version of the story is told by an author-narrator who digresses from the course of the narrative in order to belabour the point that 'yetz in der welt' / 'even today' (11) a good wife is a blessing and a bad one, like the one in this tale, is a curse (14–5). On the other hand, the fleeting depiction, if one can even call it that, of the pulling of the husband's tooth – 'sust ließ er harte pinen sich' / 'thus he submitted himself to torture' (74) – is followed by a narrative twist that turns the wife herself into the target of the audience's (putative) derision. No sooner does she get her hands on the tooth (75) and present it to her 'amiysen' / 'beau' (77) than he rejects her for fear of suffering an even worse fate at her hands ('so getar si wol ain mort began' / 'she would not shirk from committing a murder', 82) should he ever fall out of favour. In the end the deceitful woman is shown to be too crafty for her own good, and the audience's attention is directed towards her comeuppance and away from her injured husband.

Not all late-medieval German tales evince the same reluctance to engage with the motif of torturous and unnecessary dental treatment. Two different comic tales by Heinrich Kaufringer (c.1400), for example, feature analogous scenes that find new ways of accentuating the cruelty of the deception and – arguably – its comic value as part of a radical approach to storytelling that sets great store by shocking violence.[25]

In Kaufringer's *Drei listige Frauen / Three Crafty Women*, three peasant women enter a wager as to who can fool their husbands most. The first of these, Mistress Hiltigart, persuades her husband that he has died as a result of the trauma of dental treatment.[26] While some of the elements within this narrative sequence are only too familiar (Hiltigart too reveals to her husband, Perchtold, that he has such bad breath it can only be remedied by having a rotten tooth extracted), others seem 'new' and are calculated to exaggerate the heartless(?) comedy at the peasant's expense. Thus, Perchtold is at first taken aback by his wife's complaint, having always prided himself on having good teeth ('got hat mich damit begabt, das si sind stark und gesund' / 'God has blessed me with teeth that are strong and healthy', 96–7), and Perchtold it is who asks his wife's lover (their servant) to do his wife the favour of undertaking the operation (119–26). The wife then produces a fearsome set of pincers, much to her husband's distress (134–5), with which the servant is urged to tear out first one healthy tooth (138–43) and then, even more gratuitously, a second (156–67), causing Perchtold to pass out (168–70). As with the 'pranks' played by wives two and three (including tonsuring [307–10] and even castration [466–83]), a gross discrepancy becomes ever more apparent between the prize for which the three women are competing – 'den ungeraden haller' / 'an odd penny' (30) – and the physical ordeals and/or humiliation to which they subject their husbands.

For the comic effects in this text to work, the attitude of listeners (or readers) towards the victims of the peasant wives' exploits must remain devoid of sympathy; there is no room for any detail that might complicate matters by compromising our profound sense of alienation from such bestially stupid figures as these three husbands.[27] Precisely this kind of complication occurs, however, in *Die Rache des Ehemannes / The Husband's Revenge*, another of Kaufringer's comic tales.[28] Here too, yet another woman seeks to impress her lover by persuading her unsuspecting husband to have not one but two allegedly rotten teeth pulled (40–118). But in this case, problems are caused by the further characterisation of the figures involved in this apparently quite conventional narrative scenario. Not only is the lover a priest, and thus blatantly in the wrong, but the husband is a noble knight who in no way merits what happens to him.[29] The key to understanding this unexpected variation lies in the rather different narrative structure of the text, in accordance with which certain acts of extreme provocation (the assault on the knight's person) are swiftly followed by acts of even more extreme retaliation (the knight's revenge).[30] Hence, when the reckless priest goes so far as to have a pair of the finest dice manufactured from the knight's 'zwen stockzan' / 'two molars' (36), and then drunkenly teases the knight himself about what he has done (172–84), this gives the knight licence to castrate the priest and have a delicate purse made out of his 'palg' / 'scrotum' (261) and 'hoden' / 'balls' (262), before forcing the stricken cleric to bite out the woman's tongue (370–89). The loss of two teeth seems trivial by comparison.[31] If audience expectation of 'comedy' in the first part of the narrative is frustrated, it is realised all the more aggressively in the second, when, just for once, the victim of torturous dental treatment strikes back at his tormentors.

Quackery, or Festive Comedy

The rather cruel comedy of stories featuring scenes of unnecessary dental treatment is a function or consequence of a narrative type that mercilessly pits clever (superior) figures against stupid (inferior) ones, and invites listeners and/or readers to identify with the former. Other literary traditions in the fifteenth and sixteenth centuries evince different types of comic effect, and although the imagined pain of forcible tooth extraction remains a constant point of reference in later texts, there is some evidence for a growing interest in the satirical issue of the competence or otherwise of those purporting to be actual medical practitioners.[32]

Choice examples of this phenomenon are to be found in late medieval *Fastnachtspiele* or Shrovetide plays, an early form of secular 'theatre', consisting in the main of bawdy and/or scatalogically obscene sketches and role-plays that were performed in taverns (we think) as part of carnival or Shrovetide festivities in cities such as Nuremberg.[33] Extant texts reveal an apparently insatiable appetite for crude euphemism and obscene metaphor,[34] but they also show a fondness for scenarios involving quacks and fake or incompetent physicians who suggest foolish (and not infrequently obscene) remedies for the spurious (and not infrequently obscene) ailments of women and peasants.[35]

Nothing lies outside the scope of their (mock) expertise, not even teeth.[36] The absurdity of such quackery is epitomised by *Das vastnachtspil vom arzt mit den zwelf paurn / The Shrovetide Play About the Doctor and the Twelve Peasants*, where the 'physician' shrewdly diagnoses that one of a certain peasant's many ailments comes from having eaten a broth that was too hot: 'Daran hat er verprent ainn zan' / 'He has burnt a tooth on it' ([KF 82] 684,27), and all of this just from the (obligatory) analysis of the patient's urine (684,28).[37] This kind of comedy cuts both ways: no one escapes the ridicule. The patients are base and foolish peasants who invariably contaminate their urine samples with excrement, and the 'physicians' are quacks who are seen to make things up as they go along and come with a reputation of doing more harm than good.[38]

The most concentrated and detailed comic staging of quackery and dentistry occurs not in a text from Nuremberg but in one of the Tirolian (Sterzinger) plays collected, if not necessarily authored, by Vigil Raber (d.1552), entitled *Ain zendprecherey / A Teeth-Pulling* and dated 1529.[39] The burlesque tone is set by the play's opening speech, in which the wife of the quack or 'zanprecher' / 'tooth-puller' (4), having first greeted the audience ('Got grues dj Ersamenn herrn vnd frauen!' / 'God greet [you], honourable lords and ladies!', 6), extols her husband's expertise: 'mit zanprechen ist maisterlich mein Man' / 'my husband is a master at pulling teeth' (22). He is indeed so proficient, she declares, that a past patient of his did eventually recover from the botched attempt to extract one of his teeth: 'Den rechtn kund er Im nit ergreiffn; / Im gschwals maul auf wie ain sackhpfeiffn, / Er ist aber seid vill besser worn' / 'He couldn't get hold of the right tooth. / His mouth swelled up like a bagpipe, / but he has recovered well in the meantime' (26–8). This less than complimentary introduction so infuriates her husband that he needs to be reminded of the purpose of his visit: 'Ste auf bannckh vnd thue dich fleissen, / ob du mochst ain paurn vmbs geltl pscheissn' / 'Stand on a bench and do what you can / to trick a peasant out of his money' (52–3). The quack proceeds to drum up trade by describing the woes of bad teeth, including of course the traditional symptoms of swelling and bad breath (69–72); toothache, he gleefully sums up, is like a bad house-guest: it gives its 'host' no respite (73–4).

An archetypal toothache sufferer then appears in the figure of Wilbold, a peasant, who admits to suffering from a number of these very same symptoms (85–90), and whose role it is to have a tooth pulled in the course of the play. The comic performance of the extraction itself is of course lost to us now;[40] all that remains is a cursory stage direction: 'da pricht er den zannd' / 'Then he pulls the tooth' (196). What we do have, however, are the comic exchanges – involving Wilbold, his friends and the quack – which take place both before and after the operation and serve only to heighten Wilbold's discomfort. Thus, although it is perfectly obvious which of the peasant's three teeth(!) is the problem – 'O mein maister, ir sein wol drej; / der Schwartz In der mit ist der recht' / 'O my master, there are three of them, / I think. The black one in the middle is the right one' (104–5) – the quack still offers his patient a rather less than reassuring guarantee: 'ist sach, das Ich ain vnrechten thue hebn, / So tarfstu mir nicht zu lon gebn' / 'if it turns out that I have taken the wrong one, / then you don't need to pay me' (145–6). Similarly, the words of encouragement offered by the other peasants seem calculated to terrify Wilbold even more: 'Drumb, maister, machtz nit zu lang / vnd zeuch herfur ain eisn zang' / 'So, master, waste no more time / and get out your iron pincers' (131–2). The pain experienced and expressed by the patient ('ach, das dich der teufl schennt, / wie thuet mir das so leichnam we!' / 'Agh! The devil take you! This pain is killing me!', 202–3) give the lie to the quack's promises beforehand ('Ey, lieber, du wierstzn nit emphinden!' / 'Hey, friend, you won't feel a thing!', 191) and words of comfort afterwards: 'Es mues ainn ain wenig pitzln' / 'It's bound to sting a little' (210).

However much the audience is prompted to laugh at Wilbold's predicament, any sense that the quack is in some way superior to him is held strictly in check. In spite of his and his wife's intentions, and irrespective of protracted negotiations with the peasants concerning his payment (149–76), once the job is done he receives only blows as the peasants chase him away: 'da schlagens den zannprecher fur thur auß' / 'Then they kick the tooth-puller out of the door' (241–2). The mood then changes to one of collective high spirits, as the peasants start to drink wine and sing and dance, a festive scene in which Wilbold plays a full part, almost as if the preceding action had never happened. The sense of goodwill among the peasants even leads them to fetch the quack (but not his wife),[41] who is more than happy to join in and laugh at himself: 'Ich mues meins vngefell selber lachn, / seit Ir all worden seit gueter ding. / schafft, das man vns ain kuelln wein pring!' / 'I even have to laugh at my own misfortune, now that you are all making merry. Have us brought a cool wine!' (336–8). In this way, the performance ends in remarkably conciliatory fashion.

Indeed, the convergence of the dramatic action (drinking and celebrating) with the festive situation in which the text is embedded, and the real audience's celebration of Shrovetide, encourages positive identification with the experiences and sentiments, if not the social status, of the dramatis personae. As a result, the play's comic treatment of toothache and the pain of tooth extraction appears far less determined by alienation and antipathy than by a shared understanding that this peculiarly nasty ailment afflicts everyone, and that when it comes to the most drastic form of dental treatment, all are equally helpless.

Accidental Treatment, or the Comedy of Miscommunication

Further literary historical developments in the course of the sixteenth century give rise to a third type of comedy about dentistry, that of accidental treatment, in which mischance and miscommunication are of primary concern. Printed prose *Schwankbücher* / 'printed collections of amusing anecdotes in prose', a publishing sensation from around the mid-sixteenth-century onwards, came to represent the new home for comic narrative motifs and shorter literary forms of all kinds (anecdotes; *facetiae*; *Schwankmären* / 'verse-couplet comic tales'), compiled for the amusement of ever greater numbers of readers.[42] Spearheaded by Jörg Wickram's *Rollwagenbüchlein / Little Book for Travelling in a Wagon*, an assortment of 67 short narrative texts that was first printed in Strassburg in 1555 and reprinted a further 14 times by 1613,[43] these collections marked a significant functional shift away from (medieval) exemplarity towards newsworthiness, using contemporary settings to present their predominantly comic tales as 'strange but true', and encouraging their readership to laugh at human foibles and the unpredictability of the world at large.

Text no. 65 in Wickram's *Rollwagenbüchlein* is a case in point.[44] With a title designed to arouse curiosity – 'Einem ward ein Zan wider seinen willen außbrochen als er gern gessen hett' / 'Someone has a tooth pulled against his will when he would rather have eaten' (126,1–2) – the reader wonders how such a peculiar turn of events could possibly come about, before being presented with the first part of the answer in the story's opening lines (126,3–6): 'EIn Kauffmann auß dem Schwabenland schicket einen Jungen diener in Italien seine gescheft eins theils darinn außzuorichten. Dem jungen aber kam es seer übel: dann er deß Welschen gar nit bericht was' / 'A merchant from Swabia sent a young servant to Italy to take care of some business for him. But the youth suffered terribly, for he had no knowledge of Italian'. The inexperience of youth together with a lack of linguistic competence make the unfortunate fellow in question rather ill-suited for his mission in Italy; so ill-suited, it would seem, that he cannot even cope with the most basic of everyday requirements (feeding himself). Upon encountering a helpful countryman, he takes the latter's advice to the letter and enters the first premises he finds with a painted sign above the door. It is not a tavern, however, but a 'Scherhauß' / 'barber's shop' (126,16). In answer to the barber's (incomprehensible) Italian, the young man uses sign language to indicate that he is hungry, but the gesture he makes is ambiguous at best: '… deütet er auff den mund mit der hand meint er wolt gern essen' / 'he pointed with his hand to his mouth as if to say he was very hungry' (126,21–2). The master and his apprentices conclude, quite logically, that he has a bad tooth, and waste no time in going about their business: 'Bald satzt man im einen stuol dar und ein küssin darauff // hieß man in nider sitzen von stundan kam der Meister mit seinem Instrument' / 'A stool was fetched for him with a cushion on it. // He was told to sit down, whereupon the master approached with his instrument' (126,23–5). Within their 'frame' of understanding, his protestations and resistance are just more evidence of the agony of his toothache: 'Also wurffen sy in zuoruck unnd brachen im wider allen seinen willen einen zan auß' / 'So they pushed him right back and pulled out a tooth quite against his will' (126,29–30).

Story no. 65 belongs to a cluster of three texts (64–6) featuring barber-surgeons.[45] But whereas in no. 64 ('Von einem Bauren woelchem das maul unwüssend auß dem Angel kam // und wie im wider geholffen ward' / 'Concerning a peasant who had his jaw dislocated without his knowledge and how he was restored to health', 124,1–2) and no. 66 ('Von einem Scherer der seiner Mumen Senff under das Bluot schutt' / 'Concerning a barber who mixed mustard in his aunt's blood', 127,1–2), the barbers draw on their skills (dislocating a jaw; bloodletting) to teach a painful lesson to two foolish and vain individuals who fully deserve their fright and humiliation, in no. 65 the master-barber and his apprentices mean to help rather than punish the Swabian merchant's young servant. The misadventure is not explained or interpreted by the author-narrator in moral terms; nor are the consequences of the incident explored. There is no malice in those the lad encounters; the German who tries to point him in the right direction is not a spiteful trickster.[46] The story focuses instead on the outlandish consequences of a failure to communicate effectively and come to terms with a complex world, or at least with the unfamiliarity of the world beyond one's homeland.

Wickram's humour is comparatively gentle.[47] *Rollwagenbüchlein* 65 is certainly kinder on its unfortunate protagonist than the analogous text – in all likelihood known to Wickram – contained in Heinrich Bebel's *Libri facetiarum tres / Three Books of Witty Anecdotes* (1512–4), a highly influential Latin collection of over four hundred short anecdotes showcasing biting wit and/or outrageous stupidity.[48] In text III, 138, entitled 'De tribus Bavaris' / 'Concerning three Bavarians' (155), the same mishap befalls one of three companions who set off on a journey 'gratia morum in alienis terris discendorum' / 'in order to learn the customs of foreign lands' (155), and arrive in Northern Germany where they can hardly understand what is being said and where no one can understand them.[49] The folly and credulity of Bavarians is a familiar satirical theme in Bebel's work.[50] In this particular episode, however, the unwanted dental treatment is presented as deserved punishment for someone who vaunts their linguistic expertise for no good reason.[51] This moral dimension – of which there is no trace in Wickram's version – brings with it the licence for a rather more explicit and nastier reference to the process of extraction: 'dentes duos illi evulsit radicitus' / 'two of his teeth were pulled out roots and all' (156).

Less than 10 years after Wickram's *Rollwagenbüchlein*, another *Schwankbuch*, Hans Wilhelm Kirchhof's compendious *Wendunmuth / Book for Getting Rid of a Bad Mood* (1563),[52] features a reworking of Bebel's story – 'Von dreyen Baiern' / 'Concerning three Bavarians' (no. 200 [of 550!]) – in which the themes of the original Latin text are elaborated upon.[53] Thus, Kirchhof adds to Bebel's caricature of northern (Low) and southern (High) German accents by rendering the innkeeper's bafflement in direct speech: 'Wel, wel, sprach der wirt, ick verstah nich iw seuchten, dat gi qua de tanne hebben, ick schal iw helpen laten' / 'Well, well, said the innkeeper, I don't understand your words, but if there's something wrong with your teeth, I can get you help' (246). Another way is found to compound the aggressive comedy of the tooth extraction itself, when the 'patient' proves so troublesome that the barber is forced to enlist extra help to pin him down: 'Forderten der ursach halben einen starcken bauren, der auff dem marckt stund, hineyn …' / 'This obliged them to ask a strong-looking peasant, who was waiting in the marketplace, to come inside …' (247). Finally, the cultural ignorance and folly of the Bavarians is exaggerated by their response to their failed journey 'abroad', for upon returning home they tell anyone gullible enough to believe them that they travelled as far as 'die newe welt' / 'the New World' and 'der inseln America' / 'the islands of America' (247), where they encountered a savage people – 'ein genugsame anzeigung der unmenschlichkeit' / 'the ultimate proof of their inhumanity' (247) being their custom of pulling out the teeth of hungry foreigners (247). This account is meant to be blatantly far-fetched and thus ridiculous, yet on another textual level it expresses very concretely the deep-rooted fear of tooth extraction that permeates so many of the comic scenarios analysed here.

Conclusion

When a medical procedure was commonly understood to be so intrusive or violent – and by that measure 'unnatural' or inhumane – it was always likely to be regarded with some suspicion. And it is precisely this enduring suspicion that explains the recurrence and, it has to be said, success of 'teeth pulling' as a comic theme over the centuries. Of course, there are bound to be shifts of emphasis over such a long period of time. It is entirely in keeping with broader social developments, such as the rise of cities and medical professionalisation, that the sixteenth-century texts feature barber-surgeons in urban environments, for example. There would also seem to be some evidence for the diversification of types of comedy pertaining to dental treatment in the course of the fifteenth and sixteenth centuries. Yet in some ways these are relatively superficial changes that do little to mask two invariables.

First, the gender dynamics are strikingly uniform in these texts, where those who have their teeth forcibly removed are, without exception, men. The same predictable anti-feminism that casts women in the role of deceitful and scheming wife in a number of these stories also seems reluctant to envisage the pain of tooth extraction being spitefully or unintentionally inflicted on female characters. To torture a woman in this way was evidently perceived to be no laughing matter, but a scenario rather more appropriate for awful and awe-inspiring tales of martyrdom, as epitomised by the medieval legends surrounding St Apollonia. Weak and foolish male characters are quite different, however. The licence for laughing at their pain comes from the traditional expectation that men should know better, this being a fundamental tenet of conservative comedy from the Middle Ages to the present day.

Second, the drastic nature of the process of tooth extraction, the basic tools and techniques, and more importantly the mental images thereof, remained largely the same from the twelfth to the sixteenth centuries (and beyond). If toothache can be regarded as a 'psychic archetype of pain',[54] then dental treatment without pain relief represents a severe test of reason. What is at stake here is nothing less than the ability to accept pain in the present in order to avoid more pain in the future, or as the barber-surgeon in Kirchhof's story puts it: 'mit einer herterern und kürtzern [pein] die lengere zuo überwinden' / 'to put an end to the longer pain with a worse and shorter one' (247). In theory at least, to submit oneself to such treatment is to prove oneself a rational human being and to perform the operation itself is only humane, if born of the desire to lessen the suffering of others. Much of the comedy of dental treatment in medieval and early modern literature serves to deflate these twin ideals.

Notes

1. Pack, 'Entwicklung des Apollonia-Kults', 103. See also Pack, *Die historische Entwicklung des Apollonia-Kults*. Unless otherwise specified all translations in this article are mine.
2. Groß, 'Liebespfand und Höllenqual', 35.
3. '... devotam Deo offerens animam et castissimum tradens persequentibus corpus ad poenam. Igitur comprehensa beata virgine persecutores in ipsam crudeliter saevientes primo ei omnes dentes eius excusserunt ...', De Voragine. *Legenda aurea*, I, 445. Translation taken from De Voragine, *The Golden Legend*, I, 268.
4. Pack, 'Entwicklung des Apollonia-Kults', 25–30.
5. Camille, *Image on the Edge*, 76–97, especially 82–5.
6. Wells Cathedral in Somerset alone contains 11 toothache carvings according to Dunning et al., *Wells Cathedral*, 52–3.
7. This fundamental literary historical point is overlooked in the otherwise thought-provoking (if not entirely accurate) overview of the cultural significance of teeth by Ziolkowski, 'Telltale Teeth'.
8. In the courtly romance, teeth, if mentioned at all, are just another flawless feature in a beautiful lady's face; see Ziolkowski, 'Telltale Teeth', 13. In heroic epics, teeth are either ground in anger or knocked out as a function of the 'heroic' action; see also, with reference to Homer, Groß, 'Liebespfand und Höllenqual', 35–6.
9. For orientation in this extensive field, see Velten, *Scurrilitas*.
10. Ziolkowski's verdict on art history points in a similar direction: 'The paintings, drawings, and sculptures make it clear that men through the ages ... still find something grotesque, ridiculous, and degrading about toothache', 'Telltale Teeth', 15.
11. Groß, 'Liebespfand und Höllenqual', 31–5.
12. Bergson, *Le Rire*, 4.
13. Suchomski, *Lateinische Comediae des 12*, 205–35. Further references appear in the text.
14. To the extent that teeth were connotated with sexual potency, this extraction may also be understood as an attack on Decius's virility; for more on this association see Ziolkowski, 'Telltale Teeth', 11–2.
15. My thanks are due to Mererid Puw Davies for pointing this consonance out.
16. A manuscript variant for line 417 emphasises the brutality of the procedure by referring explicitly to the instrument the conspirators use: 'Incumbunt ergo torquentes forcipe dentem' / 'So they threw themselves into it and tortured the tooth with pincers', 290.
17. For more on '*Schadenfreude*' in pre-modern literary culture see Röcke, '"Schadenfreude ist die schönste Freude"'.
18. Compare the final lines of the preface or 'Argumentum' to the narrative: 'Cautius ut fugeres docui quid femina posset; / Esse potest una Lidia quoque tibi' / 'I have taught what a woman is capable of so that you may more sensibly avoid being duped. It may well be that you too have a Lidia at your side', 5–6.
19. 'Tu n'hai uno da questa parte il quale, per quello che mi paia, non solamente è magagnato ma egli è tutto fracido, e fermamente, se tu il terrain guari in bocca, egli guasterà quegli che so dallato: per che io ti consiglierei che tu il ne cacciassi fuori prima che l'opera andasse più inanzi', Boccaccio, *Decameron*, 618–9 / 'There's a tooth over here, on this side of your mouth, that as far as I can see is not only decayed, but rotten to the very core, and if it stays there much longer it will certainly contaminate the ones on either side of it. I advise you to have it out, before the damage grows worse', Boccaccio, *The Decameron*, 575. Further references follow in the text.

20. '… si ragiona delle beffe, le quali o per amore o per salvamento di loro le donne hanno già fatte a' suoi mariti, senza essersene avveduti o sì', 557.
21. '… per la qual cosa di quello che le giovani donne prendeno più piacere', 613.
22. '… che non sempre è la fortuna disposta, né sono al mondo tutti gli uomini abbagliati igualmente', 612.
23. Crane, *Exempla*, 104–5. Further references follow in the text.
24. Text taken from forthcoming critical edition by Ridder and Ziegeler, *Deutsche Versnovellistik des 13. bis 15. Jahrhunderts*, here no. 125. Further references follow in the text.
25. See Grubmüller, *Die Ordnung, der Witz und das Chaos*, 175–91.
26. Heinrich Kaufringer's *Drei listige Frauen* is one of three known versions of the text and is otherwise known as version B of the story, Kaufringer, *Werke*, I, 116–30. Further references follow in the text.
27. Compare the author-narrator's dismissive reference to the three husbands as 'geese' in the conclusion to the narrative: 'Nun lassen wir die trappen gen / ze holz, bis das si sich versten, / das si all gar trunken sind / und mit sehenden augen plind' / 'Now let's leave the ganders / to the forest until they realise / that they all are drunk / and are seeing yet blind', 543–6.
28. Kaufringer, *Werke*, I, 140–53.
29. There is consequently something of the martyr about the knight as he undergoes the torment of the (unnecessary) treatment: 'von pluot ran ain grosser pach / über sein antlutz vil clar' / 'a great stream of blood ran / over his face so fair', 112–3.
30. On this kind of narrative structure, see Bausinger, 'Bemerkungen zum Schwank'.
31. Whereas the knight's wife is never able to speak again ('die sprach nichtz dann: "läll läll läll." / also puost si ir missitat' / 'she said nothing but: "Lall, lall, lall." / That was how she made amends for her misdeed', 514–5), the knight evidently has no difficulties eating, 427–8. The injury done to his honour is what concerns him more in the rest of the narrative.
32. The presence of medical theory and practice as themes in the vernacular literature of this period has to be seen in the broader cultural context of northern European Humanism; see Coxon, 'Gelächter und Gesundheit'.
33. See Ridder, 'Fastnachtstheater'. Unless otherwise specified, the cited texts are taken from Von Keller, *Fastnachtspiele aus dem fünfzehnten Jahrhundert*. Further references follow in the text.
34. In these performances, anything and everything can acquire a euphemistic meaning, even toothache; compare *Ein hubsch vastnachtspil* ('An Amusing Shrovetide Play'), a so-called '*Gerichtsspiel*', where a man defends himself against the charge of having deflowered someone else's daughter: 'Richter, er leugt mich poslich an. / Sie klagt, ir tet gar we ein zan, / Ob ich ir mocht ein erznei geben. / Ich dacht, ir ist ein pruchwurz eben, / Die schlah ich ir pald in den munt, / So wirt sie auf der fart gesunt. / Hat sie dann seit geliden daran, / So hat es ir doch sanft getan' / 'Judge, this is a malicious accusation. / She complained of a bad toothache / [and asked] whether I could give her some medicine. / I thought that the herb in my breeches might do the trick / and that if I shoved it into her mouth, / it would cure her at once. / If she's suffered any pain since, / well, at the time it gave her plenty of pleasure', KF 24, 220, 21–8.
35. See also Wolf, 'Komische Inszenierung und Diskursvielfalt im geistlichen und im weltlichem Spiel', 301–26, especially 306–7.
36. Compare the physician's departing offer to the audience in *Des arzts vastnacht / The Doctor's Shrovetide*: 'Hört ir iemanz, der erznei wöll pflegen, / An hoher krankhait oder an nidern, / An zenn, an augen, an all seinn glidern, / Den weist zu uns, den wöll wir erzneien' / 'If you hear of anyone who needs some medicine / for a great illness or just a little one, / for their teeth, for their eyes or for all of their limbs, / point him in our direction; we want to cure him', KF 85, 699, 8–11.
37. Urine analysis per se was regarded as an entirely conventional and respectable form of medical diagnosis; see Stolberg, *Die Harnschau*.
38. Compare *Ein spil von einem arzt und einem kranken paur / A Play about a Doctor and a Sick Peasant*, where the quack is introduced to the audience by his own servant in the following dubious terms: 'Maister Viviam ist er genant, / In diesen landen unbekant, / Auch macht er die geraden lam, / Ein gut werk hat er nie getan, / Er kan die gesehenten plint Machen / Und den gesunten vertreiben das lachen, / Einen hat er bracht von dem leben, / Daruber sult ir brief und sigel sehen' / 'Master Viviam is his name, / unknown in these lands. / He can make those who walk lame. / He has never done a good deed. / He can make those who see blind; / he can rid the healthy of their laughter. / He's even taken someone's life: / he's got the document, signed and sealed, to prove it', KF 6, 59, 4–11.
39. Bauer, *Sterzinger Spiele*, 144–54. Further references appear in the text.

40. For a famous modern comic performance of tooth extraction see Laurel and Hardy's silent short film *Leave 'Em Laughing* (1928).
41. The absence of the wife at this point in the play (or the absence of any explicit evidence in the text that she is actually present) is not necessarily significant; to assume so would be perhaps to overestimate the thematic coherence of texts such as this. Nevertheless, to the modern reader at least, it is tempting to view the wife's (apparent) exclusion as a punishment for her dishonesty; her husband, the quack, is merely incompetent.
42. For an overview of the relevant texts see Dieckow, 'Um jetzt der *Katzenborischen art Rollwagenbücher* zu gedenken'.
43. Kipf, 'Schwankbuch'.
44. Wickram, *Das Rollwagenbüchlein*.
45. See also Kipf, 'Schwankbuch', 89–90.
46. More malicious or spiteful comedy was still always an option in these *Schwankbücher*; compare story no. 35 of Michael Lindener's *Katzipori* (1558), where a trickster avoids paying a merchant by leading the latter's servant to a barber-surgeon for unwanted and unnecessary tooth extraction, Lindener, *Schwankbücher*, I, 101–2.
47. Kartschoke, 'Vom erzeugten zum erzählten Lachen'.
48. Kipf, *Cluoge geschichten*, 224–94.
49. Bebermeyer, *Heinrich Bebels Facetien*, 155–6.
50. In both II, 35 ('De quodam Bavaro' / 'A Certain Bavarian') and II, 43 ('De Bavaro lentes comedente' / 'A Bavarian Eating Lentils'), Bavarians are characterised most disparagingly as foolish and hapless travellers.
51. The vanity of this individual is such that even when he returns to his two companions he lies about what happened, claiming that he would have lost more teeth if he had not been 'adeo peritus et edoctus' / 'so very proficient and learned' (156) in the local dialect.
52. See also Kipf, 'Schwankbuch', 84–5.
53. Kirchhof, *Wendunmuth*, 246–7. Kirchhof creates a cluster of all of Bebel's anti-Bavarian anecdotes at this point in his collection with his versions of Bebel II, 35 and II, 43 following immediately after 'Concerning three Bavarians' (no. 200): 'Ein Baier hatt ein wirt betrogen' / 'An innkeeper deceived by a Bavarian' (no. 201); 'Ein Baier isset linsen' / 'A Bavarian eats lentils' (no. 202).
54. Kunzle, 'The Art of Pulling Teeth', 29.

Bibliography

Bauer, Werner M., ed. *Sterzinger Spiele: Die weltlichen Spiele des Sterzinger Spielarchivs nach den Originalhandschriften (1510–1535) von Vigil Raber und nach der Ausgabe Oswald Zingerles (1886)*. Vienna: Österreichischer Bundesverlag, 1982.

Bausinger, Hermann. 'Bemerkungen zum Schwank und seinen Formtypen', *Fabula: Zeitschrift für Erzählforschung* 9, no. 1–3 (1967): 118–36.

Bebermeyer, Gustav, ed. *Heinrich Bebels Facetien: Drei Bücher*. Leipzig: Hiersemann, 1931.

Bergson, Henri. *Le Rire: Essai sur la signification du comique*. Paris: Alcan, 1900.

Boccaccio, Giovanni. *The Decameron*, translated by G.H. McWilliam. Harmondsworth: Penguin, 1972.

Boccaccio, Giovanni. *Decameron*, edited by Vittore Branca. Milan: Mondadori, 1985.

Camille, Michael. *Image on the Edge: The Margins of Medieval Art*. Cambridge, MA: Harvard University Press, 1992.

Coxon, Sebastian. 'Gelächter und Gesundheit: Humanistische Thematik im *Quacksalber* des Hans Folz?'. In *Humanismus in der deutschen Literatur des Mittelalters und der Frühen Neuzeit, XVII: Anglo-German Colloquium Hofgeismar 2003*, edited by Nicola McLelland, Hans-Jochen Schiewer and Stefanie Schmitt, 383–98. Tübingen: Niemeyer, 2008.

Crane, Thomas Frederick, ed. *The Exempla; or Illustrative Stories from the Sermones Vulgares of Jacques de Vitry*. London: Folk-Lore Society, 1890.

De Voragine, Jacobus. *The Golden Legend: Readings on the Saints*, translated by William Granger Ryan. Princeton: Princeton University Press, 1993.

De Voragine, Jacobus. *Legenda aurea*, edited by Giovanni Paolo Maggioni. 2nd ed. Florence: SISMEL-Edizioni del Galluzzo, 1998.

Dieckow, Peter C.M. 'Um jetzt der *Katzenborischen art Rollwagenbücher* zu gedenken: Zur Erforschung deutschsprachiger Prosaerzählsammlungen aus der zweiten Hälfte des 16. Jahrhunderts', *Euphorion* 90 (1996): 76–133.

Dunning, Robert, Richard Lewis and Melvyn Matthews. *Wells Cathedral: "The Minster beside the Great Spring Called Wiela"*. London: Scala, 2005.

Groß, Dominik. 'Zwischen Liebespfand und Höllenqual: Zähne, Zahnschmerzen und Zahnbehandler im Spiegel der Literatur', *Jahrbuch für Literatur und Medizin* 1 (2007): 31–49.

Grubmüller, Klaus. *Die Ordnung, der Witz und das Chaos: Eine Geschichte der europäischen Novellistik im Mittelalter: Fabliau – Märe – Novelle*. Tübingen: Niemeyer, 2006.

Kartschoke, Dieter. 'Vom erzeugten zum erzählten Lachen: Die Auflösung der Pointenstruktur in Jörg Wickrams *Rollwagenbüchlein*'. In *Kleinere Erzählformen des 15. und 16. Jahrhunderts*, edited by Walter Haug and Burghart Wachinger, 71–105. Tübingen: Niemeyer, 1993.

Kaufringer, Heinrich. *Werke*, edited by Paul Sappler. Tübingen: Niemeyer, 1972.

Kipf, Johannes Klaus. *Cluoge geschichten: Humanistische Fazetienliteratur im deutschen Sprachraum*. Stuttgart: Hirzel, 2010.

Kipf, Johannes Klaus. 'Das Schwankbuch als frühneuzeitlicher Buchtyp: Dargestellt am Beispiel von Jörg Wickrams *Rollwagenbüchlein* (1555)'. In *Ordentliche Unordnung: Metamorphosen des Schwanks vom Mittelalter bis zur Moderne: Festschrift für Michael Schilling*, edited by Bernhard Jahn, Dirk Rose and Thorsten Unger, 79–92. Heidelberg: Universitätsverlag Winter, 2014.

Kirchhof, Hans Wilhelm. *Wendunmuth*, edited by Hermann Österley. Stuttgart: Litterarischer Verein, 1869.

Kunzle, David. 'The Art of Pulling Teeth in the Seventeenth and Nineteenth Centuries: From Public Martyrdom to Private Nightmare and Political Struggle'. In *Fragments for a History of the Human Body, Part Three*, edited by Michael Feher, 28–89. New York: Zone, 1989.

Lindener, Michael. *Schwankbücher: Rastbüchlein und Katzipori*, edited by Kyra Heidemann. Bern: Peter Lang, 1991.

Pack, Dieter. 'Die historische Entwicklung des Apollonia-Kults unter besonderer Berücksichtigung des sog: "Kleinen Andachtsbildes"'. PhD thesis, Universität Würzburg, 2003.

Pack, Dieter. *Die historische Entwicklung des Apollonia-Kults unter besonderer Berücksichtigung des sog: 'kleinen Andachtsbildes'*. Würzburg: Königshausen & Neumann, 2005.

Ridder, Klaus. 'Fastnachtstheater: Städtische Ordnung und fastnächtliche Verkehrung'. In *Fastnachtspiele: Weltliches Schauspiel in literarischen und kulturellen Kontexten*, edited by Klaus Ridder, 65–82. Tübingen: Niemeyer, 2009.

Ridder, Klaus and Hans-Joachim Ziegeler, eds. *Deutsche Versnovellistik des 13. bis 15. Jahrhunderts*. Basel and Berlin: Schwabe, forthcoming.

Röcke, Werner. '"Schadenfreude ist die schönste Freude": Formen aggressiven Gelächters in der Literatur der Antike und des Mittelalters'. In *Pathos, Affekt, Emotion: Transformationen der Antike*, edited by Martin Harbsmeier and Sebastian Möckel, 277–96. Frankfurt am Main: Suhrkamp, 2009.

Stolberg, Michael. *Die Harnschau: Eine Kultur- und Alltagsgeschichte*. Cologne: Böhlau, 2009.

Suchomski, Joachim, ed. *Lateinische Comediae des 12. Jahrhunderts*. Darmstadt: Wissenschaftliche Buchgesellschaft, 1979.

Velten, Hans Rudolf. *Scurrilitas: Das Lachen, die Komik und der Körper in Literatur und Kultur des Spätmittelalters und der Frühen Neuzeit*. Tübingen: Narr Francke Attempto, 2017.

Von Keller, Adelbert, ed. *Fastnachtspiele aus dem fünfzehnten Jahrhundert*. Stuttgart: Litterarischer Verein, 1853–58.

Wickram, Georg. *Das Rollwagenbüchlein*, edited by Hans-Gert Roloff. Berlin: De Gruyter, 1973.

Wolf, Gerhard. 'Komische Inszenierung und Diskursvielfalt im geistlichen und im weltlichen Spiel: Das "Erlauer Osterspiel" und die Nürnberger Arztspiele K 82 und K 6'. In *Fastnachtspiele: Weltliches Schauspiel in literarischen und kulturellen Kontexten*, edited by Klaus Ridder, 301–26. Tübingen: Niemeyer, 2009.

Ziolkowski, Theodore. 'The Telltale Teeth: Psychodontia to Sociodontia', *PMLA* 91, no. 1 (1976): 9–22.

3

Combat, Military Medicine and Psychiatric Disorders during and after the Wars of Unification

Mark Hewitson

Preface

The Introduction to this volume draws attention to the Constitution of the World Health Organization (WHO), which was signed by 61 countries under the auspices of the United Nations (UN) on 22 July 1946. It suggests, too, that a close comparative reading of supposedly universal documents such as the Constitution, and other kinds of text, such as life-writing, can be productive for a complex understanding of the relationships between medicine and humanity (or inhumanity), as the present chapter demonstrates.

The WHO Constitution confirmed that 'Governments have a responsibility for the health of their peoples which can be fulfilled only by the provision of adequate health and social measures.' In wartime, however, governments deliberately endanger the health of their peoples by forcing citizens to fight and to suffer injury and death. This historical responsibility of states for the well-being of their populations developed in the nineteenth and twentieth centuries during a period of mass warfare and conscription, in which all men of fighting age and an increasing number of civilians faced 'rationalised slaughter'.[1] Inhumane treatment and humanity, as understood by philosophers, doctors and humanists of different kinds in the wake of the Enlightenment, often coexisted under such conditions.[2]

In the nineteenth century, most commentators and participants, including soldiers and physicians, considered war to be inevitable. What medics were seeking to do, therefore, was to lessen the suffering and heal wounds caused by states in their conflicts with each other. Their actions – and those of later military psychiatrists – are to be understood in this context. The first international codification of the conduct of war took place in the second half of the nineteenth century, after wars in Crimea (1853–6) and Italy (1859). The resulting Geneva Convention of 22 August 1864, which was signed by 12 states including Denmark and Prussia (but not Austria), only extended to care for the wounded on the battlefield by medics and stretcher-bearers, all of whom were to be treated as neutral civilians, not military enemies.[3] Treaties regulating the taking of prisoners, the definition and treatment of civilians, the use and proscription of specified weapons and shells, and the general conduct of war did not come into existence until the two Hague Conventions of 1899 and 1907. Against this background, the efforts of military doctors and early psychiatrists of war seem modest from a twentieth and twenty-first-century perspective, often overwhelmed by the scale of the violence that characterised modern warfare.[4] This chapter examines, through a reading of autobiographical literature, how medics and soldiers viewed the role of medicine at such a critical but contradictory nexus, when subjects' bodies and minds were tested in an extreme fashion.[5]

Introduction

Medical responses to injuries incurred in modern wars have been informed by broader questions about combat. Can soldiers and civilians in purportedly civilised, urban, industrial societies – or post-industrial societies – go to war in the old sense of symmetrical warfare, with combatants on each side facing similar types and risks of injury and death? This problematic hinges to a significant extent on the literature about combat readiness and combat fatigue in the Second World War, and to a lesser extent the Vietnam War and wars in Iraq (sometimes referred to as 'new wars').[6] In particular, it rests on the definition of and discussions about post-traumatic stress disorder (PTSD).[7] The degree of humanity – or inhumanity – displayed by medics has come, during the course of the last century, to rest to a considerable extent on their diagnosis and treatment of warfare's psychological and physiological effects. This chapter contrasts such a state of affairs with the medical assumptions and practices of the nineteenth century.

The term 'post-traumatic stress disorder' was first included in the *Diagnostic and Statistical Manual* (DSM) of the American Psychiatric Association in 1980, but it referred to symptoms that had been described earlier under the heading of combat stress, 'trauma', shell shock or 'war neurosis' – as the first cases in 1870–1 were labelled. The diagnostic criteria of the DSM related to someone who had:

> experienced an event that is outside the range of usual human experience and that would be markedly distressing to almost anyone, e.g., a serious threat to one's life or physical integrity; a serious threat or harm to one's children, spouse, or other close relatives and friends; sudden destruction to one's home or community; or seeing another person who has recently been, or is being, seriously injured or killed as the result of an accident or physical violence.[8]

The traumatic event had to be re-experienced in the form of 'recurrent and intrusive distressing recollections of the event', 'recurrent distressing dreams of the event', 'sudden acting or feeling as if the traumatic event were recurring' (including hallucinations, flashback episodes and reliving the experience), and 'intense psychological distress at exposure to events that symbolize or resemble an aspect of the traumatic event (for instance, anniversaries of the trauma)'.[9] It was also typical to avoid 'stimuli associated with the trauma or numbing of general responsiveness (not present before the trauma)', indicated by 'efforts to avoid thoughts or feelings associated with the trauma, ... activities or situations that arouse recollections of the trauma', 'inability to recall an important aspect of the trauma', 'markedly diminished interest in significant activities, ... feelings of detachment or estrangement from others, restricted range of affect, e.g., unable to have loving feelings', and a 'sense of a foreshortened future, e.g., does not expect to have a career, marriage, or children, or a long life'.[10] In some cases, 'symptoms of increased arousal could also be present: insomnia, 'irritability or outbursts of anger, difficulty concentrating, hypervigilance, exaggerated startle response', and 'physiologic reactivity upon exposure to events that symbolize or resemble an aspect of the traumatic event'.[11]

A study of the Vietnam War in 1990 commissioned by the Veterans' Administration found that 15 per cent of all male veterans met all criteria of PTSD, and 11 per cent partially, or 830,000 cases overall out of 2.9 million Americans who served in Vietnam. In the Second World War, 23 per cent of all US evacuations from the fighting front had taken place because of psychiatric or neurological causes.[12] Overall, 1.3 million American soldiers were diagnosed with psychological disturbances in the Second World War, compared to 613,047 German soldiers in the First World War (of whom just under 200,000 were diagnosed as 'war neurotics').[13] These are high proportions in circumstances where disclosure has traditionally been difficult, associated with charges of cowardice, weakness and lack of patriotism on the one hand, and characterised by official neglect and ignorance on the other hand. In the previous German wars – the 'wars of unification', fifty years earlier – most military doctors paid no attention at all to the psychological impact of military conflict. The first psychiatric report by the German military was published in the mid-1880s and it detailed a minuscule number of cases. Here, I investigate the grey areas that these circumstances created, considering the symptoms and treatment of those who did attract medical attention, alongside the millions of soldiers who were not diagnosed as psychiatric cases but who were profoundly affected by combat in a psychological sense.[14]

This chapter asks how differing conceptions of humanity and inhumanity were transformed by soldiers' exposure to modern forms of warfare in Germany, which were typified by artillery and dismemberment. It examines the boundaries established by psychiatrists, military doctors and other commentators between normally functioning humans and 'deviants', and between normal human responses to combat and lapses into barbarism and bestiality. Historians have already carried out extensive research into the diagnosis and treatment of the German cases of 'diseases of the nervous system' suffered by combatants between 1914 and 1918. They describe a decisive shift among psychiatrists, who were widely employed within the German army, away from theses concerning 'traumatic neuroses', which were held to be caused by physical events and mental shocks, to diagnoses of 'male hysteria', which focused on the pre-traumatic constitutional weaknesses of patients.[15] Psychoanalysts, including Sigmund Freud, contested such arguments about human weakness, positing that the physical conditions of modern warfare had removed civilised inhibitions, revealed the significance of the death wish alongside libido, and exposed the limits of humanity.[16] This study examines the relationship between doctors' and, more rarely, psychiatrists' accounts and those of soldiers themselves in the period before the First World War, asking how medics understood the impact of modern warfare between 1864 and 1871.

Military Doctors' Responses to the Injuries of Modern Warfare

The wars of unification stood in the interstices between the introduction of modern warfare and the beginnings of internationally agreed laws of war and humanitarianism. The Crimean War witnessed the exploitation of new technologies of warfare, marking it out from previous wars. More destructive, accurate and longer-range bullets and shells increased the need for skirmishers and protected positions and reduced the role of infantry formations, hand-to-hand fighting and cavalry charges, as well as producing more deadly, gruesome wounds and more effective medical means of treating such wounds.[17] At the same time, the conflict in 1864 between Prussia, Austria and Denmark, all of which were held to be civilised states, was believed by some to be the first 'humanitarian' war.[18] Jean Henri Dunant, who had published *Un Souvenir de Solférino* in 1862 about his experiences in the Franco–Austrian War of 1859, had gone on to found the International Committee for Relief to the Wounded – later becoming the Red Cross – in February 1863 with other notables from Geneva. Its first conference in October of the same year had been attended by official delegates from Prussia, Austria, Bavaria, Saxony, Baden and the Electorate of Hesse, as well as Russia, Britain, France, Italy, Spain, the Netherlands, Sweden and Norway. It had resolved, among other things, to protect and guarantee the neutrality of wounded soldiers and to use volunteers, recognisable by the red cross on their white armband, to provide relief on the battlefield. When war broke out the following year, the committee sent an envoy, Louis Appia, to Prussian and Austrian headquarters, where he dined with the Prussian commander Friedrich Heinrich Ernst von Wrangel, and was allowed free access to the fighting front.[19]

Prussian officers were unsentimental about the wounding of soldiers, but at least some commanders appear to have modified their view of the human costs of warfare, faced with new technologies of killing and changing civilian attitudes to violence and death. No war, remarked Helmuth von Moltke, 'has ever been conducted with more humanity than this one'.[20] Prussian military doctors such as the Schleswig-born Friedrich von Esmarch, one of the founders of modern field surgery, were known in the mid-nineteenth century for their innovations in first aid, bandaging, prostheses, transport for the wounded, and the use of chloroform.[21] They had also encouraged religious associations – most famously, the Order of St John – to look after soldiers in the field. Notwithstanding warnings about the impact of modern weaponry, and a long and well-known history of the agony of the wounded in battle, it was anticipated that the war between Denmark, Prussia and Austria would be more humane than previous conflicts.

In the event, the war of Prussia and Austria against Denmark was destructive, albeit on a comparatively small scale, as a result of the use of modern technologies such as breech-loading needle-guns, new types of bullet and artillery shell, ironclad steamships, trenches, fortifications and attrition.[22] The same types of warfare were typical of 1866 and 1870–1 but with much larger armies. In 1864, Appia, who had visited the main battlefield at Düppel on the afternoon of 18 April, wrote to Dunant and the International Committee for Relief to the Wounded to describe what he had witnessed: 'The streams are flooded with blood, one finds shreds of uniforms and personal things', 'here lie all sorts of grenades, spiked grenades, bullets, grapeshot cartridges, and there are shells the size of my head'.[23] 'The landscape is completely ploughed by grenade explosions', he continued:

> A bit further on, I went past twenty-five corpses, which lay on a plank, ready to be buried in a mass grave. Beside them, there are already two mass graves with a cross, on which was written, 'Here rest 308 brave soldiers, who have fallen for the fatherland.'[24]

Army doctors, who had started to record causes and types of injury and death, showed how combat had changed, but generally remained matter of fact. In his *General-Bericht* on the Danish war, the chief medical officer of the Prussian army, Gottfried Friedrich Franz Loeffler, gave an objective account of the injuries sustained, reproducing the medical notes of 197 cases. His main interest was to improve military medicine. Although he was mindful that the campaign of 1864 was 'more limited in its dimensions and was conducted under exceptionally favourable conditions', he saw it as 'the first large practical test, not only of the increase of the army's ability to strike and its energetic reforms, but also the feasibility of the principles on which the improvement of the military medical establishment rested'.[25] The report itself was explicitly connected by Loeffler to 'the wonderful achievements of a Miss Nightingale in the Crimean War' and to 'the international conference in Geneva in October 1863', the formulation of whose regulations the conflict had actually preceded.[26]

Unlike the reputedly humanist Dunant, the Prussian medical chief's interest in the incidence of injury was primarily technical, but he betrayed in passing how the physical impact of warfare had altered, with fewer deaths from illness than in the past (about a quarter of cases) and more from shrapnel and bullet wounds (nearly three quarters of cases).[27] Among the Prussians, 702 out of 738 deaths and 2,388 of 2,443 injuries were the result of gun and cannon shot rather than bayonets (1 death, 26 woundings), swords (1 death, 22 woundings), or rifle butts and clubs (no deaths, 5 woundings).[28] In this war, noted Loeffler, troops were most likely to die outright from artillery and rifle fire, or from complications arising from more severe wounding through gunshot, in contrast to the Revolutionary and Napoleonic Wars (and even the Crimean War), when they more often perished because of cold, hunger or sickness.[29] In other words, the soldiers of the wars of liberation frequently died of 'natural' causes, not far removed from those of their daily lives, while combatants in 1864 were incapacitated and died in an unaccustomed, more terrifying way, with their wounds rendered worse by new kinds of weaponry and projectiles.

The bullet wounds made by round shot had often been dismissed by the experienced soldiers of previous wars, but such shot had been 'replaced by extended shot from an extended barrel' in the wars of unification. 'For hand weapons, this change was complete in 1864', remarked Loeffler: 'Cylindrical grenades with explosive detonators were already predominant on the Prussian side.'[30] The preponderance of these weapons and shells explained, together with improvements in military medicine and 'assured connections to a nearby theatre of war in a rich land', why Prussian casualties were low.[31] Loeffler was well aware that the use of such weaponry on both sides (many Danish artillery shells were still round) in a war of movement and battles of 'annihilation' would be much more destructive.[32] 'With the extraordinary increase in the portability and accuracy of the new precision weapons – cannon as well as guns – the number of hits entered into a new relationship to the number of combatants, and serious injury becomes all the more overwhelming the greater the distances are', he warned.[33]

Much attention had already been devoted to new guns, artillery, bullets and missiles in the military literature, wrote Loeffler in 1867.[34] Less attention had been given to the physical impact of such weapons. 'Not only the number, but – much more – the type of wounding could be used to characterise each campaign, and individual actions in each campaign, if one were able to gain and to give a complete overview', he lamented: 'Until now, that has not happened. A view of *the dead on the battlefield* was thought of to such a limited extent that the injuries of the *fallen* could scarcely come into consideration.'[35] Statistics had been collected during the Crimean War and the American Civil War, but they remained incomplete, with the best figures for the former deriving from the wounded who were evacuated to Constantinople and with the principal study of the latter ignorant of the 'outcome [of treatment] for thousands' of the 77,775 soldiers suffering from artillery and gunshot wounds.[36] With modern shells, it was common for 'more or less heavy and angular pieces' to splinter, 'which cause the most terrible mutilation'.[37] The majority of Prussian wounds – about 80 per cent – were caused by rifle fire, a figure considerably higher than estimates for the Danish wounded, where dominant and more modern Prussian artillery caused a higher proportion of casualties. Like shrapnel, bullets 'change their form on hitting bone, split and, by carrying on their trajectory as separate pieces or by lying between the fragments of bone, make the wound more complicated and make healing more difficult'.[38] Prussian soldiers suffered these types of injuries in 1866 and, especially, in 1870.

Professionalism, Indifference and Disgust

Many field doctors seem to have maintained a tradition of indifference to soldiers' suffering in the wars of unification, concentrating for the good of science – when they showed any interest at all – on the diverse nature of soldiers' injuries.[39] Thus, in 1866, Ernst von Bergmann, an academic surgeon from Dorpat, was delighted finally to see about thirty wounded men in a hospital in Zittau. 'There were very nice wounds there', he wrote: 'we saw a piece of cannon shot, weighing more than three pounds, cutting its way out of a Prussian *Landwehrmann*', causing them such excitement that they had to undergo the subsequent 'pain' of missing their train towards the fighting.[40] For the army doctor Karl-Ludwig August Stahmann, the main aim of his work was the 'enrichment of his knowledge', which was hindered by his position in the front line of fighting – as a regimental medic – and his inability to follow up and study the progress of his cases.[41] These cases, as in 1864, were made up principally of shot wounds produced by bullets and shells, along with several bayonet and sabre cuts, which – although they were in the face or head in some instances – often healed.[42] The effects of wounding by shells depended on whether the shot was solid (four-pounders, six-pounders and twelve-pounders) or hollow (grenades), in which case injuries were similar to those caused by shrapnel and grapeshot. 'Of all these types of shot, fragments are rarely found in the body of the wounded', recorded Stahmann, 'because, naturally, they kill for the most part, immediately or soon'.[43] 'That many instances of death occur on the battlefield as a result of such immense wounds, we saw in the fortifications of Lipa', the doctor continued.[44] Splinters of shrapnel could travel up to 200 yards, ranging from invisible shards to large fragments that 'smash and tear bones, vessels and nerves', all of which were common in the field hospital of Sadowa on 3 July.[45]

Bullet wounds were still more commonplace, creating different incisions on entry and exit, 'in the form of a star, a slit etc.'.[46] The Austrian front-loading musket, which was based on the 'Lorenz-Wilkinson system', was effective over a range up to nine hundred yards. The Prussian needle-gun extended beyond one thousand yards and could be loaded in a lying position, which meant that infantrymen were more often hit in the head than their Habsburg counterparts, even though less frequently injured overall.[47] Austrian bullets, which more regularly split on impact, caused more tissue damage, which was 'indifferent' from a military point of view (since 'it is a question of making as large a number as possible no longer capable of fighting'), but which remained relevant from a medical one.[48] Typical cases included Musketeer K., who was shot in the upper jaw on the right-hand side, with the bullet smashing his palate and taking two incisors with it, boring a hole in the tongue, penetrating down into the left side of the throat and exiting the body near the left shoulder blade.[49] Much of the treatment of such wounds proceeded without chloroform, which was reserved for 'larger operations' such as amputation:

> For smaller operations, like the cutting out of superficially embedded bullets, the amputation of fingers and toes, scars from sabre wounds, the extraction of bullets etc., we would not use chloroform because the pain cannot be compared to the dangers which the use of chloroform brings with it.[50]

Doctors such as Stahmann appeared to be more or less inured to soldiers' suffering and to the horrors of the battlefield.

Not all medics were so indifferent.[51] Most showed concern for their patients, tempered by a sense of scientific detachment and desensitisation as a consequence of the sheer volume of injuries. One hospital inspector working in Dresden wrote on 16 July 1866 that more than fifty amputations per day were being carried out – 'for one an arm, for another a leg' – and that 'many, many tears flow here and the groaning and pain is without end'.[52] The Prussian doctor Heinrich Fritsch, working in France in 1870–1, continued to believe that 'much has got better and will become even better as a result of the Geneva Convention', yet he went on to concede that this would be of little comfort to civilians who had become 'better, milder, more compassionate and perhaps softer'.[53] Treatments had improved marginally during the 1860s for some injuries – for example, bullet wounds to the chest – but mortality from other wounds remained high: thus, for hospitalised leg wounds it varied between about 25 per cent and more than 60 per cent.[54] It has been estimated that more than 50 per cent of the wounded might eventually have died as a result of their injuries (notwithstanding official figures indicating a death rate of 25 per cent).[55] Such statistics seemed to disprove anecdotal evidence that 'seriously wounded men [had] returned after healing to duty at the front two or even three times, one after the other'.[56] Some dressing stations and field hospitals had improved, with soldiers being treated more quickly, but others were notorious for their death rates.[57] The castle at Sedan, which received more than two thousand wounded between mid-September 1870 and the end of February 1871, was said to be 'infected' and had an 'unfavourable' overall mortality rate of almost 10 per cent, with more than two thirds of operations there ending in the death of the patient.[58]

Although some modern weapons were less bloody (the bullets of *chassepots* creating only 'a small hole', for instance), others – such as the Prussian needle-gun, with its long, lead bullets – caused 'enormous wounds' and smashed bones.[59] The British guns supplied to *francs-tireurs* and the troops of Garibaldi left 'quite enormous, great holes in soft tissue' up to 7 cm in diameter.[60] The total number of such injuries had increased dramatically in 1870–1 (with between 115,000 and 135,000 dead and wounded on the German side), compared to the shorter war of 1866 and the smaller-scale, less intensive one of 1864.[61] The 'bloody work' of treating these types of cases – 'the great amount of blood and the many injuries' – transported even hardened military doctors into 'a painful mood', as Gustav Waltz described his daily experience of a field hospital.[62] In rooms full of corpses, observing barely identifiable bones protruding through tissue, Fritsch's positive expectations of war had dissolved: 'I knew of nothing that had affected me more and made me more unhappy in the entire war than these conditions' in a field hospital.[63] Soldiers' suffering in a military hospital was worse than the sight of a 'fresh battlefield', which was itself 'terrible'.[64] 'War, creating hatred, passion and the collision of duties, tore one heart from another', observed Fritsch: 'The misery and misfortune which such a time casts over a true family life together is immeasurable and endless, in great things and small. Oh – wish on no one that a time like this returns!'[65] 'Anyone with any fantasy' would prefer to be blind or to veil 'the cold skeleton of facts', which 'such hardship, suffering and heart-felt pain' had 'spread amongst people'.[66] The painfulness of modern warfare was difficult even for doctors – with their professional experience of pain – to ignore.

Doctors were generally more detached from the suffering of soldiers than many combatants. Julius Naundorff, a doctor working under the aegis of the 'red cross', was one exception who demonstrated – in 1866 – what conditions were like without the filter of medical professionalism. His hope was to bring an end to the conditions that had characterised battle until then. In previous conflicts, soldiers remained 'behind on the bloody battlefield with burning pain, calling out for refreshment and help'.[67] In Naundorff's ideal war, 'help and care for their wounds would not be lacking, which they need and without delay, and which itself is so often deadly or can at least have the loss of the wounded limb as a consequence'. Further, soldiers should not have 'the worse fate of expecting to become the terrible victim of those creatures greedy for booty – the hyenas of the battlefield – who fall on the defenceless for plunder, murdering those still living in order to be able to rob them all the more securely, as they do the dead'.[68] Such conditions were not 'pictures of fantasy' or 'from long ago', but 'how it has been in recent times'.[69] Naundorff's impression of war was based on his experiences of 1866. 'Whoever has not seen a battle himself can only with difficulty summon up a picture of the apparent disorder, the wild on-top-of-each-other, which predominates within its sphere', and is kept in check only by 'the power of discipline' of 'good soldiers', degenerating into chaos with the involvement of 'truly disciplined troops' or with any divergence from the 'mechanical norms' of 'an unchangeable order'.[70] 'Under the impression of indescribable horrors', the soldier began to 'fail in his duty' and the 'machine, whose action is not regulated precisely for every case, starts to falter'.[71]

As they approached the 'hot point of a battle', Naundorff and a group of medics were surrounded by all kinds of wounded men:

> Kugeln umschwirren sie so dicht, daβ man sie zu sehen glaubt. Es ist als befänden sie sich inmitten eines summenden Bienenschwarmes. Über ihnen, neben ihnen, überall die pfeifenden Töne, die Musik der Schlacht, nur unterbrochen durch das tiefere Summen und Rauschen der Voll- und Hohlkugeln, welche die Geschütze schleudern.
>
> Geschlossene Bataillone rücken an ihnen vorüber, zum Sturm; sie werden bald genug ihre Trümmer von der Erde auszusuchen haben… .
>
> Die Erde zittert, wie bei einem tobenden Orkan. Sie stäubt hier und dort empor, wenn die in Dampf gehüllte Kugel sie aufwühlt… . 'Vorwärts, Kameraden,' sagt der Unteroffizier zu seinen stutzenden Leuten, – sie beugen dann und wann ihre Häupter. Dem Einen streift eine Kugel den Arm. Man legt einen Verband an. Wer fragt weiter darnach? Einem Andern wird die Verbandtasche von einem Granatsplitter zerrissen. 'Besser, als wenn es der Leib gewesen wäre,' meint sein Kamerad… . Sie achten dessen nicht, sie eilen vorwärts, getreu ihrer Pflicht. An Todten vorüber,

denen sie nicht mehr zu helfen vermögen, vorbei an Hügeln von Leichen. Einige dieser Todten haben den Ausdruck der Ruhe auf ihrem Antlitz. Es sind die, welchen die Kugeln ein schnelles Ende, den wahren seligen Soldatentod im 'Jubel der Schlacht' gaben. Aber eine weit größere Zahl trägt die Spur eines entsetzlichen Todeskampfes an sich. Mit starren ausgestreckten Gliedern, die Hände in die Erde gebohrt, die Augen weit und unnatürlich geöffnet, die Haare des Bartes borstig aufgerichtet und mit einem unheimliches und kramphaftes Lächeln um den Mund, welches die zusammengepreßten Zähne sehen läßt, – so liegen sie da, hier, dort, überall, Bilder des Todes, welche eine lange Zeit hindurch, wachend und schlafend, vor unserm geistigen Auge zu schweben scheinen.

An den Hängen der Hügel, in den Hohlwegen liegen sie aufgetürmt, und eine träge, dunkle Fluth sickert von ihnen aus und sammelt sich in den Senkungen des Bodens zu blutigen Lachen, welche dampfen. Es riecht nach Pulver und nach Blut und es ist nicht ohne Grund, wenn man diesem eigentümlich spezifischen Blutgeruch eine betäubende und wilderregende Kraft zuschreibt. Indem er durch die Sinne zu dem Gehirn und bis zu den Quellen des Lebens steigt, gießt er die in Adern eine fieberhafte Aufregung.

Die wilden Völker trinken Blut, ehe sie sich mit der Wuth und der Gier des Tigers in ihre grausamen Kämpfe stürzen.

Bullets whizz around them so thickly that one thinks one sees them. It is as if they found themselves in the middle of a buzzing swarm of bees. Above them, around them, everywhere the whistling tones, the music of battle, only interrupted by the humming and din of solid and hollow shells which the cannon hurl out. Closed battalions push forward towards them; soon enough, they will have to pick out their own rubble from the earth....

The earth shakes, as during a raging hurricane.... 'Forwards, comrades,' says an NCO to his men in support – they lower their heads now and then. A bullet glances the arm of one. One puts on a bandage. Who asks anything about it? The bag of bandages was ripped from another by grenade splinter. 'Better than if it had been the body', says my comrade.... They pay no attention to it, they rush forwards, true to their duty. Past the dead, whom they are no longer able to help, past hills of corpses. Some of these have an expression of calm on their faces. They are the ones who have been given a quick end, the true, ecstatic death of the soldier in 'the joy of battle'.

But a far greater number carry the trace of a terrible struggle with death. With rigid, outstretched limbs, their hands drilled into the earth, their eyes distant and unnaturally wide open, the hair of their beards bristling on end and covered with a sticky slime, often a haunting and desperate smile on their lips, which allows their teeth to be seen, pressed together – they lie here, there and all over, images of death, which seem to flicker before our spiritual eyes, waking and sleeping, for a long time.

On the rise of the hills and in hollows, they lie piled up, and a sluggish, dark flood seeps from them and collects in the depressions of the ground to form bloody puddles, which steam. It smells of gunpowder and blood, and it is not without reason when one attributes an intoxicating and wild, inflaming energy to this unusual, particular smell of blood. By climbing from the senses to the brain and to the sources of life, it pours into the arteries a feverish excitement.

Wild peoples drink blood before they leap into their cruel battles with the rage and hunger of a tiger.[72]

Parts of Naundorff's account fused fantasy and streams of consciousness, as doctors – 'covered over and again with blood' – could 'no longer carry out their difficult work', since they, too, were humans, and what they were being asked to do was 'beyond the power of humanity'.[73] In other parts, the medic revealed unimagined horrors ('sometimes, from a piled-up wall of dead bodies, one sees an arm stretch out and flail around, trying to grab something') and expressed hopes of religious redemption (in a chapter on 'The Coming Dawn', for instance).[74] Citing Dante's vision of hell and Dunant's description of Solferino, he gave a description of a war that might be necessary for the existence of the state, but which was nerve-shattering and 'unnatural'.[75]

War Psychosis

In modern wars, it seemed, courage had become 'passive', hinting at the new strains felt by combatants. Richard Martin, a Saxon student who chose deliberately to remain in the ranks, revealed what this meant:

Die *Tapferkeit* freilich, welche *der Soldat der modernen Heere* zeigen muβ, ist von *anderer Art*, als es die unserer Vorfahren oder die der griechischen und römischen Heroen gewesen ist. Zu ihrem gröβten Teile kann sie heutzutage nur in der *Verachtung der Todesgefahr* bestehen; nur in den seltensten Fällen kommt es in den modernen Schlachten zu einem Kampf von Mann gegen Mann, denn das todbringende Geschoß erreicht die meisten schon vorher aus weiter Entfernung. Ja, in den Schlachten des letzten deutsch-französischen Krieges sind viele verwundet und getötet worden, ohne daß sie nur einen einzigen Feind zu Gesicht bekommen haben. Wie soll sich da eine heroische Gesinnung anders bethätigen als in der Bezwingung der Todesfurcht? Der schwächlichste und militärisch schlechtest geschulte Mann kann darin größer sein als mancher Riese von Gestalt, der bei dem Gedanken an das Tod geschossen werden von unvorhergesehener Stelle aus sich ängstlich und scheu benimmt. Ich glaube also darin Recht zu behalten, wenn ich die Tapferkeit unserer modernen Soldaten als eine vorwiegend *passive Tugend* bezeichne.

Immerhin fordert *auch diese Art von Heldentum* unsere Achtung heraus, den sie zeugt von großer Seelenstärke und Selbstbeherrschung. Es gilt dabei, gegen den stärksten Trieb im Innern des Menschen anzukämpfen, das ist der Trieb der Selbsterhaltung. Die Liebe zum Leben ist ja jedem Menschen angeboren; ebenso tief eingwurzelt ist ihm damit zugleich die Furcht vor dem Tode, und das Auflehnen seiner individuellen Natur gegen das Vernichtetwerden ist etwas ganz Natürliches.

Der gemeine Mann, der in sich selbst vielleicht nicht immer moralische Kraft finden würde, dieser instinktiven Regung Herr zu werden, schaut in der Schlacht auf seine Vorgesetzten, auf das Verhalten, das diese inmitten des Kugelregens an den Tag legen. Und da muß ich denn sagen, *daß die Haltung unserer Offiziere mit ganz wenigen Ausnahmen über alles Lob erhaben war*… . Man könnte getrost *jedem* deutschen Offizier einen Totenkopf, wie bei den braunschweigischen Husaren, an seine Kopfbedeckung heften, den jeder muß sich eigentlich schon von dem Augenblicke an als dem Tode geweiht betrachten, wo er überhaupt die Offizierscarriere einschlägt.

Admittedly, the *courage* that the *soldier of the modern army* must show is of *a different kind* from that of our ancestors or that of Greek and Roman heroes. For the most part, it can only exist today in *contempt for the risk of death*; in modern battles, it only comes to a struggle of man against man in the rarest cases, for death-bringing bullets reach the majority beforehand from a great distance. Yes, in the battles of the last Franco-German war, many were wounded and killed without ever having seen a single enemy in the face. How should heroic attitudes manifest themselves here other than in the suppression of the fear of death? The weakest and militarily worst-schooled man can be greater in this respect than many of gigantic stature who show themselves to be anxious and timid when they think of being shot dead from an unexpected position. I believe that I am right to designate the courage of our modern soldiers as a predominantly *passive virtue*.

> Nevertheless, *this type of heroism*, too, deserves our respect, for it betrays a great strength of soul and self-control. It is a question of struggling against the strongest internal urge of man, the urge for self-preservation.... The common man, who perhaps will not always find the moral strength in himself, looks in battle to his superiors, to the conduct which they display in a hail of bullets. And, there, I must say that *the conduct of our officers, with very few exceptions, was beyond all praise*.... One could assuredly stick a death's head on the helmet of *every* German soldier, as amongst the Brunswick hussars, for every one of them must have seen themselves devoted to death from the moment that they began the career of an officer.[76]

There are some signs that soldiers broke down when confronted – in a 'passive' state – by such conditions. Many admitted they were unable to banish recollections of battle and its aftermath when they returned to civilian life.[77] Leonard Heiners, an ordinary soldier at the battle of Gravelotte in August 1870 was so overwhelmed by the sensations of battle – 'the persistent thunder of cannon from both sides, the peculiar rattle of *mitrailleuse*, the constant small arms fire of the infantry, the roar of the cavalry, the cries of pain of the wounded, the groaning of the dying' – that he was unable to banish them after the event.[78] Looking back on the battle, after which he was sent home wounded, he was unable to find words for it: 'Dear God, the sights of a battlefield cannot be described. They are too terrible.'[79] In a similar fashion, Georg von Bismarck, a junior officer in 1866, 'was deeply shaken by the view, beyond all measure', of a field hospital that he visited on the evening of 3 July, commenting that 'whoever sees all that for the first time will be shaken to his core', even those with 'good nerves' like himself.[80] Like many other soldiers, Bismarck had fallen asleep on the battlefield, waking up in the middle of the night to wander between the corpses, not bothered – apparently – that he stumbled and fell several times on top of them: 'my receptiveness for otherwise terrifying impressions was so cauterised that I hardly paid attention to the plaintive cries from the nearby dressing station nor the marrow-penetrating shrill neighing of the horses, suffering from open wounds'.[81] All the same, 'all the impressions of that night have remained in my memory in the most vital way', he concluded: clearing the field of bodies gave rise to scenes that shook 'even those with the strongest nerves and which stick in the memory forever'.[82] Soldiers' inability to forget or, at least, to control the recollection of combat – hinted at by many troops in 1864, 1866 and 1870–1 – was later seen as a critical symptom of PTSD.

Occasionally, combatants referred to other symptoms that seem close to those displayed by soldiers in later conflicts whose actions were monitored more extensively. Caspar Honthumb, a rank-and-file soldier who took part in the storming of Danish fortifications at Düppel in April 1864, became completely immobile, for instance. After storming and taking Fort 3, he wrote later, 'the fire was not spent' and 'the call of "forwards" echoed through the ranks', prompting 'the braver ones to storm from fort to fort in wild, victorious jubilation, more and more audacious, more and more certain of victory and further and further forwards', and to take part 'in the often bitter fighting'.[83] Honthumb was swept forwards in the same movement, yet he quickly fell to the ground, having seen – in his own words – 'a tremor to the left and to the right': 'As clear as if it had just happened, this moment and the thoughts and experiences which I had then stand before my eyes now.'[84] He 'felt' that he had been wounded in the left hip, but he was not sure whether the bullet had 'grazed it or gone right in'.[85] When he realised that it was 'a rather insignificant glancing blow', he wanted to get up again and advance.[86] 'This attempt failed; I had no more strength to stand up, which I don't attribute to the injury – in itself, small – but largely to my previous endeavours and violent excitement.'[87] His situation, as a consequence, was 'disagreeable in the highest degree', exposed to a 'persistently violent rain of bullets' and surrounded by 'a great number of dead and wounded', whose 'moaning and groaning helped to make up the unpleasantness of his position'.[88] Worst of all, he was forced to watch 'inactively' as his comrades stormed the other forts, before eventually being moved by the sight of Danes retreating with impunity from the fort in front of him to re-enter the battle, 'since I could not forego the pleasure, thirsting for amusement', of sending all 'my bullets … towards the Danes'.[89] 'I can assure you', he wrote to his civilian friend, 'that I now experience as much pleasure in thinking about these manifold acts of killing as I would if I had saved as many human lives as I have now destroyed.'[90] This overpowering combination of emotions was further confused by the disgusting sight of the battlefield, visible as the fighting subsided in the afternoon: 'God, what a view! Wherever the eye looked, corpses; wherever the foot trod, blood. I will not further illuminate these sad groups, these painfully contorted faces, these glassy, broken eyes.'[91] He was only happy, 'and first breathed in again', as he finally left 'this site of misery and devastation' at around four o'clock.[92] Few other combatants were completely overcome by their emotions during the fighting itself, to the point of lying motionless on the ground, but many recorded similar types of feeling. To such veterans, news of more fighting after the lapsing of the armistice in late June 1864 came as a 'message of terror'.[93]

Horror and heroism coexisted in many memoirs of the wars, with the latter constituting the framework by means of which combatants' experiences could be ordered in a meaningful and socially recognised fashion, and with the former often comprising the core or a disruptive element, which could not be ignored or repressed completely.[94] Psychiatrists were not employed by the German armies during the wars of unification, and psychiatric diagnoses or psychological explanations of the effects of combat played little role in 1864, 1866 or 1870–1, even though the official military report on the medical consequences of the Franco–German War, published in the late 1880s, commented extensively on mental and nervous conditions.[95] The concluding section of the report on 'War Psychoses', which was non-committal and seemingly reassuring, began:

> Die früher sehr allgemein gehegte Annahme, dass grosse politische Umwälzungen und Kriege vorzugsweise geeignet seien, das Seelenleben der mit nur minder widerstandsfähiger Psyche Begabten zu trüben, somit die Zahl der Geisteskranken in der Bevölkerung des betreffenden Landes überhaupt zu vermehren, ist neuerdings vielfach in Zweifel gezogen.
>
> The previously very generally held view that great political upheavals and wars are extremely well suited to trouble the life of the soul of those with a less robust psyche, thereby increasing the number of mentally ill in the population of the affected country overall, has recently come to be doubted in many respects.[96]

Given that 'a relatively high number of the mentally ill have come to a demise on the battlefields and barricades, or in prisons for some individuals, one should treat the question of whether wars increase the number of lunatics in the *population as a whole* … as an open one, as previously'.[97] The report went on:

> Im Gegensatz zu der Neigung, die Vermehrung der Geisteskrankheiten in der Bevölkerung während kriegerischer Zeitläufe zu bezweifeln, findet sich in Verhandlungen psychiatrischer Gesellschaften und anderen Veröffentlichungen meist die Ueberzeugung

ausgesprochen, dass, wie schon das Soldatenleben überhaupt, so noch mehr das Kriegsleben der Heeresangehörigen allerdings dazu angethan sei, zu psychischen Störungen Veranlassung zu geben und dass solche sowohl während der kriegerischen Ereignisse als namentlich nach Ablauf derselben verhältnissmässig häufig zur Entwickelung und Ausbildung kommen.

In opposition to the tendency to doubt the increase of mental illnesses in the population during the course of wars, one finds in the bulletins of psychiatry associations and other publications the conviction voiced, in the main, that the life of the soldier in general, and even more the wartime life of members of the army, tends to cause mental disturbances, and that these develop and are reinforced relatively frequently both during the events of wartime and after them.[98]

Yet such disagreements were presented as the disciplinary disputation of a handful of experts, with the army summary citing in opposition only a lecture by the Rhenish psychiatrist Karl Friedrich Werner Nasse and the contribution of the Prussian academic Rudolf Arndt – who had served as a military doctor in the war – to the psychiatry section of the meeting of natural scientists in Leipzig in August 1872.[99] The report's own figures for 'the mobile Prussian army', based on admissions to military hospitals, showed that 53 per 100,000 of the average strength of the army and 37 per 100,000 of all those mobilised had been admitted for 'mental disturbances' during the period of the war, compared to 51 to 64 per 100,000 in 1867–9.[100] The statistical analysis of the report confirmed:

Danach hat es freilich den Anschein, als ob dem allmäligen Abklingen einer durch den Feldzug von 1866 bedingten Steigerung der Geisteskrankheiten in der Armee eine neue in dem 2. Halbjahr 1871 und dem Jahr 1872 gefolgt sei, welche schon 1873 wesentlichen Nachlass zeigt, während 1874 der Zugang weit unter den Durchschnitt sinkt, um alsdann langsam aber stetig wieder anzusteigen.

Accordingly, it seems, it is true, as if the gradual decline after the increase in mental illnesses in the army caused by the campaign of 1866 was followed by a new one [increase] in the second half of 1871 and 1872, which was already showing considerable signs of relenting in 1873, whilst 1874 sank far below the average, and then slowly but steadily began to climb again.[101]

The recovery of soldiers seemed to have been rapid, with the majority recorded as 'healed', and the absolute numbers – 316 men admitted from a total force of approximately 1.5 million – were small.[102] Taking into account late admissions and other statistical anomalies, 'a moderate increase of the mentally ill during the duration of wartime activities could be deduced with considerable probability', ran the *Sanitäts-Bericht*'s cautious conclusion.[103]

The army hierarchy generally ignored psychiatrists' notions of 'war' or 'military psychosis', which were discussed from the 1870s onwards.[104] Nevertheless, some doctors were aware that combatants betrayed symptoms of trauma or, at least, acute psychological and physiological distress, unable to pick themselves up or to move on the battlefield, for instance. At the battle of Mars-la-Tour on 16 August 1870, one doctor even claimed to have witnessed 'the first person that I have seen die from anxiety': 'The person screamed out of anxiety and, with contempt, we let him lie where he was. After two hours, he was brought to us at the dressing station, still unwounded but with rasping breath and open eyes which did not blink when one touched the eyeball; he died shortly afterwards.'[105] Most suffered milder reactions, but ones that they termed 'terrible' and that they were unable to forget. Many attempted to banish them.[106] One chaplain reassured himself in 1870 that it was 'good that the implicated relatives at home don't get to see the suffering and misery of their own here', for 'even the doctors admit that the sight of this horror almost wears them down over the long term'.[107]

What happened when soldiers (and doctors) returned home themselves? It is not known how many experienced 'nervous cramps, in which they broke down in tears', like one evangelical pastor, but it can be surmised that a large number had at least some difficulties, which they endeavoured to conceal.[108] Few, though, made much fuss, rarely referring in writing to their reintegration into interrupted civilian lives. Georg von Siemens, coming back in 'proud virility' (Manneskraft) and giving his father his 'last great joy', was probably closer to the norm.[109]

Conclusion

Military doctors and, later (from the 1880s onwards), a handful of military psychiatrists (or doctors with some training in psychiatry), treated their patients in the 1860s and 1870s within a broader paradigm of warfare deriving from previous conflicts. Some of the most illuminating literature on this topic is that on the American Civil War, which tends to emphasise 'voluntary' reasons for continuing to fight; either the 'cause' that soldiers took up or a 'constellation of values' including duty, honour, godliness, chivalry and masculinity, all of which supposedly contributed to troops' 'courage' – or 'heroic action undertaken without fear'.[110] Such soldiers refused to show fear or to hide from bullets and shrapnel (in demonstrations of courage). As one common saying went: 'A brave man dies but once', whereas 'a coward dies a thousand times'.[111] These types of explanation of fighting, it can be held, derive from the particular nature of the conflict in the United States – it was, after all, a civil war involving militia armies composed of volunteers. However, research on the other wars of the 1860s – those in Schleswig, Bohemia and Germany, which were more typical of interstate conflicts involving mass armies of conscripts and reservists – has also found evidence of such 'character' or constellations of values – and indeed patriotic and national 'causes' – as reasons for fighting.[112] Overall, though, historians have found far more evidence in the German wars of the 1860s and early 1870s of hardiness, matter-of-factness and unthinking acceptance of both war and the military, frequently followed by shock and disgust at the conditions and outcomes of combat.[113]

Doctors noted the damaging effects of new military technologies at the same time as maintaining a professional distance from them, in contrast to combatants, including many officers. Their desire to record cases and ameliorate the provisions of military medicine usually belonged to this conception of their scientific vocation. The external reports of the International Committee for Relief to the Wounded were markedly less optimistic (or, even, matter of fact) than those of German military doctors. German medics were – partly as a consequence of this broader detachment, partly as a result of their training – relatively indifferent to the psychological impact of modern warfare on soldiers. Troops had continued to fight in the wars of unification, going on to be celebrated – and to remember their own deeds – within a heroic narrative of military glory.[114] Field doctors remained for the most part behind the fighting front and appear only infrequently – Naundorff was an exception – to have shared the experiences of combatants. They had little reason to challenge the dominant, heroic narrative and break with the traditions of the medical profession, which had been established during the 1830s, 1840s and 1850s.[115] Although questions were posed after the fighting, in the 1880s, about the psychiatric effects of combat, with some soldiers having symptoms that resembled those of PTSD, they remained – in these circumstances – unanswered.[116] As Hermann Oppenheim developed his theory of 'traumatic neurosis', and rivals such as Willy Hellpach and

Alfred Hoche put forward an opposing thesis about predispositions to mental illness, at a time when the number of asylum inmates in Prussia increased from 27,000 in 1880 to 143,000 in 1910, they did so with no reference to the traumas of the wars of unification.[117]

The neglect of psychiatric cases in nineteenth-century wars allowed specialists in the First World War to advance their theses about 'male hysteria' among those with weak constitutions and other predispositions, rather than those suffering physical and emotional shocks, with relatively little opposition, referring back only to 'accident trauma' and 'pension hysterics' during the 1890s.[118] In this sense, the professional 'objectivity' – rather than more active 'inhumanity' – of medics combined with the avoidance of 'bad news' by the army as a whole to wipe soldiers' suffering from the official record of the German wars.

Notes

1. Pick, *War Machine*. All translations are mine unless otherwise indicated.
2. Bullock, *The Humanist Tradition in the West*; Davies, *Humanism*; Gay, *The Enlightenment*, vol. I, *The Rise of Modern Paganism*.
3. Ganschow, 'Kriegsvölkerrechtliche Aspekte', 181.
4. See, for example, Strachan, 'Essay and Reflection'.
5. I have written more extensively about the relationship between 'war literature' and ego documents in Hewitson, '"I Witnesses"'. For the wider context, see Pethes and Richter, *Medizinische Schreibweisen* and Micale, *The Mind of Modernism*.
6. Many of the classic texts come from studies of the US Army: Marshall, *Men against Fire*; Stouffer et al., *The American Soldier*; Grossman, *On Killing*; and Grossman and Christensen, *On Combat*. See also Shils and Janowitz, 'Cohesion and Disintegration'; Wessely, 'Twentieth-Century Theories of Combat Motivation and Breakdown'; and Watson, 'Culture and Combat in the Western World, 1900–1945'.
7. The main debates concern the 'invention' of PTSD and its cultural heterogeneity: see Young, *The Harmony of Illusions*; for a recent summary, see Hinton and Good, *Culture and PTSD*.
8. 'Diagnostic criteria for 309.89 Post-Traumatic Stress Disorder', *Diagnostic and Statistical Manual*, cited in Binneveld, *From Shellshock to Combat Stress*, 191.
9. Binneveld. *From Shellshock to Combat Stress*. See also, on the German case, Komo, *Für Volk und Vaterland*; Küchenhoff and Warsitz, 'Psychiatrie und Psychoanalyse nach den Weltkriegen'; Riedesser and Verderber, *"Maschinengewehre hinter der Front"*; Riedesser and Verderber, *Aufrüstung der Seelen*; Ulrich, 'Nerven und Krieg'.
10. Binneveld, *From Shellshock to Combat Stress*, 191.
11. Binneveld, *From Shellshock to Combat Stress*, 191.
12. Tiffany and Allerton, 'Army Psychiatry in the Mid-'60s'.
13. Lerner, 'From Traumatic Neurosis to Male Hysteria', 140–1.
14. This approach is consistent with Young's case in *The Harmony of Illusions*, 3–42, about cultural and historical heterogeneity and specificity, but it leaves open the possibility that the specific physical and emotional 'shocks' of modern warfare could have effects that were at least partly separable from contemporaries' understanding of them.
15. See, for instance, Lerner, *Hysterical Men*; Kaufmann, 'Science as Cultural Practice'; Eckart, *Man, Medicine, and the State*; Eckart, *Medizin und Kolonialimperialismus*; Eckart, '"The Most Extensive Experiment"'; Eckart, 'Medizin und kolonialer Krieg'; Eckart, '"Eiskalt mit Würgen und Schlucken"'; Eckart, 'Aesculap in the Trenches'; Eckart, 'Medizin und imperialistischer Krieg'; Eckart and Gradmann, *Die Medizin und der Erste Weltkrieg*.

16. Freud, 'Introduction to *Psycho-Analysis and the War Neuroses*'.
17. On the strategic shifts, see 'Die vier Armeen in der Krim' *Grenzboten* 13/4 (1854): 361–70, and 14/2 (1855): 56–63, 143–52.
18. Loeffler, *General-Bericht*; J. Zechmeister, *Die Schusswunden und die gegenwärtige Bewaffnung der Heere*. Munich: J.J. Lentner'schen Buchhandlung, 1864.
19. Buk-Swienty, *Schlachtbank Düppel*, 83.
20. Embree, *Bismarck's First War*, 42–3.
21. Officers, at least, expected chloroform to be used and were now shocked when it was not available. See, for example, Von Gründorf, *The Danish Campaign of 1864*, 23, on the wounding of the Prince of Württemberg at Oeversee: 'His heel-bone was shattered, and the head doctor of the Belgians had to work with very limited means in his personal first-aid kit to resection the bone, or in other words to saw out its splintered part. There was no chloroform, and Württemberg suffered excruciating pain.'
22. Some authors, such as Epstein, 'Patterns of Change and Continuity', 375–88, have contended that, 'although the mid-nineteenth century saw the advent of technological change regarding strategic deployment and communication on the one hand, and the introduction of new tactical weapons on the other, the operational conduct of warfare remained remarkably consistent with that of 1809–15. This was due to the similarity of the size of the forces committed to operations, their organization and structure.' The physical and psychological impact of technological changes, which is what concerns us here, was much greater, however. See, for instance, Phillips, 'Military Morality Transformed', 579. The debate about the impact of modern military technology and associated transformations of combat is an old one: Howard, *War in European History*; Gooch, *Armies in Europe*; Strachan, *European Armies and the Conduct of War*; Wawro, *Warfare and Society in Europe, 1792–1914*. More specifically, see Wirtgen, *Das Zündnadelgewehr*.
23. Louis Appia, *Les blessés dans le Schleswig pendant la guerre de 1864* (1864), in Buk-Swienty, *Schlachtbank Düppel*, 308.
24. Appia in Buk-Swienty, *Schlachtbank Düppel*, 308–9.
25. Loeffler, *General-Bericht*, viii, xvi.
26. Loeffler, *General-Bericht*, ix.
27. Loeffler, *General-Bericht*, ix.
28. Loeffler, *General-Bericht*, 1, 10, 36, 46.
29. Loeffler, *General-Bericht*, 21.
30. Loeffler, *General-Bericht*, 42.
31. Loeffler, *General-Bericht*, 2.
32. Loeffler, *General-Bericht*, 44.
33. Loeffler, *General-Bericht*, 44.
34. Loeffler, *General-Bericht*, 42. For example, J. Zechmeister, *Die Schusswunden und die gegenwärtige Bewaffnung der Heere* (Munich, 1864).
35. Loeffler, *General-Bericht*, 35.
36. Loeffler, *General-Bericht*, 53. Chenu, *Rapport au Conseil de santé des armées*; Scrive, *Relation medico-chirurgicale de la Campagne d'Orient*. See also the United States Surgeon-General's Office, *Reports on the Extent and Nature of the Materials Available for the Preparation of a Medical and Surgical History of the Rebellion*.
37. Loeffler, *General-Bericht*, 43.
38. Loeffler, *General-Bericht*, 44.
39. See accounts such as those of Fischer, *Militärärztliche Skizzen* and Peltzer, *Militärartzliche Kriegserinnerungen*.
40. Buchholtz, *Ernst von Bergmann*, 207.
41. Stahmann, *Militärärztliche Fragmente und Reminiscenzen*, 1.
42. Stahmann, *Militärärztliche Fragmente und Reminiscenzen*, 90–4.
43. Stahmann, *Militärärztliche Fragmente und Reminiscenzen*, 97.
44. Stahmann, *Militärärztliche Fragmente und Reminiscenzen*, 97.
45. Stahmann, *Militärärztliche Fragmente und Reminiscenzen*, 97–9.
46. Stahmann, *Militärärztliche Fragmente und Reminiscenzen*, 103.
47. Stahmann, *Militärärztliche Fragmente und Reminiscenzen*, 152–3. Most of the wounded still had shots to the upper and lower extremities: Stahmann, *Militärärztliche Fragmente und Reminiscenzen*, 128.
48. Stahmann, *Militärärztliche Fragmente und Reminiscenzen*, 153.

49. Stahmann, *Militärärztliche Fragmente und Reminiscenzen*, 103.
50. Stahmann, *Militärärztliche Fragmente und Reminiscenzen*, 147.
51. Von Werder, *Erlebnisse eines Johanniter-Ritters*, 30–44, 65–102.
52. Herr Blittowsky, 16 July 1866, *Kriegsbriefe* Archive, Universitäts- und Landesbibliothek Bonn.
53. Fritsch, *1870/71: Erinnerungen und Betrachtungen*, 166–7.
54. Billroth, *Chirurgische Briefe*, 192–4, 266–75.
55. Steinbach, *Abgrund Metz*, 45.
56. Fritsch, *1870/71: Erinnerungen und Betrachtungen*, 167.
57. Billroth, *Chirurgische Briefe*, 10–14, reported that the *Johanniter* and other volunteer hospitals received casualties 'very much more quickly' than the reserve field hospitals, for instance.
58. Stromeyer, *Erinnerungen eiens deutschen Arztes*, 420.
59. Fritsch, *1870/71: Erinnerungen und Betrachtungen*, 168.
60. Fritsch, *1870/71: Erinnerungen und Betrachtungen*, 169.
61. Steinbach, *Abgrund Metz*, 45, argues convincingly that many tallies of the dead need to be revised upwards, since initial figures are cited that subsequently increased because of death as a result of wounds. For example, Bazaine estimated 5,000 dead and 23,500 wounded for the Army of the Rhine between 14 August and 7 October 1870, but the number of deaths probably rose by 6,000–10,000.
62. Waltz, *Erlebnisse eines Feldarztes*, 14.
63. Fritsch, *Erinnerungen und Betrachtungen*, 133.
64. Fritsch, *Erinnerungen und Betrachtungen*, 133.
65. Fritsch, *Erinnerungen und Betrachtungen*, 263.
66. Fritsch, *Erinnerungen und Betrachtungen*, 263.
67. Naundorff, *Unter dem rothen Kreuz*, 73; also, 'Da werden Weiber zu Hyänen', in Petsch, *Heldenthaten Preußischer Krieger*, 19–22.
68. 'Da werden Weiber zu Hyänen', in Petsch, *Heldenthaten Preußischer Krieger*, 19–22.
69. Naundorff, *Unter dem rothen Kreuz*. This was confirmed, among others, by officers in Deitl, *Unter Habsburg Kriegsbanner*, vols. 1–6.
70. Naundorff, *Unter dem rothen Kreuz*, 108.
71. Naundorff, *Unter dem rothen Kreuz*, 108.
72. Naundorff, *Unter dem rothen Kreuz*, 120–1.
73. Naundorff, *Unter dem rothen Kreuz*, 136.
74. Naundorff, *Unter dem rothen Kreuz*, 161, 168–75.
75. Naundorff, *Unter dem rothen Kreuz*, 136–7, 165, 177.
76. Martin, *Kriegserinnerungen eines 105ers*, 176–7. See also Stier, *Unter Prinz Friedrich Karl*, 62, who labelled the troops – himself included – 'leaderless sheep', once their officer had been killed.
77. Stier, *Unter Prinz Friedrich Karl*.
78. See Leonard Heiners, 'Tagebuch und Erlebnisse aus meiner Dienstzeit', 27, *Kriegsbriefe* Archive, Universitäts- und Landesbibliothek Bonn.
79. Heiners, 'Tagebuch und Erlebnisse', 28.
80. Von Bismarck, *Kriegs-Erlebnisse*, 49–50.
81. Von Bismarck, *Kriegs-Erlebnisse*, 51.
82. Von Bismarck, *Kriegs-Erlebnisse*, 52.
83. Honthumb, *Mein Tagebuch*, 86.
84. Honthumb, *Mein Tagebuch*, 87.
85. Honthumb, *Mein Tagebuch*, 87.
86. Honthumb, *Mein Tagebuch*, 87.
87. Honthumb, *Mein Tagebuch*, 87.
88. Honthumb, *Mein Tagebuch*, 87.
89. Honthumb, *Mein Tagebuch*, 87–8.
90. Honthumb, *Mein Tagebuch*, 88.
91. Honthumb, *Mein Tagebuch*, 89.
92. Honthumb, *Mein Tagebuch*, 89.
93. Honthumb, *Mein Tagebuch*, 118.
94. Krüger, 'German Suffering in the Franco-German War, 1870/71', 417 makes a similar point. The argument here militates against those put forward by Becker, *Bilder von Krieg und Nation* and Mehrkens, *Statuswechsel*.

95. Militär-Medizinal-Abtheilung des Königlich Preussischen Kriegsministeriums, *Sanitäts-Bericht*, see especially VII: *Erkrankungen des Nervensystems* (1885). Lengwiler, 'Psychiatry beyond the Asylum'; Lengwiler, *Zwischen Klinik und Kaserne*; Lerner, *Hysterical Men*, begins his study twenty years after the end of the Franco–German War and with no reference to it.
96. Militär-Medizinal-Abtheilung des Königlich Preussischen Kriegsministeriums, *Traumatische, idiopathische und nach Infektionskrankheiten beobachtete Erkrankungen*, 412.
97. Militär-Medizinal-Abtheilung des Königlich Preussischen Kriegsministeriums, *Traumatische, idiopathische und nach Infektionskrankheiten beobachtete Erkrankungen*, 413.
98. Militär-Medizinal-Abtheilung des Königlich Preussischen Kriegsministeriums, *Traumatische, idiopathische und nach Infektionskrankheiten beobachtete Erkrankungen*, 413.
99. Militär-Medizinal-Abtheilung des Königlich Preussischen Kriegsministeriums, *Traumatische, idiopathische und nach Infektionskrankheiten beobachtete Erkrankungen*, 413.
100. Militär-Medizinal-Abtheilung des Königlich Preussischen Kriegsministeriums, *Traumatische, idiopathische und nach Infektionskrankheiten beobachtete Erkrankungen*, 413.
101. Militär-Medizinal-Abtheilung des Königlich Preussischen Kriegsministeriums, *Traumatische, idiopathische und nach Infektionskrankheiten beobachtete Erkrankungen*, 413.
102. Militär-Medizinal-Abtheilung des Königlich Preussischen Kriegsministeriums, *Traumatische, idiopathische und nach Infektionskrankheiten beobachtete Erkrankungen*, 413. The calculations (53 and 37 per 100,000) are taken from the lower totals of the actual fighting force.
103. Militär-Medizinal-Abtheilung des Königlich Preussischen Kriegsministeriums, *Traumatische, idiopathische und nach Infektionskrankheiten beobachtete Erkrankungen*, 414.
104. Lengwiler, 'Psychiatry beyond the Asylum', 48–9.
105. Von Hase, *Feldarztbriefe*, 13.
106. Cited in Rak, *Krieg, Nation und Konfession*, 193.
107. Martin Schall to his bride, 30 August 1870, cited in Rak, *Krieg, Nation und Konfession*, 190.
108. Cited in Rak, *Krieg, Nation und Konfession*, 194.
109. Helfferich, *Georg von Siemens*, vol. 1, 187–8.
110. The quotation comes from Barton, *Goodmen*, 17. Scholars emphasising 'causes' voluntarily defended include Hess in his study of the *Union Soldier in Battle* and McPherson, *What They Fought For, 1861–1865* and *For Cause and Comrades*. Historians looking at constellations of values include Barton himself and Linderman, *Embattled Courage*.
111. Barton, *Goodmen*, 62.
112. I have written about this at greater length in Hewitson, *The People's Wars*, 312–472.
113. See especially Müller, *Soldaten in der deutschen Revolution von 1848/49*; Buk-Swienty, *Schlachtbank Düppel*; Kühlich, *Die deutschen Soldaten im Krieg von 1870/71*; Rak, *Krieg, Nation und Konfession*; Steinbach, *Abgrund Metz*; Krüger, *'Sind wir denn nicht Brüder?'*; Mehrkens, *Statuswechsel*; and Meteling, *Ehre, Einheit, Ordnung*.
114. The work of Frank Becker is particularly useful: Becker, *Bilder von Krieg und Nation*.
115. Huerkamp, *Der Aufstieg der Ärzte im 19*; Berg and Cocks, *Medicine and Modernity*, 17–34; Frevert, *Krankheit als politisches Problem 1770–1880*, 36–44, 116–84. On surgery, see Lawrence, 'Democratic, Divine and Heroic'; Porter, 'Hospitals and Surgery'.
116. This does not mean that PTSD lacked cultural inflections, merely that some symptoms referred to combatants were consistent with later descriptions of 'trauma', 'shell-shock' and 'post-traumatic stress disorder': Good and Hinton, 'Introduction: Culture, Trauma and PTSD', in Hinton and Good, *Culture and PTSD*, 3–49.
117. Lerner, 'From Traumatic Neurosis to Male Hysteria', 143–54.
118. Lerner, *Hysterical Men*, 62–74. Many theories formulated during the First World War combined physical (or somatic) and psychological 'shocks': see Leese, 'Essay Review: Making Shell-Shock'.

Bibliography

Barton, Michael. *Goodmen: The Character of Civil War Soldiers*. University Park: Pennsylvania State University Press, 1981.

Becker, Frank. *Bilder von Krieg und Nation: Die Einigungskriege in der bürgerlichen Öffentlichkeit Deutschlands 1864–1913*. Munich: Oldenbourg, 2001.

Berg, Manfred and Geoffrey Cocks, eds. *Medicine and Modernity: Public Health and Medical Care in Nineteenth- and Twentieth-Century Germany*. Cambridge: Cambridge University Press, 1997.

Billroth, Theodor. *Chirurgische Briefe aus den Kriegs-Lazarethen in Weissenburg und Mannheim 1870: Ein Beitrag zu den wichtigsten Abschnitten der Kriegschirurgie, mit besonderer Rücksicht auf Statistik*. Berlin: Hirschwald, 1872.

Binneveld, Hans. *From Shellshock to Combat Stress: A Comparative History of Military Psychiatry*, translated by John O'Kane. Amsterdam: Amsterdam University Press, 1997.

Buchholtz, Arend. *Ernst von Bergmann: Mit Bergmanns Briefe von 1866, 1870/71 und 1877*. 2nd ed. Leipzig: F.C.W. Vogel, 1911.

Buk-Swienty, Tom. *Schlachtbank Düppel: 18. April 1864: Geschichte einer Schlacht*. Berlin: Osburg Verlag, 2011.

Bullock, Alan. *The Humanist Tradition in the West*. New York: Norton, 1985.

Chenu, Jean-Charles. *Rapport au Conseil de Santé des Armées sur les résultats du service médico-chirurgical aux ambulances de Crimée et aux hôpitaux militaires français en Turquie, pendant la campagne d'Orient en 1854, 1855, 1856*. Paris: Masson, 1865.

Davies, Tony. *Humanism*. 2nd ed. London: Routledge, 2008.

Deitl, F. *Unter Habsburgs Kriegsbanner*. Dresden: Piersons, 1898–1900.

Eckart, Wolfgang U. 'Medizin und kolonialer Krieg: Die Niederschlagung der Herero-Nama-Erhebung im Schutzgebiet Deutsch-Südwestafrika, 1904–1907'. In *Studien zur Geschichte des deutschen Kolonialismus in Afrika*, edited by Peter Heine and Ulrich van der Heyden, 220–35. Pfaffenweiler: Centaurus-Verlagsgesellschaft, 1995.

Eckart, Wolfgang U. 'Aesculap in the Trenches: Aspects of German Medicine in the First World War'. In *War, Violence and the Modern Condition*, edited by Bernd Hüppauf, 177–93. Berlin: De Gruyter, 1997.

Eckart, Wolfgang U. 'Medizin und imperialistischer Krieg: Kaiserliche Sanitätstruppen bei der Niederschlagung der "Boxer"-Erhebung (1900–1901)'. In *Medizingeschichte und Gesellschaftskritik: Festschrift für Gerhard Baader*, edited by Michael Hubenstorf, Hans-Uwe Lammel, Ragnhild Münch, Sabine Schleiermacher, Heinz-Peter Schmiedebach and Sigrid Stöckel, 135–55. Husum: Matthiesen Verlag, 1997.

Eckart, Wolfgang U. *Medizin und Kolonialimperialismus: Deutschland 1884–1945*. Paderborn: Schöningh, 1997.

Eckart, Wolfgang U. '"The Most Extensive Experiment that the Imagination Can Conceive": War, Emotional Stress, and German Medicine, 1914–1918'. In *Great War, Total War: Combat and Mobilization on the Western Front, 1914–1918*, edited by Roger Chickering and Stig Förster, 133–49. Cambridge: Cambridge University Press, 2000.

Eckart, Wolfgang U., ed. *Man, Medicine, and the State: The Human Body as an Object of Government Sponsored Medical Research in the 20th Century*. Stuttgart: Franz Steiner Verlag, 2006.

Eckart, Wolfgang U. '"Eiskalt mit Würgen und Schlucken": Körperliches und seelisches Trauma in der deutschen Kriegsliteratur, 1914–1939', *Trauma und Gewalt* 1, no. 3 (2007): 186–99.

Eckart, Wolfgang U. and Christoph Gradmann, eds. *Die Medizin und der Erste Weltkrieg*. Pfaffenweiler: Centaurus-Verlagsgesellschaft, 1996.

Embree, Michael. *Bismarck's First War: The Campaign of Schleswig and Jutland 1864*. Solihull: Helion and Company, 2006.

Epstein, Robert M. 'Patterns of Change and Continuity in Nineteenth-Century Warfare', *Journal of Military History* 56, no. 3 (1992): 375–88.

Fischer, K. *Militärärztliche Skizzen aus Süddeutschland und Böhmen*. Aarau: H.R. Sauerländer, 1867.

Freud, Sigmund. 'Introduction to *Psycho-Analysis and the War Neuroses* (1919)'. In *The Standard Edition of the Complete Psychological Works of Sigmund Freud, Volume XVII (1917–1919): An Infantile Neurosis and Other Works*, edited by James Strachey, 205–10. London: Hogarth Press, 1955.

Frevert, Ute. *Krankheit als politisches Problem 1770–1880: Soziale Unterschichten in Preußen zwischen medizinischer Polizei und staatlicher Sozialversicherung*. Göttingen: Vandenhoeck und Ruprecht, 1984.

Fritsch, Heinrich. *1870/71: Erinnerungen und Betrachtungen*. Leipzig: Reclam, 1900.

Ganschow, Jan. 'Kriegsvölkerrechtliche Aspekte'. In *Der Deutsch-Dänische Krieg 1864: Vorgeschichte – Verlauf – Folgen*, by Jan Ganschow, Olaf Haselhorst and Maik Ohnezeit. Graz: Ares Verlag, 2013.

Gay, Peter. *The Enlightenment: An Interpretation*. New York: Norton, 1966.

Gooch, John. *Armies in Europe*. London: Routledge and Kegan Paul, 1980.

Grossman, Dave. *On Killing: The Psychological Cost of Learning to Kill in War and Society*. Boston: Little, Brown and Company, 1995.

Grossman, Dave and Loren W. Christensen. *On Combat: The Psychology and Physiology of Deadly Conflict in War and in Peace*. Belleville, IL: PPCT Research Publications, 2004.

Helfferich, Karl. *Georg von Siemens: Ein Lebensbild aus Deutschlands großer Zeit*. Berlin: Springer, 1923.

Hess, Earl J. *The Union Soldier in Battle: Enduring the Ordeal of Combat*. Lawrence: University Press of Kansas, 1997.

Hewitson, Mark. '"I Witnesses": Soldiers, Selfhood and Testimony in Modern Wars', *German History* 28, no. 3 (2010): 310–25.

Hewitson, Mark. *The People's Wars: Histories of Violence in the German Lands, 1820–1888*. Oxford: Oxford University Press, 2017.

Hinton, Devon E. and Byron J. Good, eds. *Culture and PTSD: Trauma in Global and Historical Perspective*. Philadelphia: University of Pennsylvania Press, 2016.

Honthumb, Caspar Alexander. *Mein Tagebuch*. Münster: Theissing, 1865.

Howard, Michael. *War in European History*. Oxford: Oxford University Press, 1976.

Huerkamp, Claudia. *Der Aufstieg der Ärzte im 19. Jahrhundert: Vom gelehrten Stand zum professionellen Experten: Das Beispiel Preußens*. Göttingen: Vandenhoeck und Ruprecht, 1985.

Kaufmann, Doris. 'Science as Cultural Practice: Psychiatry in the First World War and Weimar Germany', *Journal of Contemporary History* 34, no. 1 (1999): 125–44.

Komo, Günter. *Für Volk und Vaterland: Die Militärpsychiatrie in den Weltkriegen*. Münster: Lit, 1992.

Krüger, Christine G. *"Sind wir denn nicht Brüder?": Deutsche Juden im nationalen Krieg 1870/71*. Paderborn: Schöningh, 2006.

Krüger, Christine G. 'German Suffering in the Franco-German War, 1870/71', *German History* 29, no. 3 (2011): 404–22.

Küchenhoff, Joachim and Peter Warsitz. 'Psychiatrie und Psychoanalyse nach den Weltkriegen'. In *HardWar/SoftWar: Krieg und Medien 1914 bis 1945*, edited by Martin Stingelin and Wolfgang Scherer, 47–80. Munich: Wilhelm Fink Verlag, 1991.

Kühlich, Frank. *Die deutschen Soldaten im Krieg von 1870/71: Eine Darstellung der Situation und der Erfahrungen der deutschen Soldaten im Deutsch-Französischen Krieg*. Frankfurt am Main: Peter Lang, 1995.

Lawrence, Christopher. 'Democratic, Divine and Heroic: The History and Historiography of Surgery'. In *Medical Theory, Surgical Practice: Studies in the History of Surgery*, edited by Christopher Lawrence, 1–47. London: Routledge, 1992.

Leese, Peter. 'Essay Review: Making Shell-Shock', *British Journal of Psychology* 92, no. 2 (2001): 411–15.

Lengwiler, Martin. *Zwischen Klinik und Kaserne: Die Geschichte der Militärpsychiatrie in Deutschland und der Schweiz 1870–1914*. Zurich: Chronos, 2000.

Lengwiler, Martin. 'Psychiatry beyond the Asylum: The Origins of German Military Psychiatry before World War I', *History of Psychiatry* 14, no. 1 (2003): 41–62.

Lerner, Paul. 'From Traumatic Neurosis to Male Hysteria: The Decline and Fall of Hermann Oppenheim, 1889–1919'. In *Traumatic Pasts: History, Psychiatry, and Trauma in the Modern Age, 1870–1930*, edited by Mark S. Micale and Paul Lerner, 140–71. Cambridge: Cambridge University Press, 2001.

Lerner, Paul. *Hysterical Men: War, Psychiatry, and the Politics of Trauma in Germany, 1890–1930*. Ithaca, NY: Cornell University Press, 2003.

Linderman, Gerald F. *Embattled Courage: The Experience of Combat in the American Civil War*. New York: Free Press, 1987.

Loeffler, Gottfried Friedrich Franz. *General-Bericht über den Gesundheitsdienst im Feldzuge gegen Dänemark 1864*. Berlin: Hirschwald, 1867.

Marshall, S.L.A. *Men against Fire: The Problem of Battle Command in Future War*. New York: William Morrow, 1947.

Martin, Richard. *Kriegserinnerungen eines 105ers*. Plauen: Wieprecht, 1896.

McPherson, James M. *What They Fought For, 1861–1865*. Baton Rouge: Louisiana State University Press, 1994.

McPherson, James M. *For Cause and Comrades: Why Men Fought in the Civil War*. New York: Oxford University Press, 1997.

Mehrkens, Heidi. *Statuswechsel: Kriegserfahrung und nationale Wahrnehmung im Deutsch-Französischen Krieg 1870/71*. Essen: Klartext, 2008.
Meteling, Wencke. *Ehre, Einheit, Ordnung: Preußische und französische Städte und ihre Regimenter im Krieg, 1870/71 und 1914–19*. Baden-Baden: Nomos, 2010.
Micale, Mark S., ed. *The Mind of Modernism: Medicine, Psychology, and the Cultural Arts in Europe and America, 1880–1940*. Stanford: Stanford University Press, 2004.
Militär-Medizinal-Abtheilung des Königlich Preussischen Kriegsministeriums, ed. *Sanitäts-Bericht über die deutschen Heere im Krieg gegen Frankreich*. Berlin: Mittler, 1884–91.
Militär-Medizinal-Abtheilung des Königlich Preussischen Kriegsministeriums, ed. *Traumatische, idiopathische und nach Infektionskrankheiten beobachtete Erkrankungen des Nerven Systemen bei den Deutschen Heeren im Kriege gegen Frankreich 1870/71*. Berlin: Hirschwald, 1885.
Müller, Sabrina. *Soldaten in der deutschen Revolution von 1848/49*. Paderborn: Schöningh, 1999.
Naundorff, Julius. *Unter dem rothen Kreuz: Fremde und eigene Erfahrungen auf böhmischer Erde und den Schlachtfeldern der Neuzeit*. Leipzig: Veit, 1867.
Peltzer, M. *Militärärztliche Kriegserinnerungen an 1866 und 1870/71*. Berlin: Springer, 1914.
Pethes, Nicolas and Sandra Richter. *Medizinische Schreibweisen: Ausdifferenzierung und Transfer zwischen Medizin und Literatur (1600–1900)*. Tübingen: Niemeyer, 2008.
Petsch, Wilhelm. *Heldenthaten Preußischer Krieger und Charakterbilder aus dem Feldzuge von 1866*. Berlin: Schlesier, 1867.
Phillips, Gervase. 'Military Morality Transformed: Weapons and Soldiers on the Nineteenth-Century Battlefield', *Journal of Interdisciplinary History* 41, no. 4 (2011): 565–90.
Pick, Daniel. *War Machine: The Rationalisation of Slaughter in the Modern Age*. New Haven: Yale University Press, 1996.
Porter, Roy. 'Hospitals and Surgery'. In *The Cambridge History of Medicine*, edited by Roy Porter, 176–210. Cambridge: Cambridge University Press, 2006.
Rak, Christian. *Krieg, Nation und Konfession: Die Erfahrung des Deutsch-Französischen Krieges von 1870/71*. Paderborn: Schöningh, 2004.
Riedesser, Peter and Axel Verderber. *Aufrüstung der Seelen: Militärpsychiatrie und Militärpsychologie in Deutschland und Amerika*. Freiburg im Breisgau: Dreisam-Verlag, 1985.
Riedesser, Peter and Axel Verderber. *"Maschinengewehre hinter der Front": Zur Geschichte der deutschen Militärpsychiatrie*. Frankfurt am Main: Fischer Taschenbuch Verlag, 1996.
Scrive, Gaspard. *Relation médico-chirurgicale de la campagne d'Orient du 31 mars 1854, occupation de Gallipoli, au 6 juillet 1856, evacuation de la Crimée*. Paris: Masson, 1857.
Shils, Edward A. and Morris Janowitz. 'Cohesion and Disintegration in the Wehrmacht in World War II', *Public Opinion Quarterly* 12, no. 2 (1948): 280–315.
Stahmann, Karl-Ludwig August. *Militärärztliche Fragmente und Reminiscenzen aus dem östreichisch-preussischen Feldzuge im Jahre 1866*. Berlin: Hirschwald, 1868.
Steinbach, Matthias. *Abgrund Metz: Kriegserfahrung, Belagerungsalltag und nationale Erziehung im Schatten einer Festung 1870/71*. Munich: Oldenbourg, 2002.
Stier, Ernst. *Unter Prinz Friedrich Karl: Erlebnisse eines Musketiers vom X. Armeekorps im Feldzug 1870–71*. Munich: C.H. Beck, 1883.
Stouffer, Samuel. *The American Soldier*. Princeton: Princeton University Press, 1949.
Strachan, Hew. *European Armies and the Conduct of War*. London: Allen and Unwin, 1983.
Strachan, Hew. 'Essay and Reflection: On Total War and Modern War', *International History Review* 22, no. 2 (2000): 341–70.
Stromeyer, Georg Friedrich Louis. *Erinnerungen eines deutschen Arztes*. 2nd ed. Hannover: Rümpler, 1874.
Tiffany, William J. and William S. Allerton. 'Army Psychiatry in the Mid-'60s', *American Journal of Psychiatry* 123, no. 7 (1967): 810–21.
Ulrich, Bernd. 'Nerven und Krieg: Skizzierung einer Beziehung'. In *Geschichte und Psychologie: Annäherungsversuche*, edited by Bedrich Loewenstein, 163–92. Pfaffenweiler: Centaurus-Verlagsgesellschaft, 1992.
United States Surgeon-General's Office. *Reports on the Extent and Nature of the Materials Available for the Preparation of a Medical and Surgical History of the Rebellion*. Philadelphia: Lippincott, 1865
Von Bismarck, Georg. *Kriegs-Erlebnisse: 1866 und 1870/71*. 2nd ed. Dessau: C. Dünnhaupt, 1907.
Von Gründorf, Wilhelm. *The Danish Campaign of 1864: Recollections of an Austrian General Staff Officer*. Solihull: Helion and Company, 2010.

Von Hase, Paul. *Feldarztbriefe 1870/71*. Leipzig: Breitkopf und Härtel, 1895.
Von Werder, Bernhard. *Erlebnisse eines Johanniter-Ritters auf dem Kriegsschauplatze in Böhmen*. Halle: Mühlmann, 1867.
Waltz, Gustav. *Erlebnisse eines Feldarztes der badischen Division im Kriege 1870–71*. Heidelberg: Winter, 1872.
Watson, Alexander. 'Culture and Combat in the Western World, 1900–1945', *Historical Journal* 51, no. 2 (2008): 529–46.
Wawro, Geoffrey. *Warfare and Society in Europe, 1792–1914*. London: Routledge, 2000.
Wessely, Simon. 'Twentieth-Century Theories of Combat Motivation and Breakdown', *Journal of Contemporary History* 41, no. 2 (2006): 268–86.
Wirtgen, Rolf. *Das Zündnadelgewehr: Eine militärtechnische Revolution im 19. Jahrhundert*. Herford: Mittler, 1991.
Young, Allan. *The Harmony of Illusions: Inventing Post-Traumatic Stress Disorder*. Princeton: Princeton University Press, 1995.
Zechmeister, J. *Die Schusswunden und die gegenwärtige Bewaffnung der Heere*. Munich: J.J. Lentner'schen Buchhandlung, 1864.

4 From Neurosis to a New Cure of Souls: C.G. Jung's Remaking of the Psychotherapeutic Patient

Sonu Shamdasani

Preface

In the twentieth century, one of the main vehicles through which medicine came to redefine the human was through the rise and spread of the practice of psychotherapy. Such practices proposed to transform subjects, and in so doing generated new conceptions of what it means to be human. One critical vector in this development was a shift in the early decades of the twentieth century from conceptions of psychotherapy being solely oriented to the cure of pathology to also being vehicles for facilitating new forms of well-being.[1]

A number of psychotherapies came to offer a series of competing 'optional' ontologies: conceptions not only of the reasons for one's maladies and how to be cured of them, but of how to be well and take up one's place in society and the world.[2] These were not only illness narratives in Arthur Kleinman's sense,[3] but also what one could call transformation narratives. The psychotherapeutic encounter became a site for the proposal and acceptance of new conceptions of what it is to be human.

One prominent figure in this regard was the Swiss psychiatrist, psychologist and founder of analytical psychology, C.G. Jung. This chapter looks at how this occurred through studying the transformations in his practice from around the time of the First World War onwards on the basis of his own self-experimentation, as a case history within these wider developments. From this time onwards for Jung, psychotherapy was reformulated into a practice to facilitate the higher psychological and spiritual development of the individual, which he termed the process of individuation.

Psychotherapy became a vehicle for formulating and proposing a new notion of humanity. In this view, humanity was still in the making, and psychotherapy could provide a means towards its future evolution.

This chapter studies a series of cases of Jung, demonstrating how he reformulated the 'offer' of psychotherapy, how individuals took it up, and how this helped to shape the evolving contours of the social role of the psychotherapeutic patient. Like Hewitson's contribution in this volume, it looks at patients' accounts alongside those of their physicians.

The recovery of a religious orientation was central to this offer, and Liebscher's contribution in this volume opens up this question and goes into further detail regarding Jung's relation to contemporaneous movements in German Protestantism. Other contributions to this volume, such as those by Coxon, Davies, Ring, Schonfield and Wilks study representations and mediations of dental, medical and psychotherapeutic practices in literary texts. This chapter concentrates on forms of life-writing: in particular, letters and analytic diaries.

In the twentieth century, analytic diaries formed an important subterranean literary genre, as the silent accompaniment of therapeutic practices. In not a few cases, individuals undergoing psychotherapy spent more time writing in analytic diaries than actually seeing their therapists, and this process continued, as a form of self-analytic activity into a lifetime mode of notation and self-reflection.

This chapter also charts the evolution of a social network of patients, and the role this played in the development of Jung's movement. In the context of this volume, this forms an example of how developments in the German-speaking world were transmitted to and taken up in the English-speaking world.

In 1922, the ethnologist and linguist Jaime de Angulo issued a 'challenge to all brother-neurotics – go, my brethren, go to the Mecca, I mean to Zürich, and drink from the fountain of life, all ye who are dead in your souls, go and seek new life.'[4] It was of course, to Jung that de Angulo was exhorting his 'brother-neurotics' to go. By 1912, Jung's fame had spread, and an increasing number of neurotics wound their way to Jung. What de Angulo and his 'brother-neurotics' were seeking in Jung's psychotherapy was no medical cure, but a way out of a widespread cultural and spiritual malaise.

Since its rise in the last quarter of the nineteenth century, in line with general medical practice, the various forms of psychotherapy had maintained a privative concept of health, as being the absence of nervous and psychological disorder. This was linked with a negative notion of the aim of psychotherapy, as being the removal of pathology and the restoration of normal living. While schools of psychotherapy had different conceptions of mental disorders, as well as of the means for their removal, this was generally one common denominator. From the time of the First World War onwards, Jung began to depart from this and reformulate the practice of psychotherapy as one having as its goal the higher spiritual development of the individual. This reformulation was to have far-reaching consequences on the subsequent development of psychotherapy, as well as on the plethora of humanistic, new age and alternative therapies that rose up. While claiming that his psychotherapy remained part of 'medical psychology', this reformulation offered a new definition of the human, which many individuals came to take on. Jung was not alone in proposing more melioristic possibilities for psychotherapy. From the 1930s onwards, a number of other figures in the field also did so. Significantly, these reformulations were coupled with competing conceptions of what it meant to be human. What follows, then, can be considered as a case study within a wider transformation of the field.[5]

This shift away from a then conventional medical view of the aims of psychotherapy opened the question of the relation of psychotherapy to religious practices. In 1904, the French psychologist Pierre Janet had made the observation that when patients found a friend or someone whom they could obey, their problems ceased. Priests had formerly fulfilled this function, and doctors could now do the same. Priests had done this in a haphazard manner, and no longer had the authority that they once had. He noted that it was 'une caractéristique de notre temps que ce travail de direction morale soit parfois effectué par un médecin à qui est souvent attribué ce rôle de direction morale lorsque le patient ne trouve plus suffisament de soutien autour de lui.' / 'a characteristic of our time that this work of moral direction has sometimes returned to the doctor, who is now often charged with this role of moral direction when the patient does not find enough support around him.'[6] In 1912, Jung discussed the parallels between psychoanalysis and the practice of religious confession. He argued that the psychological value of religious confession lay in the fact that it enabled the sufferer to re-enter into human community from isolation and to form a moral bond, which he identified with the psychoanalytic 'transference'. The moral value that the Church set on confession was justified by the fact that 'der größte Teil der Menscheit nicht nur der Führung bedürftig ist, sondern auch nichts Besseres sich wünscht, als geführt and bevormundet zu werden.' / 'the greater part of humanity not only needs guidance, but wishes for nothing better than to be guided and held in tutelage.'[7] Through confession, the priest stood in for the individual's parents, and so helped them to free themselves from the family. For fifteen hundred years, this had functioned as an effective means of education. However, for contemporary developed individuals, it had lost this educative value – 'sobald sich die Kirche als unfähig erwies, ihre Führerschaft auf geistigem Gebeit zu behaupten.' / 'as soon as the Church proved incapable of maintaining her leadership in the intellectual sphere.'[8] Modern individuals wanted understanding, and not the sacrifice of the intellect. Their goal was to achieve moral autonomy and to be able to guide themselves. When faced with this demand, the doctor had to analyse the transference, which the priest did not have to do. Thus, in Jung's view, the decline of the confessional formed an essential context for the possibility of psychoanalysis, which presented itself as a modernised cure of souls.

If the doctor was now to take up the role being increasingly vacated by the priest, this reopened the question of the role of suggestion in psychotherapy. In the first decade of the twentieth century, a reaction set in against the use of suggestion and hypnosis in psychotherapy. 'Catharsis', 'interpretation', 'persuasion' and 'analysis' became the new buzzwords. Jacqueline Carroy has noted that in the hypnotic literature, suggestion functioned as a heterodox, umbrella term, which, as well as imperative suggestion, included paradoxical injunctions and interpretations.[9] In a similar manner, if one studies psychoanalytic and psychotherapeutic cases in the twentieth century, one finds that 'interpretation' functioned in a similar catch-all manner. While the theoretical account of practices changed considerably, the same was not the case in the practices themselves, and under the rubric of interpretation in the psychoanalytic literature, it is not hard to find some of the best examples of authoritarian directives. Freud had claimed that the practice of psychoanalysis was free from suggestion. In 1913, Jung argued that this was simply an impossibility:

> Wie bie der kathartische Methode Suggestibilität und Suggestion vermieden werden könnten, ist dem kritischen Verstand undenkbar. Die sind überall vorhanden … selbst bei Dubois und den Psychoanalytikern, die alle rein rational zu verfahren glauben. *Da hilft keine Technik und kein Sichverbergen – der Arzt wirkt nolens volems, vielleicht in erster Linie, durch seine Persönlichkeit, das heißt suggestiv.*
>
> It is unthinkable to critical understanding that suggestibility and suggestion can be avoided in the cathartic method. They are

> present everywhere ... even with Dubois and the psychoanalysts, who all believe they are working purely rationally. *No technique and no self-effacement help here; the doctor works nolens volens, and perhaps most of all, through his personality, that means suggestively.*[10]

The therapist's conduct ineluctably became an exemplary paragon for the patient. Being impossible to escape, the only solution lay in attaining sufficient self-knowledge. Jung wrote: 'Ich habe viele Male die Gelegenheit gehabt, zu sehen, daß der Analytiker mit seiner Behandlung immer gerade so weit kommt, als er in seiner eigenen moralischen Entwicklung gelangt ist.' / 'I have had the opportunity of seeing many times that the analyst always gets just as far with his treatment as he has succeeded in his moral development.'[11] The goal, however, lay not in directing the patient, but in assisting the patient in attaining self-governance and self-knowledge. We will shortly see how these issues were played out in Jung's practice.

From 1913 onwards, Jung commenced in a process of self-experimentation that he termed his 'confrontation with the unconscious' and his 'confrontation with the soul'. At the heart of this project was his attempt to get to know his own 'myth' as a solution to the mythless predicament of secular modernity. This took the form of provoking an extended series of waking fantasies in himself. He elaborated, illustrated and commented on these fantasies in a work that he called *Liber Novus*, or *The Red Book*, which was at the centre of his later work.[12] This depicted the process through which he regained his soul and overcame the contemporary malaise of spiritual alienation, which was achieved through enabling the rebirth of a new image of God in his soul and developing a new world view in the form of a psychological and theological cosmology. *Liber Novus* presented the prototype of Jung's conception of the individuation process, which he held to be the universal form of individual psychological development.

However, there has been little study of what was taking place in Jung's practice during this critical period, or how he attempted to develop a replicable form of psychotherapy from his own self-experimentation. In what follows, I intend to explore this through utilising unpublished letters and accounts of some of his patients. As Jung did not publish his case material, or write about his practice other than in general terms, these documents allow us to fill this lacuna.

In retrospect, Jung stated that after his break with Freud, he found it necessary to develop a new attitude towards his patients:

So beschloß ich, zunächst einmal vorraussetzungslos abzuwarten, was sie von sich aus erzählen würden. Ich stellte also darauf ab, was der Zufall brachte. Bald zeigte es sich, daß sie spontan ihre Träume und Phantasien berichteten, und ich stellte lediglich ein paar Fragen: 'Was fällt Ihnen dazu ein?' Oder 'Wie verstehen Sie das?' 'Woher kommt das?' Aus den Anworten und Assoziationen ergaben sich die Deutungen wie von selber. Theoretische Gesichtspunkte ließ ich beiseite und war den Patienten nur behilflich, die Bilder aus sich heraus zu verstehen.

I decided for the present to wait presuppositionless for what they would tell by themselves. I also took account of what chance brought. It soon appeared that they spontaneously reported their dreams and phantasies and I only asked a few questions, 'What occurs to you in connection with that?' 'How do you understand that?' 'Where does that come from?' The interpretations rose by themselves from the answers and associations. I left all theoretical viewpoints by the side, and only helped the patients to understand the dream-images by themselves.[13]

This suggests that Jung's practice with his patients followed the same procedure with which he attempted to understand his own dreams and visions at this time: setting aside theoretical presuppositions to allow the images and figures to explain themselves. He maintained that it was for the sake of his patients that he undertook his self-exploration, as he thought that he could not expect them to do something that he did not dare to do himself. He made one other comment about his clinical work at this time:

Ich habe ein Ärztediplom, ich muß meinen Patienten helfen, ich habe eine Frau und fünf Kinder, und ich wohne an der Seestraße 228 in Küsnacht – das waren Tätsachlichkeiten, die mich anforderten. Sie bewiesen mir Tag für Tag, daß ich wirklich existierte ... So waren meine Familie und mein Beruf immer eine beglückende Realität und eine Garantie, daß ich normal und wirklich existierte.

I have a medical diploma, I must help my patients, I have a wife and five children, I live at 228 Seestrasse in Küsnacht – these were actualities which made demands upon me. They proved to me day by day that I really existed ... So my family and my profession always remained a joyful reality and a guarantee that I was normal and really existed.[14]

Here, he states what his patients did for *him*: convince him of his normality. The general impression this gives is that his clinical practice was not seriously affected by the turmoil of his self-experimentation during this period.

In the autumn of 1911, the American psychoanalyst and neurologist James Jackson Putnam sent his cousin Fanny Bowditch Katz to be analysed by Jung. After the death of her father, Henry Bowditch, she had fallen into a prolonged depression. Katz wrote letters to Putnam detailing the development of the analysis, and Putnam replied back with advice. It is widespread today for therapists to be supervised, but it seems that Katz was one of the first supervised patients. Jung approved of this, and Katz would often read Jung her letters to Putnam for his approval. When Jung met Putnam, he discussed her situation with him. Katz's family seemed to be rather suspicious of Jung. On 10 December 1912 Putnam wrote to Katz: 'I suppose it is not to be wondered that your nice aunt ... should think Dr. Jung's ideas strange & reprehensible. You know, I imagine, that even the majority of the doctors are very much down on the whole business.'[15] At the same time, Putnam relayed advice to Jung via Katz: 'Tell Dr. Jung you will get well & strong & he must find means to help you.'[16] Putnam provided his own analysis of Jung to Katz:

> It is a fault in Dr. Jung [entre nous] that he is too self-assertive & I suspect that he is lacking in some needful kinds of imagination & that he is, indeed, a strong but vain person, who might & does do much good but might also tend to crush a patient. He is to be learned from but not followed too implicitly.[17]
>
> I suspect that Dr. Jung's very masterful ways may affect some of his patients more strongly than he realizes himself & you must not get dependent on him or hesitate to form critical judgements of him in your mind.[18]
>
> I cannot but suspect that you are suffering in part from the influence of Dr. Jung's personality & tendency to excessive too personal way of taking things. Perhaps I am wrong, but there will be no harm in realizing that he also is no God but a blind man trying to lead the blind, & that you are as much at liberty to criticize him as he is to criticize you.[19]

Putnam relayed Katz's account of her analysis with Jung to Ernest Jones, who was highly critical of Jung's procedures. As ever, indiscretion was the fundamental rule of psychoanalytic politics.[20]

Jung did not seem to be concerned with keeping strict confidentiality. At the Burghölzli hospital, it had been common procedure for psychiatrists to correspond with the families of patients. In the case of Katz, Jung continued in this vein, writing letters to Katz's mother reporting on her progress. In 1915, he informed her that her daughter needed to undergo a maturational process to reach the full independence necessary for health. He added that he could not describe this process to her, as it would require writing a large book.[21]

Jung was also not bound by the 50-minute hour. On one occasion while he was on military service in 1915, he arranged to meet Katz to have a two-and-a-half hour session at the train station.[22] James Kirsch, who had analysis with Jung at the end of the 1920s recalled that some of his interviews with Jung took place walking in the hills around Küsnacht.[23] In the summer months, Jung would sometimes practice in his garden.

While he was analysing Katz, Jung sent her to be concurrently analysed by his assistant, Maria Moltzer.[24] At the beginning of 1913, Moltzer and Toni Wolff had been admitted as members of the Zürich Psychoanalytical Society as lay members.[25] When Moltzer started to practice, she was supervised by Jung. He described his supervision to the American psychiatrist Smith Ely Jeliffe:

> I trusted the cases entirely to her with the only condition, that in cases of difficulties she would consult me or send the patient to me in order to be controlled by myself. But this arrangement existed in the beginning only. Later on Miss M. worked quite independently and quite efficiently. Financially she is quite independent being paid directly by her patients ... I arranged weekly meetings with my assistant, where everything was settled carefully and on an analytical basis.[26]

The practice of analysis in tandem subsequently became a standard feature of classical Jungian technique, it being held to be desirable for an individual to be analysed by a man and a woman.

Jung's self-exploration took the form of inducing and entering into waking fantasies, dialoguing with the characters that appeared, and drawing and painting the images that appeared.[27] He suggested these same practices to his patients. In 1916, he described his procedure in an unpublished paper, 'The Transcendent Function'.[28] This paper in effect charts how Jung was attempting to develop a generalisable psychotherapeutic method from his self-experimentation. He later termed this 'active imagination'. He noted that one commenced by concentrating on a particular mood, and attempting to become as conscious as possible of all fantasies and associations which came up in connection with it. The aim was to allow fantasy free play, but without departing from the initial affect in a free associative process. This led to a concrete or symbolic expression of the mood, which had the result of bringing the affect nearer to consciousness, hence making it more understandable. The mere process of doing this could have a vitalising effect. Individuals could write, draw, paint or sculpt, depending on their propensities. Once these fantasies had been produced and embodied, two approaches were possible: creative formulation and understanding. Each needed the other, and both were necessary to produce the transcendent function, which arose out of the union of conscious and unconscious contents, and resulted in a widening of consciousness.

In his practice at this time, Jung encouraged his patients to undertake similar forms of self-investigation. In her sessions with Katz, Moltzer talked openly about her own experiences, and taught Katz about Jung's new conceptions. In one session, Katz noted in her diary that:

> In speaking of God, [Moltzer] spoke of Dr. Jung's conception of 'Abraxas' the Urlibido, which she also accepts; using the word Libido and Horme alike for the individual force. The Abraxas is the great cosmic force behind each God (the God embracing the devil is dualistic – Abraxas a monotheistic conception – the one power. Very difficult to understand and have remembered little.[29]

It is not surprising that Katz found this difficult to understand, for it appears that in this session Moltzer was giving her a digest of the first of Jung's *Septem Sermones ad Mortuos.* Like Jung, Moltzer had a book in which she wrote and painted. She called this her Bible, and also encouraged Katz to do the same. Katz noted in her diary: 'Everyone must write his Bible and in working out mine I shall find my adaptation to R. [Rudolf Katz, her husband].'[30] Moltzer thought that it was only through art that one could constellate the unconscious.[31] Katz eventually returned to America, living till the age of 93. In 1956, she informed Jung that she owed her unusually good health and the originality of her silver jewellery to her years in Zürich.[32]

In 1912, Tina Keller had been sent for analysis by her husband, Adolf Keller, one of the first pastors to become interested in psychoanalysis, and a member of Jung's circle. Adolf Keller was the pastor of St Peter's Church in Zürich, and had found psychoanalysis to be a valuable tool in pastoral counselling. In her childhood, Tina Keller had suffered from anxious fears, and these re-emerged in her marriage, despite it being a happy one. Adolf Keller asked Jung for advice, and he recommended analysis. Tina Keller began her analysis with Maria Moltzer. As a result of a dream, Moltzer sent her to Jung.[33] Keller recalled that Jung told her that '"you are very fortunate that you come to analysis after the Freudian ideas have been enlarged," and I was quite sure that I would not have stayed in a Freudian analysis.'[34] She described her situation in the following way:

> My husband's concern was that I should be freed from fear, but Dr. Jung knew he could not take my fears away. He said so to me and added that fear and anxiety were only symptoms, that I was in an 'individuation process' and the symptoms would only diminish as the individuation proceeded … Dr. Jung challenged my faith and tried to expose my unconscious doubts … He was sure that modern persons must come to a personal religious experience and such an experience can only come, when one has nothing to hold onto.[35]

From this it is clear that Jung conceived of the task of analysis as being more than just symptom removal: it was the higher development of the personality. For this to be possible, individuals needed direct religious experience. Nothing could be further from Freud's virulently atheistic attitude.

Jung not only encouraged his patients to talk spontaneously about their experiences, he spontaneously told them of his own. Patients appeared to have been quite aware of what Jung was undergoing. Keller recalled:

> At the time I was in analysis with Dr. Jung, he was still strongly under the impression of that period of irruption from the unconscious … It was during the First World War and Dr. Jung would occasionally allude to his overwhelming experiences. Once he mentioned that they had caused his hair to begin to turn grey … He often spoke of himself and his own experiences.[36]

Jung did not conceal the creative work of his ongoing self-experimentation from his patients:

> In those early days, when one arrived for the analytic hour, the so-called 'red book' often stood open on an easel. In it Dr. Jung had been painting or had just finished a picture. Sometimes he would show me what he had done and comment upon it. The careful and precise work he put into these pictures and into the illuminated text that accompanied them were a testimony to the importance of this undertaking. The master thus demonstrated to the student that psychic development is worth time and effort.[37]

On one such occasion, Jung showed her a painting in the *Red Book* and related it to his relations with his wife and Toni Wolff. Keller recalled:

> [Jung] said, 'see these three snakes that are intertwined. This is how we three struggle with this problem.' I can only say that it seemed to me very important that, even as a passing phenomenon, here three people were accepting a destiny which was not gone into just for their personal satisfaction.[38]

If the psychic process of the therapist affected the patient, Jung had no reluctance in openly sharing his. Keller noted:

> One felt accepted into the very special atmosphere of the discovery of the inner world and of its mystery ... Whenever Dr. Jung spoke of these experience I could feel his emotion. Coming to analysis at that time one entered a very special atmosphere. One felt that Dr. Jung stood in awe before fragments that 'were coming to him,' and that he must try to understand, but that were quite beyond what the human brain can grasp. Everything was fluid, what he said was tentative, paradoxical and full of seeming contradictions.[39]

Jung developed a set of specific principles that he urged upon his patients. Keller noted:

> Dr. Jung insisted on preparation. We were taught to write out our dreams and association to each of its elements ... The most important technique I learned in the sessions with Dr. Jung was writing 'from the unconscious.' Early in my analysis Dr. Jung said, 'You must at once begin to prepare for the time you will no more be coming to me. Each time, as you are leaving, even as you are going downstairs, you have more questions. Write these down as if they were letters to me. You do not need to send these letters. When you ask a question, in the measure that you really want an answer, and you are not afraid of that answer, there is an answer deep inside you. Let it come up.' I tried and nothing came, and I told Dr. Jung. But he insisted. He even said, 'Surely you know how to pray!'[40]

The role of prayer as one of the sources for Jung's analytic technique has not been commented upon. It is important to realise that the psychology of prayer was an important subject in the psychology of religion and in psychical research. The new psychology of suggestion, autosuggestion and telepathy was invoked to explain prayer. Frederic Myers attempted to put forward a spiritual but non-theological definition of prayer or supplication, broadly defined as the appeal to the unseen. It was 'an attempt to obtain benefits from unseen beings by an inward disposition of our own minds.'[41] Judging by Keller's description of Jung's counsel, what seems to have been at issue here is a nondenominational form of prayer. The unconscious was the unseen, the higher power to which one appealed for instruction and healing.

Indications of Jung's interest in prayer may be found in his fantasies at the beginning of 1914. In a fantasy on 1 January 1914, Jung's 'I' found himself in a desert valley, where he met an anchorite called Ammonius.[42] The latter told him that he should not forget his morning prayer. Jung's 'I' realised that we had lost our prayers. In a fantasy of 14 January 1914, Jung's 'I' wanted to borrow a copy of *The Imitation of Christ*, with the 'aim of prayer, or something similar', as there were moments when science left us sick.[43]

At the same time, Jung held back from advocating traditional prayer in sessions. One of his students, Kurt Binswanger recalled: '[Alphonse] Maeder believed it to be good to pray with his patients during the (analytical) hour. And that was for Jung something he couldn't go on with.'[44]

During the course of the analysis, Tina Keller felt love and hatred towards Jung:

> Dr. Jung never spoke of 'transference' but obliged me to face the fact that I was 'in love.' It would have been easier to use a technical term. Dr. Jung's theory was that I was 'in love' with some quality (or archetype) which he represented, and had touched in my psyche. If and in measure that I would be able to realize this quality or this unknown element in myself, then I would be free of him as a person.[45]

Not only did Jung dispense with technical language to describe his patient's relation to him, he appears to have done the same with respect to his relations to his patients, and been quite open to speak of what he felt:

> He was convinced of the meaning of such a manifestation, and he said that what I brought was such an openness that he owed me some spiritual value that would fertilize my psyche and my 'individuation' would be a 'spiritual child.' This sounded good. He sincerely meant it, but it did not prove true.[46]

Here, Jung openly avows the active agency of the therapist in the therapeutic encounter, fertilising the patient's psyche, giving rise to the patient's individuation. After her analysis with Jung, Keller had analysis with Toni Wolff.

Far from being a solitary endeavour, Jung's confrontation with the unconscious was a collective endeavour, in which he took his patients along with him. Those around Jung formed an avant-garde group engaged in a social experiment that they hoped would transform their lives, and the lives of those around them.[47] Keller noted:

> During the First World War, in the midst of the feeling of catastrophe, when cultural values were breaking down, when there was general consternation and disillusionment, a small group around Dr. Jung participated in his vision of an inner world unfolding. Many of us were later disappointed. The vision was too vast and leads into the future.[48]

Tina Keller subsequently became a psychotherapist. For decades, she was Jung's main representative in Geneva. She would turn to Jung for supervision. On one occasion, she discussed a borderline case she had taken on. Jung told her, 'You have not the right to experiment in the same way as I have because I have now my name. If something happens to me, you see, it is different than if something happens to you.'[49] Jung was quite aware of the experimental nature of his practice, and the protection accorded by his status and medical qualification. Another of Jung's patients during this period, Emil Medtner claimed that were it not for Jung, he would have shared Friedrich Nietzsche's fate and 'gone mad'. Medtner likened analysis to what Goethe had once referred to as a 'psychic cure in which insanity is let in to heal insanity'.[50]

In 1913, Edith Rockefeller McCormick went to Zürich to have analysis with Jung, together with her husband. The McCormicks wrote letters home to Edith's father, John D. Rockefeller, apprising him of their progress, and expressing their deep admiration for Jung. On 15 June 1915, Harold McCormick wrote to him:

> This is not a tabernacle of joy, but a shrine to which seekers only address themselves, and it was in this spirit that I have postponed again my sailing and Edith still finds herself held. With both of us, every day counts. This is not a place (the School of Zurich) which encourages remaining here beyond the right or normal time but the whole question is one of degree at best, for no one who is really interested in analytical psychology and finds it of help ever drops it, because if it is one thing, – it is to be lived, and the more one

studies the more one is prepared to live on its basis. So one must strike out again in life else it (analytical psychology) defeats its own purpose. The fundamental idea of it is to teach one, one's self – and this is not always easy, and still more difficult, owing to conscious resistances, to follow one's path when it has been laid out by one's own self. But there is a natural tendency, which one must guard against, of preferring the ease of this life here to the hardships and difficulties of life and living in general, but neither Edith nor I have reached this point yet, and when it is reached I have no doubt it will be effectively met.[51]

This letter conveys that for the McCormicks, as for many others during this period, Jung's analysis was becoming not only a form of therapy but also the basis for a new way of life grounded in psychology.

The first phase of Jung's self-experimentation had consisted in a 'return' to himself, a reconnection with his soul. From Harold McCormick's letters, it appears that he was successful in aiding some of his patients to do likewise. On 1 September 1915, Harold McCormick wrote to John D. Rockefeller:

> We are doing our best and are deeply appreciating the opportunity of the work under the beautiful inspiration and guidance – only as to showing us ourselves and enabling us to better know ourselves – of Dr. Jung. It seems a trite thing to say, but I do most sincerely say that I am surprised how little I have known myself heretofore or how little I have cared for the society & acquaintance and intimacy of myself. I am told there is a wealth of opportunity in this direction, without in any way meaning self-adulation.[52]

Their son, Fowler McCormick, also had analysis with Jung in the winter of 1916–7. He recalled that in many of the sessions he had, 'Jung would occupy himself by carving in wood while we talked.'[53]

We have seen that Jung recommended that his patients write letters to him without sending them. I have come across others who did just this.[54] The following is from such a letter by Cary de Angulo, which gives further indication of Jung's handling of the rapport. Cary de Angulo (née Fink) was of the first generation of women to take a medical degree in the United States, although she never practised. After the collapse of her marriage to the brilliant linguist and ethnologist, Jaime de Angulo, she went to Zürich to work with Jung in 1921. In 1923 she described their therapeutic relationship in the following way:

> The essential fact is that wandering about the universe completely detached, I have met you and entered into an indissoluble union with you. It took place automatically without any willing or not-willing on my part just on account of your being what you are. To this 'you' I can write because this 'you' gives me a place in your life – a unique place of great intimacy and yet extreme aloofness. That is the way I define a symbolical relationship. I am at one and the same time inside your being and forever and completely separated from you.... Every hour I spend with you has holiness in it for me, not because I am worshipping you, but because I am reaching toward certain values which you express more patently than anyone else.[55]

Cary de Angulo was more receptive than Tina Keller to what Jung was proposing, and sensitively describes the sincerity of the endeavour, and the manner in which the aim was for her to recover her sense of religious values, rather than to worship Jung. Appreciating her intelligence and judgement, Jung turned to her for advice concerning the *Red Book*. She noted:

> You had the night before had a dream in which I appeared in a disguise and was to do work on the *Red Book* and you had been thinking about it all that day and during Dr. Wharton's hour preceding mine especially (pleasant for her I must say) ... As you had said you had made up your mind to turn over to me all of your unconscious material represented by the *Red Book* etc. to see what I as a stranger and impartial observer would say about it. You thought I had a good critique and an impartial one ... For yourself, you said you had always known what to do with your ideas, but here you were baffled. When you approached them you became enmeshed as it were and could no longer be sure of anything. You were certain some of them had great importance, but you could not find the appropriate form – as they were now you said they might come out of a mad-house.[56]

Jung asked her to transcribe the *Red Book*. He saw this task as also having a pedagogical value. She noted that he said he 'would explain things to me as I went along ... In this way we could come to discuss many things which never came up in my analysis and I could understand your ideas from the foundation.'[57]

Jung also conducted analyses by correspondence. Jaime de Angulo sent his ex-wife his dreams. She discussed these in her sessions with Jung, and sent Jaime back Jung's interpretations. In a session on 14 February

1924, she presented Jung with notes which Jaime de Angulo had written about himself and some dreams that he had sent. On the following day, she wrote to him Jung's general comments:

> He said that he would indeed want to 'moderate' you were you with him, and that the way he would do it would be to see that you understood thoroughly the concepts before you rushed ahead into the processes … In as much as he is not in a position to put the brakes on you personally, he suggested that you read the 'Psychology of the Unconscious' again very carefully, and also the 'Types' making notes and discussions on the parts you do not understand, and sending these notes to me for criticism.[58]

She continued to give Jung's interpretations of four of his dreams. While Jung directed Jaime de Angulo to closely study his writings, this was not a general procedure. In the same letter, she conveyed Jung's advice concerning a case which Jaime de Angulo had taken on:

> he said you should not by any means have tried to explain any theory to him, but if you were going to handle him as a case, the transference should have been made to do the ploughing of the ground, and the theory only administered with great caution and attention to his capacity to take it in.[59]

Patients in analysis with Jung quite naturally wrote to their friends about their experiences in Zürich. In the mid-1920s, the American theatre set designer Robert Edmond Jones came to Jung for analysis. He wrote about his experiences to Mabel Dodge:

> I have been working with this man for two weeks and I have already begun to move in a world of the most ancient and magical visions of soul-states and the beginnings of Time. This is no psychoanalysis or any of those things. This man is a wise man possessed of the secrets … This work is not merely curative. It is serene and austere and disciplinary. There is a good deal of Gurdjieff in it. I wish I could describe this experience to you but it is of no use. It is really more esoteric than anything else, an initiation into manhood. There is no trace of medicine or (therapeutics)? in it. A subtle deep terrible mystical journey, torments, vigils, illuminations. I think we have a very good working combination. I got in right at the start by not hanging back the way lots of patients do; and it was such a blessed relief to me to find that I

wasn't a homosexual and didn't have to be one of those. Jung says that I have the most remarkable gift for animating other people that he has ever seen. His nickname for me is Burster of Shells because I have yanked about half a dozen of his patients right out of their [shells] and made them admit. And he sometimes called me a Giver of Life.[60]

Dodge also received accounts from Mary Foote of her analysis with Jung. Drawn into the magic circle, she sent Foote her own dreams to take to be analysed by Jung.[61] These correspondence networks played a critical role in the dissemination of analysis, and shaped the expectations of prospective patients. As Foote informed Dodge, 'Jung doesn't remove your complexes & he thinks all progress comes from conflict so I suppose one will go on conflicting for the rest of one's life.'[62] 'Letters home' from Zürich did much to promote analysis in America and England, and helped it gain social acceptance. Through such trade routes, developments in the German-speaking world spread throughout the English-speaking world.

Jung's instructions to his patients on how to conduct active imagination were quite specific. To explain it, he would recount his own experiences. In 1926, Christiana Morgan came to Jung for analysis. She had been drawn to Jung's ideas on reading *Psychological Types*, and turned to Jung for assistance with her problems with relationships and her depressions. In a session in 1926, Christiana Morgan noted Jung's advice to her about how to produce visions:

> Well, you see these are too vague for me to be able to say much about them. They are only the beginning. You only use the retina of the eye at first in order to objectify. Then instead of keeping on trying to force the image out you just want to look in. Now when you see these images you want to hold them and see where they take you – how they change. And you want to try to get into the picture yourself – to become one of the actors. When I first began to do this I saw landscapes. Then I learned how to put myself into the landscape, and the figures would talk to me and I would answer them.[63]

Jung described his own experiments in detail to his patients, and instructed them to follow suit. His role was one of supervising them in experimenting with their own stream of images. Morgan noted Jung saying:

> Now I feel as though I ought to say something to you about these phantasies.... The phantasies now seem to be rather thin and full of

> repetitions of the same motives. There isn't enough fire and heat in them. They ought to be more burning ... You must be in them more, that is you must be your own conscious critical self in them – imposing your own judgements and criticisms.[64]

Jung went so far as to suggest that his patients prepare their own *Red Books*. Morgan noted him saying:

> I should advise you to put it all down as beautifully as you can – in some beautifully bound book. It will seem as if you were making the visions banal – but then you need to do that – then you are freed from the power of them. If you do that with these eyes for instance they will cease to draw you. You should never try to make the visions come again. Think of it in your imagination and try to paint it. Then when these things are in some precious book you can go to the book & turn over the pages & for you it will be your church – your cathedral – the silent places of your spirit where you will find renewal. If anyone tells you that it is morbid or neurotic and you listen to them – then you will lose your soul – for in that book is your soul.[65]

With Morgan's permission, Jung used her material in an extended seminar, which ran from 1930 to 1934.[66] Morgan found Jung's treatment of her material inspiring:

> The seminar notes have arrived for which I thank you. I have read them – and I closed the book with a prayer – (a hymn) of gratefulness to you for not having detracted from – indeed for having enhanced – the august quality of those visions. I wish it were possible to convey how completely such an experience can change a life – how in fact, it works in actuality. How the meaning of life is the necessity to embody forth those very visions (or perhaps one should say to act under their sign). / I particularly liked all that you said about the animal face. I lost connection with it this winter.[67]

While patients such as these responded wholeheartedly to Jung's suggestions, others were more critical. In 1919, the English psychologist William McDougall went to have analysis with Jung. During the course of the analysis, McDougall, Jung and his assistant Peter Baynes went sailing together and had dinner together. Amy Allenby, a student of Jung's, later recalled:

> Baynes and Jung noticed that McDougall was firmly entrenched behind his persona, and that one could never get to the real person underneath. So Jung suggested that they should invite McDougall to an evening by the lake and ply him with wine until he would get a little drunk; they did, and it happened.[68]

By contemporary standards of psychotherapy, such practices would be seen as unprofessional 'boundary breaking'. Such a judgement is anachronistic. Jung never held such a conception of boundaries. In his view, there was no strict division between analysis and life. Analysis was conceived as leading to the psychological reformulation of society through fostering new attitudes and values in the individual. Foremost among these were freedom from hypocrisy, coupled with openness and honesty in personal relations.

McDougall was not convinced by his analysis. Shortly after, he wrote in one of his books:

> I have put myself into the hands of Doctor Jung and asked him to explore the depths of my mind, my 'collective unconscious' ... And the result is – I 'evermore came out by that same door wherein I went.' ... I seem to find in myself traces or indications of Doctor Jung's 'archetypes', but faint and doubtful traces. Perhaps it is that I am too mongrel-bred to have clear-cut archetypes; perhaps my 'collective unconscious' – if I have one – is mixed and confused and blurred.[69]

In 1926, he published *An Outline of Abnormal Psychology*.[70] In his chapter on Jung's theories, he reproduced some of his dreams, Jung's analysis of them, and his own interpretations. Intrigued by this account, Smith Ely Jeliffe asked Jung for more information concerning his treatment of McDougall. Jung replied:

> I don't know whether I am bound to medical discretion in McDougall's case, as he designates himself as a hopelessly normal personality. I probably had no right to consider his case as one that would fall under the concept of medical discretion. There isn't much to be indiscreet about anyway. It was really as he states it: a very few dreams taken to Dr. Jung in order to have an argument about it, and withholding if possible all reactions which could be disagreeable. It was, as you suspect, a very modest number of conversations and anything else but a submission to the actual procedure of analysis of which, I'm afraid, Prof. McDougall has not the faintest idea. I like

however his experiments with rats and wouldn't argue that point with him, but people who are absolutely innocent of psychology, I find, are usually profoundly convinced of their psychological competence.[71]

Jung's insistence that his patients prepare themselves for analysis also took the form of requiring patients to undergo analysis with one of his followers prior to seeing him, and also of being tutored in analytical psychology. In the 1920s, Jung turned to Cary de Angulo to tutor some of his patients. On one occasion, he asked her to take on one of his patients, Dr Bond, for tutoring during his absence. As she was an 'introvert of the nth degree', she needed much general preparatory knowledge.[72]

In addition to tutoring, preparation took the form of prior analyses with one of Jung's pupils. To the American writer, Leonard Bacon, he wrote that patients had first to begin their analysis with one of them so as to get a 'decent preparation' before seeing him.[73]

The significance of preparation was that it enabled Jung to concentrate on fostering the higher development or individuation of his patients. From the 1920s, individuals did not come to Jung not knowing what to expect: they were selected and primed. The social role of the analytic patient – in this context, of a patient of Jung – had to be created. If they had extensive personal problems to sort out, Jung would generally leave this to his assistants. This indicates that what ensued was the result of quite unusual procedures. Of his practice, Jung noted that he had very few new cases, and that most of them had had prior experience of psychotherapy. In 1954, he wrote that just as with surgery, there was minor and major psychotherapy, and that his concern here was with the latter: 'Es handelt sich um eine Minderzahl von Patienten mit gewissen geistigen Ansprüchen, und nur solche durchlaufen eine Entwicklung, welche dem Arzt Probleme von der hier geschilderten Art aufgeben.' / 'It is a question of a minority of patients with certain spiritual demands, and only these patients undergo a development which presents the doctor with problems of the nature described here.'[74]

In his subsequent published writings, Jung insisted that his patients' individuation was not a product of suggestion, but a natural spontaneous process, which was simply quickened by the analysis. Some saw it otherwise. Tina Keller recalled:

> I believe it was a kind of contagion because of the dynamic process that Dr. Jung was still involved in, and that those close to him were identifying with. This poses the question, whether a pioneer in an

'exceptional' state can safely work as a therapist? Or is there perhaps a special quality in such a man, so stimulating to the privileged persons, that the advantages outweigh the dangers?[75]

In her analysis with Jung, she, and others around her, were drawn into the process that Jung himself was undergoing. His experiment with himself was at the same time an experiment on them. In 1929, Jung explicitly described his aim as being one of bringing about 'eines seelischen Zustandes, in welchem mein Patient anfängt, mit seinem Wesen zu experimentieren.' / 'a psychic state in which my patient begins to experiment with his own being'.[76] Their interactions with him played a critical role in establishing analytical psychology as a social movement. Through this, the results of Jung's self-experimentation began to have a transformative effect on an ever-growing number of people, as they took on his conceptions, and let him change their lives. The willingness of a number of individuals to accept the invitation to experiment with their lives in such a manner and embrace his new conceptions convinced Jung that the latter were not merely idiosyncratic, but were replicable, and had general significance.

The consequence of this expansion of the remit of psychotherapy beyond the cure of pathology was that what was formerly a 'medical method of treatment' had become a 'method of self-education', no longer bound to the consulting room.[77] This brought it into proximity with Eastern esoteric traditions on the one hand, and European spiritual practices on the other. Consequently, Jung spent much time from the 1930s onwards engaged in the comparative study of these practices.[78] He maintained that his fantasies, and those of his patients, stemmed from the mythopoetic imagination, which was missing in the present rational age. Reconnecting with this could form the basis for cultural renewal. The task of moderns was one of establishing a dialogue with the contents of the collective unconscious and integrating them into consciousness. This was to play an important part in the popular 'mythic revival'. He held that cultural renewal could only come about through self-regeneration of the individual, in other words, through the individuation process. What he was proposing was a new 'image of man'. As he saw it, the task with which his patients were confronted was one of recovering a sense of meaning in their life, made more pressing with the secularisation and rationalisation of contemporary culture. Consequently, he held that individuals who managed to recover a sense of meaning in their lives were healing not only themselves but also the culture. Thus, the aim of the therapeutic cure was not one of helping the patient adapt to existing social norms, but to foster a process of self-realisation that would ultimately contribute to reshaping society. The psychotherapeutic patient had become the doctor of society.

Notes

1. See Shamdasani, 'Psychotherapy in Society'.
2. See Shamdasani, 'Psychologies as Ontology-Making Practices'; Shamdasani, 'Questioning the Unconscious'.
3. Kleinman, *The Illness Narratives*.
4. Jaime de Angulo to Chauncey Goodrich, 28 August 1922, Goodrich papers, Bancroft Library, University of California at San Francisco.
5. On this wider context, see Shamdasani, 'Psychotherapy in Society'.
6. Pierre Janet, *Les obsessions et la psychasthénie*, *I*, 727.
7. Jung, *Versuch einer Darstellung der psychoanalytischen Theorie*, in Jung, *Gesammelte Werke* (hereafter, *GW*), 4, § 433; Jung, *An Attempt at an Account of Psychoanalytic Theory*, in *Collected Works* (hereafter, *CW*), 4, § 433.
8. Jung, *Versuch einer Darstellung der psychoanalytischen Theorie*, § 434.
9. Carroy, *Hypnose, suggestion et psychologie*, 179–200.
10. Jung, 'Psychotherapeutische Zeitfragen', *GW* 4, § 584; Jung 'Timely Psychotherapeutic Questions', *CW* 4, § 584. On Jung's use and understanding of hypnosis and suggestion, see Shamdasani, '"The Magical Method That Works in the Dark"'.
11. Jung, 'Psychotherapeutische Zeitfragen', § 587.
12. Jung, *The Red Book*.
13. Jaffé and Jung, *Erinnerungen, Träume, Gedanken*, 174; Jaffé and Jung, *Memories, Dreams, Reflections*, 194.
14. Jaffé and Jung, *Erinnerungen, Träume, Gedanken*, 193; Jaffé and Jung, *Memories, Dreams, Reflections*, 214.
15. Putnam to Bowditch Katz, 10 December 1912, Katz papers, Countway Library of Medicine.
16. Putnam to Bowditch Katz, 12 December 1912.
17. Putnam to Bowditch Katz, 7 January 1912.
18. Putnam to Bowditch Katz, 10 December 1912.
19. Putnam to Bowditch Katz, 10 December 1913.
20. Putnam cited a reply from Jones in an undated letter to Bowditch Katz.
21. Jung to Mrs Katz, 27 February 1912.
22. Jung to Bowditch Katz, 11 January 1915.
23. James Kirsch, interview with Gene Nameche, 1968, Jung Biographical Archive, Countway Library of Medicine.
24. On Bowditch Katz's analyses, see also Taylor, 'C.G. Jung and the Boston Psychopathologists 1902–1912'. On Bowditch Katz, Moltzer and Jung, see Shamdasani, *Cult Fictions*.
25. 30 January 1913, 'Protokolle des Psychoanalytischen Vereins', archives of the Psychological Club, Zürich.
26. Jung to Jelliffe, July 1915, in Burnham and McGuire, *Jelliffe*, 198.
27. On the evolution of the techniques of Jung's self-experimentation, see Shamdasani, 'Jung's Practice of the Image'.
28. Jung, 'Die Transzendente Funktion', *GW* 8, §§ 170–1; Jung, 'The Transcendent Function,' *CW* 8, §§ 170–1.
29. Bowditch Katz, entry for August 1917, Diary, Katz papers.
30. 17 August 1917, Diary.
31. 7 May 1917, Diary.
32. Fanny Bowditch Katz to Jung, 17 January 1956, Jung archive, Swiss Federal Institute of Technology, Zürich.

33. Swan, *The Memoir of Tina Keller-Jenny*, 17.
34. Swan, *The Memoir of Tina Keller-Jenny*, 19.
35. Keller, 'C.G. Jung', 5.
36. Tina Keller, 'Recollections of my encounter with Dr. Jung', Jung Biographical Archive, Countway Library of Medicine, A2.
37. Swan, *The Memoir of Tina Keller-Jenny*, 21.
38. Tina Keller interview with Gene Nameche, 1969, R.D. Laing papers, University of Glasgow, 27.
39. Tina Keller, 'Recollections of my encounter with Dr. Jung', B12, A2.
40. Swan, *The Memoir of Tina Keller-Jenny*, 23.
41. Myers, *Human Personality and its Survival after Bodily Death*, vol. 2, 310.
42. Jung, *The Red Book*, 269.
43. Jung, *The Red Book*, 292.
44. Kurt Binswanger, interview with Gene Nameche, Jung Biographical Archive, Countway Library of Medicine, 14.
45. Tina Keller, 'Recollections of my encounter with Dr. Jung', B19.
46. Tina Keller, 'Recollections of my encounter with Dr. Jung', B19.
47. For a study of another important case at this time, see De Moura, 'Learning from the Patient'.
48. Tina Keller, 'Recollections of my encounter with Dr. Jung', A5.
49. Tina Keller interview with Gene Nameche, 18.
50. Cited in Ljunggren, *The Russian Mephisto*, 91.
51. Harold McCormick to John D. Rockefeller, 15 June 1915, Rockefeller Archive Centre, Terrytown, NY.
52. Harold McCormick to John D. Rockefeller, 1 September 1915, Rockefeller Archive Centre.
53. Fowler McCormick interview with Gene Nameche, Jung Biographical Archive, Countway Library of Medicine, 8.
54. One example being Rivkah Scharf (I thank Nomi Kluger Nash for enabling access to her papers).
55. Cary Baynes (née de Angulo), 14 January 1923, letter drafts, Baynes papers, Contemporary Medical Archives, Wellcome Library, London.
56. 26 January 1924, letter drafts.
57. 26 January 1924, letter drafts.
58. Cary de Angulo to Jaime de Angulo, 15 February 1924, Cary Baynes papers.
59. Cary de Angulo to Jaime de Angulo, 15 February 1924.
60. Robert Edmond Jones to Mabel Dodge, 1926, Dodge papers, Beinecke library, Yale University.
61. Mary Foote to Mabel Dodge, November 1925, Dodge papers. On Mary Foote, see Trousdell, 'The Lives of Mary Foote'.
62. Mary Foote to Mabel Dodge, 1929.
63. Christiana Morgan, 8 July 1926, analysis notebooks, Countway Library of Medicine.
64. Analysis notebooks, 12 October 1926.
65. Analysis notebooks, 12 July 1926.
66. Jung, *Visions*.
67. Morgan to Jung, 31 June 1931, Jung Archive, Swiss Federal Institute of Technology, Zürich.
68. Amy Allenby, interview with Gene Nameche, Jung Biographical Archive, Countway Library of Medicine, 3.
69. McDougall, *National Welfare and National Decay*, 134.
70. McDougall, *An Outline of Abnormal Psychology*, 181–205.
71. Jung to Jeliffe, 7 June 1932, in Burnham and McGuire, *Jeliffe*, 326.
72. Jung to Cary de Angulo, 17 August 1925, Baynes papers.
73. Jung to Leonard Bacon, 26 July 1926, Bacon papers, Beinecke Library, Yale University.
74. Jung, *Mysterium Coniunctionis*, *GW* 14, 2 § 178; *CW* 14, § 514.
75. Tina Keller, 'Recollections of my encounter with Dr. Jung', B17-8.
76. Jung, 'Ziele der Psychotherapie', *GW* 16, § 99; 'The Aims of Psychotherapy', *GW* 16, § 99.
77. Jung, 'Die Probleme der modernen Psychotherapie'. (1929), *GW* 16, § 174; 'The Problems of Modern Psychotherapy', *CW* 16, § 174.
78. For the former, see Jung, *The Psychology of Kundalini Yoga*; for the latter see Martin Liebscher's contribution to this volume.

Bibliography

Burnham, John C. and William McGuire, eds. *Jelliffe: American Psychoanalyst and Physician; and His Correspondence with Sigmund Freud and C.G. Jung*. Chicago: University of Chicago Press, 1983.

Carroy, Jacqueline. *Hypnose, suggestion et psychologie: L'invention de sujets*. Paris: Presses Universitaires de France, 1991.

De Moura, Vicente. 'Learning from the Patient: The East, Synchronicity and Transference in the History of an Unknown Case of C.G. Jung', *Journal of Analytical Psychology* 59, no. 3 (2014): 391–409.

Jaffé, Aniela and C.G. Jung. *Erinnerungen, Träume, Gedanken*. Düsseldorf: Walter Verlag, 1989.

Jaffé, Aniela and C.G. Jung. *Memories, Dreams, Reflections*, translated by Richard Winston and Clara Winston. London: Fontana, 1990.

Janet, Pierre. *Les obsessions et la psychasthénie, I*. Paris: Alcan, 1903.

Jung, C.G. *The Collected Works of C.G. Jung*, edited by Gerhard Adler, Michael Fordham and William McGuire. Princeton: Princeton University Press, 1953–76.

Jung, C.G. *Gesammelte Werke*, edited by Marienne Niehus-Jung, Lena Hurwitz-Eisner and Franz Jung. Düsseldorf: Walter Verlag, 1995.

Jung, C.G. *Versuch einer Darstellung der psychoanalytischen Theorie*. In *Gesammelte Werke* 4, edited by Marienne Niehus-Jung, Lena Hurwitz-Eisner and Franz Jung, §§ 203–26. Düsseldorf: Walter Verlag, 1995.

Jung, C.G. *An Attempt at an Account of Psychoanalytic Theory*. In *The Collected Works of C.G. Jung* 4, edited by Gerhard Adler, Michael Fordham and William McGuire, §§ 203–26. Princeton: Princeton University Press, 1953–76.

Jung, C.G. 'Die Transzendente Funktion'. In *Gesammelte Werke* 8, edited by Marienne Niehus-Jung, Lena Hurwitz-Eisner and Franz Jung, §§ 131–91. Düsseldorf: Walter Verlag, 1995.

Jung, C.G. 'The Transcendent Function', In *The Collected Works of C.G. Jung* 8, edited by Gerhard Adler, Michael Fordham and William McGuire, §§ 131–91. Princeton: Princeton University Press, 1953–76.

Jung, C.G. 'Ziele der Psychotherapie'. In *Gesammelte Werke* 16, edited by Marienne Niehus-Jung, Lena Hurwitz-Eisner and Franz Jung, §§ 66–131. Düsseldorf: Walter Verlag, 1995.

Jung, C.G. 'The Aims of Psychotherapy', In *The Collected Works of C.G. Jung* 16, edited by Gerhard Adler, Michael Fordham and William McGuire, §§ 66–131. Princeton: Princeton University Press, 1953–76.

Jung, C.G. 'Die Probleme der modernen Psychotherapie'. In *Gesammelte Werke* 16, edited by Marienne Niehus-Jung, Lena Hurwitz-Eisner and Franz Jung, §§ 114–74. Düsseldorf: Walter Verlag, 1995.

Jung, C.G. 'The Problems of Modern Psychotherapy'. In *The Collected Works of C.G. Jung* 16, edited by Gerhard Adler, Michael Fordham and William McGuire, §§ 114–74. Princeton: Princeton University Press, 1953–76.

Jung, C.G. *Mysterium Coniunctionis*. In *Gesammelte Werke* 14, edited by Marienne Niehus-Jung, Lena Hurwitz-Eisner and Franz Jung. Düsseldorf: Walter Verlag, 1995.

Jung, C.G. *Mysterium Coniunctionis*. In *The Collected Works of C.G. Jung* 14, edited by Gerhard Adler, Michael Fordham and William McGuire. Princeton: Princeton University Press, 1953–76.

Jung, C.G. 'Psychotherapeutische Zeitfragen: Ein Briefwechsel zwischen C.G. Jung und R. Loÿ'. In *Gesammelte Werke* 4, edited by Marienne Niehus-Jung, Lena Hurwitz-Eisner and Franz Jung, §§ 576–669. Düsseldorf: Walter Verlag, 1995.

Jung, C.G. 'Timely Psychotherapeutic Questions: A Correspondence between C.G. Jung and R. Loÿ'. In *The Collected Works of C.G. Jung* 4, edited by Gerhard Adler, Michael Fordham and William McGuire, §§ 576–669. Princeton: Princeton University Press, 1953–76.

Jung, C.G. *The Psychology of Kundalini Yoga: Notes of the Seminar Given in 1932*, edited by Sonu Shamdasani. Princeton: Princeton University Press, 1996.

Jung, C.G. *Visions: Notes of the Seminar Given in 1930–1934*, edited by Claire Douglas. Princeton: Princeton University Press, 1997.

Jung, C.G. *The Red Book. Liber Novus*, edited by Sonu Shamdasani; translated by Mark Kyburz, John Peck and Sonu Shamdasani. New York: W.W. Norton, 2009.

Keller, Tina. 'C.G. Jung: Some Memories and Reflections', *Inward Light* 35 (1972): 1–18.

Kleinman, Arthur. *The Illness Narratives: Suffering, Healing, and the Human Condition*. New York: Basic Books, 1988.

Ljunggren, Magnus. *The Russian Mephisto: A Study of the Life and Work of Emilii Medtner*. Stockholm: Almqvist and Wiksell International, 1994.
McDougall, William. *National Welfare and National Decay*. London: Methuen, 1921.
McDougall, William. *An Outline of Abnormal Psychology*. London: Methuen, 1926.
Myers, Frederic W.H. *Human Personality and Its Survival of Bodily Death*. London: Longmans, 1903.
Shamdasani, Sonu. *Cult Fictions: C.G. Jung and the Founding of Analytical Psychology*. London: Routledge, 1998.
Shamdasani, Sonu. 'Psychologies as Ontology-Making Practices: William James and the Pluralities of Psychological Experience'. In *William James and the Varieties of Religious Experience*, edited by Jeremy Carrette, 27–46. London: Routledge, 2004.
Shamdasani, Sonu. 'Jung's Practice of the Image', *Journal of Sandplay Therapy* 24, no. 1 (2015): 7–21.
Shamdasani, Sonu. 'Psychotherapy in Society: Historical Reflections'. In *The Routledge History of Madness and Mental Health*, edited by Greg Eghigian, 363–78. London: Routledge, 2017.
Shamdasani, Sonu. 'Questioning the Unconscious', *Annals of the New York Academy of Sciences* 1406, no. 1 (2017): 86–89.
Swan, Wendy K., ed. *The Memoir of Tina Keller-Jenny: A Lifelong Confrontation with the Psychology of C.G. Jung*. New Orleans: Spring Journal Books, 2011.
Taylor, Eugene. 'C.G. Jung and the Boston Psychopathologists 1902–1912'. In *Carl Jung and Soul Psychology*, edited by E. Mark Stern, 131–44. New York: Haworth Press, 1986.
Trousdell, Richard. 'The Lives of Mary Foote: Painter and Jungian', *Journal of Analytical Psychology* 61, no. 5 (2016): 588–606.

5

C.G. Jung and the Berneuchen Movement: Meditation and Active Imagination in Jungian Psychotherapy and Protestant Spiritual Practice in the 1930s

Martin Liebscher

Preface

The Introduction to this volume shows that the twentieth century's conceptualisation of humanity was strongly based on the materialist understanding of the human body defined by biomedical science, and individual contributions explore tensions in the history and literary reception of biomedicine, between the dichotomies of human and inhuman, humane and inhumane. This chapter argues that this fourfold semantic field of medicine, revolving around the corporeal, has always been encompassed by a *quinta essentia*, a fifth element that is the non-human other, namely God: according to the Swiss pastor and theologian Karl Barth, 'the pure and absolute boundary and beginning of all that we are and have and do', yet also 'the Unknown, who is never a known thing in the midst of other known things'.[1] The psychiatrist and philosopher Karl Jaspers used the term 'transcendence' to denote a mode of being that is the complete other, a mode in which we do not have a share, but on which we are nonetheless based and to which we relate.[2]

It was another psychiatrist, C.G. Jung, contemporary of Jaspers, who attempted to bridge the separation between the scientific medical discourse of the mind on the one hand, and philosophical and theological theories of transcendence on the other hand. By arguing for the ability of the human soul to recognise and even integrate transcendent content, Jung opposed Kantian or post-Kantian notions of religious agnosticism. Following Sonu Shamdasani's contribution to this volume on Jung's psychological self-experiment and the consequent shift of his psychotherapy from being solely a cure for pathology, to becoming a theory of higher psychological and spiritual awareness, this chapter in turn outlines the key role Jung attributed to spiritual meditation as part of the psychological process of individuation. Jung describes the aim of psychological individuation as the Ego experiencing the archetype of the Self, or the unity of the individual with the collective unconscious.

Such an idea invites reflection as to what extent a psychotherapeutic treatment is justified in incorporating such a practice as spiritual meditation that expands or even dissolves the boundaries of the Ego. The psychological incorporation of the hitherto non-human other, that is, God, experienced in an ecstatic union through meditation or other spiritual practices, challenges our understanding of what it is to be human, which in modern Western thought is firmly rooted in the subject–object duality. In the last analysis, such a notion raises the question of whether integration of the non-human other leads to an inhuman illusion or even delusion in the Freudian sense, or brings with it a heightened responsibility for creation and humanity.

Introduction

> Ich bin Arzt. [*Directeur de conscience* zu sein] ist die natürliche Berufung des Geistlichen; er sollte es tun. Deshalb wünsche ich mir, daß eine neue Generation von Geistlichen heranwachsen möge, die das gleiche tun wie die in der katholischen Kirche: die den Versuch wagen, die Sprache des Unbewussten, ja selbst die Sprache der Träume, in die gewöhnliche Sprache zu übersetzen. Ich weiß, zum Beispiel, daß es jetzt in Deutschland den Berneuchener Kreis, eine liturgische Bewegung, gibt; und einer ihrer Hauptvertreter ist eine Mann, der eine umfassende Kenntnis der Symbolik besitzt. Er hat mir eine ganze Reihe von Beispielen geliefert, die ich nachprüfen konnte, wo er die Traumfiguren mit größtem Erfolg in die dogmatische Sprache übersetzt hat, und diese Leute sind in aller Stille in die kirchliche Ordnung zurückgeglitten: sie gehören einer Kirche an, und wenn man ihnen helfen kann, wieder bei der Kirche unterzuschlüpfen, so ist ihnen geholfen.

> I am a doctor; I have no preparation for [being a *directeur de conscience*]. It is the natural calling of the clergyman; he should do it. Therefore, I wish that a new generation of clergymen would come in and do the same as they do in the Catholic Church: that they would try to translate the language of the unconscious, even the language of dreams, into proper language. For instance, I know that there is now in Germany the 'Berneuchener Circle', a liturgical movement; and one of the main representatives is a man who has a great knowledge of symbolism. He has given me quite a number of instances, which I am able to check, where he translated the figures in dreams into dogmatic language with the greatest success, and these people quietly slipped back into the order of the Church. They have no right to be neurotic. They belong to a church, and if you can help them to slip back to the Church you have helped them.
>
> Carl Gustav Jung (1939)[3]

What is the relation between Jungian psychotherapy and *Seelsorge*?[4] As outlined by Sonu Shamdasani in his contribution to this volume, C.G. Jung's understanding of psychotherapy changed around the time of the beginning of the First World War from being a mere treatment of neurotic ailments to a practice aimed at reaching a higher spiritual development. Jung's change of direction was mainly triggered by the effects of the psychological self-experimentation that he undertook at the time. During an intense process of active imagination, he engaged with visionary images that seemed to point the way towards not only psychological healing, but some kind of elaborate state of self-awareness. He later called this the process of individuation.

In the following decades, Jung embarked on research into the fields of anthropological, historico-cultural, mythological and religious studies, in a quest to find human experiences similar to the psychological individuation process that he had discovered. One practice that seemed to have much in common with his own experiences was spiritual meditation, as depicted in various sacred texts of the East and Christian spiritual exercises in the West. But whereas the Buddhist and tantric sutras were part of a living tradition of meditation, Christianity, according to Jung, had no equal to them, with the exception of the *Exercitia Spiritualia* of Ignatius of Loyola (1491–1556). In the following, I will argue that Jung's claim was not only wrong, but that his understanding of Christian meditation was directly shaped by his contacts with members of the Berneuchen movement, a High Church movement that attempted to reintroduce meditation into German Protestantism. Hitherto unknown letters between founding members of the Berneuchen movement and Jung will show how this intellectual exchange formed their respective understanding and practice of meditation and active imagination.

From 1938 to 1940, Jung's weekly lectures at the Swiss Federal Institute of Technology Zürich (ETH) were dedicated to the role that spiritual meditation could play in the psychological process of individuation. He contrasted the yogic understanding of meditation in texts such as the *Amitâyur-dhyâna-sûtra*, *Shrî-Chakra-Shambhâra Tantra* or Patanjali's *Yoga Sutra* with Christian meditative practice as depicted in works by mystics such as Ignatius of Loyola, Meister Eckhart (c.1260–c.1328) or Richard of Saint Victor (d.1173). The aim of the spiritual practice of meditation in the Buddhist and Yogic tradition is to reach a higher state of awareness that will overcome the duality between subject and object (*samadi*). By contrast, the practitioner of Ignatius's *Exercitia Spiritualia* is looking for the 'discernment' (*discretio*), the realisation of the difference between good and evil that will ultimately lead to a mystical self-abandonment in God. Jung describes this process as the aim of psychological individuation, when the Ego encounters the archetype of the Self, which is the unity of the individual with the collective unconscious.

Thus, Jung's psychotherapeutic treatment accepts the incorporation of a practice that aims to expand the boundaries of the Ego as defined by the Freudian model of the psyche. The psychological incorporation of the hitherto non-human (and also in-human) Other, experienced in an ecstatic union through meditation or other spiritual practices, questions the understanding of what it means to be human, an understanding that in the tradition of enlightened Western thought has been firmly rooted in the subject–object duality. By contrast, Jung argues for the psychological wholeness of the soul that transcends this divide, resorting to examples from medieval Christian mysticism.

Jung, the Society of Jesus and Roman Catholicism

In June 1939, Jung followed up his lecture series on Eastern meditation with one on Ignatius of Loyola's *Exercitia Spiritualia* as an example of Christian meditative practice. His interest in the Society of Jesus and its founder is already evident in his encounters with the unconscious, as noted in his *Black Books*, where he cites on 19 April 1914 the Jesuit motto *In majorem Dei gloriam*. Or one can go even further back to Jung's earliest childhood memories, a time when he developed an intense fear connected to the image of a Jesuit priest. One day, the young boy was gazing at a figure with 'breitem Hut und langem schwarzen Gewand vom Wald herunter kommen' / 'a strangely broad hat and a long black garment coming down from the wood':

> Bei seinem Anblick befiel mich Furcht, die rasch zu tödlichem Schrecken anwuchs, denn in mir formte sich die entsetzenerregende Erkenntnis: 'Das ist ein Jesuit!' Kurz zuvor hatte ich nämlich einem Gespräch zugehört, das mein Vater mit einem Amtskollegen über die Umtriebe der 'Jesuiten' führte. Aus dem halb ärgerlichen, halb ängstlichen Gefühlston seiner Bemerkungen erhielt ich den Eindruck, daß 'Jesuiten' etwas besonders Gefährliches, sogar für meinen Vater, darstellten. Im Grunde wußte ich nicht, was 'Jesuiten' bedeutete. Aber das Wort Jesus kannte ich aus meinem Gebetlein.
>
> At the sight of him I was overcome with fear, which rapidly grew into deadly terror as the frightful recognition shot through my mind: 'That is a Jesuit.' Shortly before, I had overheard a conversation between my father and a visiting colleague concerning the nefarious activities of the Jesuits. From the half-irritated, half-fearful tone of my father's remarks I gathered that 'Jesuits' meant something specially dangerous, even for my father. Actually I had no idea what Jesuits were, but I was familiar with the word 'Jesus' from my little prayer.[5]

From 1933 onwards, Jung had an opportunity to discuss the *Exercitia Spiritualia* with theologians such as Ernesto Buonaiuti (1881–1946) at the annual Eranos conferences in Ascona. At those conferences, the former Catholic priest and historian of Christianity, who due to his defence of Catholic modernism was excommunicated in 1925, lectured on topics such as 'Meditation and Contemplation in the Roman Catholic Church' (1933) and 'The Exercises of Saint Ignatius of Loyola' (1935). But it was probably after 1945 that Jung's interest in Roman Catholicism was strongest, when he befriended the Dominican priest and Professor of Dogmatic Theology in Oxford, Victor White (1902–60). In his first letter to White, Jung writes:

> I am highly interested in the point of view the church takes with reference to my work. I had many discussions with catholic priests in this country too and it is on my instigation that catholic scholars have been invited to the Eranos lectures of which you presumably have heard.[6]

One of those scholars was the Jesuit, theologian and Church historian Hugo Rahner (1900–68), one of the leading experts on Ignatius of Loyola at the time, and Jung had ample time to discuss the *Exercitia Spiritualia* with him. Jung was also in contact with the mystic Père Bruno de Jésus-Marie (1892–1962), the editor of the *Etudes Carmélitaines*, who came to see Jung in June 1946 together with Hans Schnyder von Wartensee (1895–1987), senior lieutenant of the Swiss Guard and later founder of the Swiss section of the Equestrian Order of the Holy Sepulchre of Jerusalem.[7]

Jung, Reformed Protestantism and Dialectical Theology

Although some of Jung's close allies were reformed Protestant theologians such as Hans Schär (1910–67), Professor of Science of Religion, Psychology of Religion, and Pastoral Theology at the University of Bern, and the pastor and theologian Adolf Keller (1872–1963),[8] Jung held a strong, although ambivalent fascination with Roman Catholicism. As Jung remarked in his memoirs:

> Jahrelang konnte ich keine katholische Kirche mehr betreten ohne geheime Angst vor Blut, Hinfallen und Jesuiten. Das war der Ton oder die Atmosphäre, von der sie umwittert war. Aber immer hat sie mich fasziniert. Die Nähe eines katholischen Priesters war womöglich noch unbehaglicher. Erst in meinen Dreißigerjahren, als ich den Stephansdom in Wien betrat, konnte ich die Mater Ecclesia ohne Beschwernis fühlen.
>
> (*ETG*, 23)

> For years afterward I was unable to set foot inside a Catholic church without a secret fear of blood and falling and Jesuits. That was the aura or atmosphere that hung about it, but at the same time it always fascinated me. The proximity of a Catholic priest made me even more uneasy, if that were possible. Not until I was in my thirties was I able to confront Mater Ecclesia without this sense of oppression. The first time was in St Stephen's Cathedral in Vienna.
>
> (*MDR*, 17)

But Roman Catholicism also presented Jung with the opportunity to encounter a living Christian tradition of meditative practice that he could compare with Eastern meditation. According to Jung, Protestantism did not offer any equal to that tradition. As a child, he had experienced the spiritual helplessness of his father Johann Paul Achilles Jung (1842–96), a reformed Protestant pastor, who instead of addressing and solving the child's religious anxieties, resorted to learned formulas and even admitted that he did not understand doctrines such as the Holy Trinity (*ETG*, 58; *MDR*, 53). In hindsight, Jung would interpret his father's failure as part of a serious crisis of faith, to which Johann Paul Achilles Jung reacted with an ever-firmer subscription to the dogmas of the church, rather than with openness to the possibilities of personal religious experience. What Jung saw in the case of his father was the weakening of his faith by the historical-critical method of liberal theology.

The controversial debates surrounding the appointment of Wilhelm Martin Leberecht de Wette (1780–1849) as Professor of Theology at Basel University in 1822 – Wette's critical account of the Bible was heavily rejected by members of pietistic circles close to the 'Deutsche Christentumsgesellschaft' – left their mark on the city of Basel.[9] The attempt to hold a fragile balance between pietism on one hand and critical theology at the university on the other hand was to find a late echo in Jung's description of his father's struggle and his own preference for mysticism. By the end of the First World War, the Basel-born pastor and theologian Karl Barth (1886–1968) published his *Der Römerbrief / The Epistle to the Romans* (1918), which in its second edition of 1922 can be regarded as the swansong of the age of liberal theology. Disappointed by the theological justification for the Great War offered by his former professors, Barth argued against the possibility of any personal experience of God in the sense of the philosopher Friedrich Schleiermacher's 'absolute feeling of dependence'.[10] According to Barth, God was transcendent:

> Gott, die reine Grenze und der reine Anfang alles dessen, was wir sind, haben und tun, in unendlichem qualitativem Unterschied dem Menschen und allem Menschlichen gegenüberstehend, nie und nimmer identisch mit dem, was wir Gott nennen, als Gott erleben, ahnen und anbeten, das unbedingte Halt! gegenüber aller menschlichen Unruhe und das unbedingte Vorwärts! gegenüber aller menschlichen Ruhe, das Ja in unserm Nein und das Nein in unserm Ja, der Erste und der Letzte und als solcher der Unbekannte, nie und nimmer aber eine Größe unter andern in der uns bekannten Mitte, Gott der Herr, der Schöpfer und Erlöser – das ist *der lebendige Gott!*

> God, the pure and absolute boundary and beginning of all that we are and have and do; God, who is distinguished qualitatively from

> men and from everything human, and must never be identified with anything which we name, or experience, or conceive, or worship, as God; God, who confronts all human disturbance with an unconditional command 'Halt', and all human rest with an equally unconditional command 'Advance'; God the 'Yes' in our 'No' and the 'No' in our 'Yes', the First and the Last, and consequently, the Unknown, who is never a known thing in the midst of other known things; God, the Lord, the Creator, the Redeemer – that is *the living God*.[11]

It is Barth's view of a transcendent God that Jung found to be the most unacceptable aspect of his dialectical theology. As a psychologist, Jung was primarily interested in the individual psychological experience of a God image. Around the time Barth began to write his commentary on Paul's epistle, Jung was deeply involved in his own spiritual journey. Archetypal images of a new-born God called Abraxas emerged from the collective unconscious, a God who seemed to be personal and transcendent at the same time.[12] Jung described these experiences in his notebooks known as the *Black Books*.[13] Ultimately, these encounters with what he at first called primordial images formed the basis of his analytical psychology.

Barth's theology of the transcendent God and his consequent rejection of any mystical experience stood in sharp contrast to Jung's God image as the archetype of the Self. But Jung shunned an open debate with the representatives of dialectical theology. It was only some thirty years later, in the preface to *Psychology and Alchemy* (1944), that Jung argued against the concept of a 'transcendent God', albeit without mentioning Barth explicitly: 'aber auf alle Fälle muß die Seele eine Beziehungsmöglichkeit, das heißt eine Entsprechung zum Wesen Gottes in sich haben, sonst könnte ein Zusammenhang nie zustande kommen. Diese Entsprechung ist, psychologisch formuliert, der *Archetypus des Gottesbildes*.' / 'at all events the soul must contain in itself the faculty of relationship to God, i.e., a correspondence, otherwise a connection could never come about. This correspondence is, in psychological terms, the *archetype of the God-image*.'[14] But in a corresponding footnote, the addressee of this remark becomes obvious when Jung writes that it was 'psychologically quite unthinkable for God to be simply the "wholly other"', a term associated with Barth's understanding of the transcendental God, for a "wholly other" could never be one of the soul's deepest and closest intimacies – which is precisely what God is.'[15]

In a letter of 12 July 1947, Jung described his critical relationship with dialectical theology as follows:

> Es wäre mir tatsächlich auch eine große Überraschung, dass von Seiten der dialektischen Theologie überhaupt etwas, was den Menschen praktisch interessieren könnte, kommen sollte. Es ist mir nie gelungen, irgend ein Verhältnis zu dieser Theologie zu finden, und es ist mir dunkel geblieben, worin denn eigentlich der Dialog bestehen soll. Der scheint mir ja vollkommen zu fehlen. Ich habe mehr Beziehung zu Gegnern der dialektischen Theologie und auch zu katholischen Theologen, was mir besonders interessant ist.
>
> It would be a big surprise indeed if there came anything from the side of dialectical theology that could be of practical interest to man. I have never been able to find any connection to this theology and the actual nature of the dialogue has remained obscure to me. That seems to be missing completely. I have more connection with opponents of dialectical theology, even with Catholic theologians, what I find particularly interesting.[16]

This letter was addressed to the German Lutheran pastor and theologian Walter Uhsadel (1900–85), who would in later years occupy chairs for practical theology at the universities of Hamburg and Tübingen. It is no surprise that Jung's critical remark on dialectical theology appeared in a letter to Uhsadel, who was a member of the Evangelische Michaelsbruderschaft, an offshoot of the Berneuchen movement, which was in turn part of the Lutheran High Church movement.

The Berneuchen Movement and the Brotherhood of Saint Michael

The Berneuchen movement originated from the German youth movement of the nineteenth century. In the 1920s, German Lutheran clergy and laymen sought to develop a new way forward for Protestantism. The failure of liberal theology and the end of the state church in Germany prompted a series of annual meetings between 1923 and 1928 on a country estate in Berneuchen in the Neumark (also known as East Brandenburg; today Lubuskie in Poland). In contrast to Barth, this group saw a new path for the church in a renewal and deepening of its spiritual life. The results of the meetings were published in the *Berneuchener Buch* (1926) by Karl Bernhard Ritter (1890–1968), Wilhelm Stählin (1883–1975), Ludwig Heitmann (1880–1953) and Wilhelm Thomas (1896–1978).[17] The group's programme had seventy signatories, including the philosopher and theologian Paul Tillich (1886–1965). According to the Berneuchen movement, restoration of spiritual life in German Protestantism demanded the renewal of liturgical practice with a stronger emphasis on the celebration of the Eucharist, the practice of daily office and the study of the Bible. The idea of a return to early aspects of liturgical and spiritual practices also brought the Berneuchen group closer to Roman Catholicism, and in the years to come it formed an important cornerstone of the ecumenical movement in Germany.

At Michaelmas 1931, 22 members of the Berneuchen movement met in the Upper Chapel of the University Church of Marburg to form the Evangelische Michaelsbruderschaft. They shared in the conviction that it was not sufficient only to discuss the renewal of the Church, but that first and foremost such a renewal needed to be practised as part of the committed togetherness of a Christian brotherhood.[18] The principles of the Brotherhood were based on the *trias* of *martyria* (witness), *leiturgia* (church service) and *diakonia* (service in society).

The Brotherhood was led by an elder. The first of these was Karl Bernhard Ritter, who initiated the foundation when he invited the brothers to the ceremony of 1931 at the University Church of Marburg, where he was pastor at the time.[19] Ritter had studied theology and philosophy in Heidelberg, Halle and Erlangen before he volunteered as a soldier at the front in 1914. After the war, he became a member of the Prussian *Landtag* for the Deutschnationale Volkspartei, a national-conservative party that was founded in 1918. He was also a founding member of the Jungdeutscher Bund, a national-conservative offshoot of the Wandervogel movement. There he first met Wilhelm Stählin, later Bishop of Oldenburg, who was slightly older than Ritter. Stählin had studied theology in Erlangen, Rostock and Berlin. His strong interest in psychology and pastoral care led him to found the Gesellschaft für Religionspsychologie / Society of Religious Psychology and the journal *Archiv für Religionspsychologie / Archive of Religious Psychology* in 1914. These two pastors shared wartime military experience. When Ritter and Stählin were invited to join the foundation of the Jungdeutscher Bund, they encountered young Germans who were highly critical of the church. This younger generation regarded the church as having been stripped bare of its spiritual qualities; for them the church had lost its appeal as a place where words could form the unmediated expression of concrete life.[20] Thus, both Ritter and Stählin thought that if the Church was ever to attract this younger generation, it would need to reflect on its authentic values rather than merely engaging with ideological questions: 'Die Kirche entfaltet ihre stärkste werbende Kraft, sie ist dann am meisten ein wirkliches Zeugnis für die Welt, wenn sie als

Kirche da ist.' / 'The church unfolds its strongest attraction and is the most real witness to the world, if it is there as a church.'[21] Ritter recollected the mood of the times as follows:

> Auch Stählins Schrift über den 'Sinn des Leibes' gehört in diesen Zusammenhang. Dass das bloß intellektuelle Wort bei den Menschen unserer Zeit nicht mehr ankommt, weil es nicht hineingenommen ist in den tragenden Zusammenhang einer vom Bilde gesättigten Anschauung, erfuhren wir im Umgang mit dieser Jugend, lange ehe die psychologische Forschung die Bedeutung der Bilder für den seelischen Haushalt herausstellte und etwa am Singen, am Tanz und Spiel die Bedeutung der leiblichen Gebärde, der Einbeziehung des ganzen leibhaften Menschen in alle echte und wirksame Erfahrung von Wirklichkeit erkennbar machte.
>
> Zusammenhänge, die in der ärztlichen Wissenschaft des letzten Jahrzehnts immer klarer geworden sind und den kranken Menschen an Stelle des bloßen erkrankten körperlichen Organgefüges entdecken ließen, kurz und gut, die Einbettung des Menschen in den Kosmos, theologisch gesprochen, die Wahrheit und das Gewicht des ersten Artikels, der Lehre von der Schöpfung, wurden uns unmittelbar zum Erlebnisinhalt.
>
> Stählin's text about the 'meaning of the body' also belongs in this context. In conversation with this young generation we experienced that the mere intellectual word is no longer effective for contemporary man as it has not been incorporated in the fundamental context of a perception saturated by images – and this was long before psychological research had highlighted the significance of images for the soul's balance as well as, through the examples of song, dance or play, the importance of the physical gesture and the inclusion of the whole physical human being as part of any true and effective experience of reality.
>
> These are connections that have become significantly clearer in the medical science of the last decade and that have allowed us to see the ill human being rather than a mere diseased physical assemblage of organs. In summary, the embeddedness of man in the cosmos, in theological terms, the truth and the weight of the first article, that is to say the doctrine of creation, became for us an unmediated experience.[22]

In these recollections of Ritter's from 1953, clear reference to Jungian psychology can be detected when he writes about the psychological research that emphasised the importance of psychological images (*Bilder*) for the economy of the soul or the wholeness of man. However, Ritter also claimed that this emphasis on the image was discovered prior to and independently from psychology, including Jungian psychology.

Carl Happich, Pastoral Advisor and Spiritual Guide

Another important aspect linking the spiritual practice of these theologians to Jung's psychology was the practice of meditation. The introduction of meditation into the Michaelsbruderschaft was an initiative of another founding father, the medical doctor Carl Happich (1878–1947). Ritter and Happich shared political views. Happich was a member of the Stahlhelm Bund der Frontsoldaten, a right-wing paramilitary organisation with close ties to the Deutschnationale Volkspartei. Both men were also Freemasons at the Lodge of St John Zum flammenden Schwert in Darmstadt. Happich presided over this Christian-oriented Masonic lodge from 1921 to 1930. He was also an active participant in Hermann Graf Keyserling's Schule der Weisheit, where Jung lectured on a number of occasions. There Jung first met Richard Wilhelm (1873–1930) in the early 1920s, and also became acquainted with Erwin Rouselle (1890–1949). Both men were friends of Happich's, and Rouselle was even a member of the same Masonic lodge as Happich. Other friends in common included Rudolf Otto (1869–1937) and Heinrich Zimmer (1890–1943). Although his father was a Lutheran pastor, Happich's understanding of Christianity soon exceeded the limitations of his own denomination and opened his faith to the spiritual wealth of Catholicism and to ecumenical dialogue.[23] This openness, and the desire to help his patients, led him to experiment with forms of therapy that combined physical, psychological and spiritual elements. Ritter described Happich's approach as follows:

> Neben einem ganz ursprünglichen Interesse für alle Erscheinungsformen des seelischen Lebens war es wohl vor allem anderen sein leidenschaftliches Arzttum, sein Wille zu helfen, das ihn in der Erforschung und praktischen Erprobung jener uralten Wege zur Herzmitte des menschlichen Seins, zu der verborgenen, fruchtbaren Welt der Bilder und Gesichte Schritt für Schritt weiterführte. In seiner ärztlichen Praxis erschloss sich ihm sowohl die diagnostische wie vor allem die therapeutische Seite der Meditation. Mit wenigen überaus glücklich gewählten Leitbildern gelang es ihm in ungezählten Fällen, ordnend, heilend auf das Innere seiner

> Patienten einzuwirken. Es ging ihm nicht um Analyse der seelischen Verfassung, sondern um wirksame Synthese, um Befruchtung des seelischen Mutterbodens für neues, gesundes Wachstum, um Anregung seelischer Kristallisationsvorgänge. Das Gesunde muss das Kranke, das Gebild alles Chaos überwinden.
>
> Besides his natural interest in all forms of spiritual life, it was probably his passion for being a doctor, his will to help, that gradually led him on to discover and probe, in practice, those ancient paths to the heart's centre of human existence, to the hidden and fruitful world of images and visions. In his medical practice, the diagnostic and especially the therapeutic sides of meditation revealed themselves to him. With a few remarkably well-chosen guiding images he was able in countless cases to have a structuring and healing effect on the internal life of his patients. He did not care as much about an analysis of the mental state as about an effective synthesis, a fertilisation of the spiritual mother soil for new and healthy growth, a stimulus for a process of crystallisation. That which is healthy must overcome that which is sick, and structure must overcome chaos.[24]

Happich introduced the method of meditation that he used to treat his patients to a selected group of the Brothers at an Easter retreat at the Westerburg in Rhineland-Palatinate in 1931. According to Ritter, Happich had derived his method from his comprehensive knowledge of the meditative practises of the East and of the Christian Middle Ages, in connection with extensive practical research that had led him to remarkable spiritual discoveries.[25] Happich's initial introduction to his method of meditation initiated the Brotherhood's deeper engagement with the meditative tradition of the Church and a revitalisation of meditation in German Protestantism. As Ritter wrote:

> So half er uns durch Jahre hindurch vorwärts, auch als wir dann dazu übergingen, meditative Übungen zur Vertiefung des geistlichen Lebens zu schaffen, die Brücken zu schlagen von der Meditation zum Kultus, zur versenkenden Betrachtung in das Schriftwort und zur andächtigen Schau der 'Zeichen' und 'Gleichnisse'. Er ermutigte, warnte vor Irrwegen, machte auf Gefahren aufmerksam und ließ uns so in der Meditation eine unvergleichliche Schule der Andacht, des Gebets, des 'Gehorsams' entdecken. So schuf er schließlich die Voraussetzung dafür, daß wir nicht hilflos und verständnislos vor den Dokumenten einer meditativen Tradition

> standen, die im deutschen Protestantismus jedenfalls seit langem abgerissen ist, obwohl die Reformatoren selbst, wie es z. B. nicht wenige Äußerungen Luthers verraten, in ihrem Frömmigkeitsleben zweifellos mit von dieser Tradition geprägt waren.
>
> For many years he helped us progress, including when we began to create meditative exercises for a deepening of the spiritual life and to build bridges between meditation and *cultus*, immersive reflection on the scriptures and devout contemplation of 'signs' and 'similes'. He encouraged us, warned of erroneous paths, hinted at the dangers, and thus enabled us to discover in meditation an incomparable school of devotion, prayer and 'obedience'. Thus he ultimately created the conditions which preserved us from a helpless and uncomprehending encounter with the documents of a meditative tradition that had long since been cut off in German Protestantism, at least, although the pious lives of the reformers, as e.g. not a few of Luther's statements reveal, were without any doubt shaped in part by this tradition.[26]

Happich summarised his experience of meditation with the Michaelsbruderschaft in a small book entitled *Anleitung zur Meditation / Guide to Meditation* in 1938.[27] As early as 1932, he had published the outlines of this method in an article for the *Zentralblatt für Psychotherapie und ihre Grenzgebiete / Review of Psychotherapy and Related Areas*, in which he differentiated between two kinds of consciousness: one of images and the other of thinking.[28] The image-consciousness is said to form an early state in the development of human consciousness, forming a layer of experience between the imageless unconscious and rational consciousness.[29] Thinking in images, according to Happich, provides a different form of knowledge from rational thought.

Happich criticised the one-sidedness of the Western mind that failed to attain the refinement of Indian and Eastern Asian meditation.[30] Rational thinking had disconnected the Western mind from image-consciousness. According to Happich, the only comparable method to Eastern forms of meditation was the *Exercitia Spiritualia* as taught by Ignatius of Loyola, something that Jung would also claim in his ETH lectures on Active Imagination at the end of the 1930s. Happich recommended his own method of meditation for finding access to the images and their symbolic meaning. Alongside breath awareness he used visualisation to enter this realm of image consciousness: a meadow, a mountain and a chapel were used as symbolic representations of three stages of spiritual development, which consisted in a return to one's origins, taking part in life's quest and finding creative ways to overcome obstacles, with the ultimate goal of complete renewal. The final stage touched on the religious aspect of healing. From this starting point, Happich continued to work with the Michaelsbruderschaft on meditations concerning Christian symbols such as the cross.[31]

Of crucial importance for the development of his theory was the work of Herbert Silberer (1882–1923), a Viennese psychoanalyst and, like Happich, a Freemason, especially his *Probleme der Mystik und ihrer Symbolik / Problems of Mysticism and Its Symbols* (1914). This text was also well known to Jung. Happich discovered in Silberer's work not only a similar concept to image consciousness, but a link to Eastern and Yogic mysticism. Although Happich could not have known about Jung's personal experiments with active imagination, he found a comparable notion in what Silberer called the spontaneous production of symbols. Jung's assistant and close collaborator Marie Louise von Franz acknowledged Happich's independent achievement:

> Als Jung den inneren Weg der aktiven Imagination zuerst an sich selbst und später mit seinen Analysanden ausprobierte, waren alle solchen innersten Möglichkeiten der Psychotherapie noch weitgehend unbekannt. Seither aber ist eine ziemliche Wandlung in diesem Gebiet geschehen. Man verwendet zum Beispiel die Methode Carl Happichs, eine vom Arzt dirigierte Bildmeditation, René Desoille hat die Technik des *rêvé éveillé* eingeführt … Zum Schritt der ästhetischen Gestaltung hat die Psychotherapie heute weitgehend den Weg gefunden, noch nicht aber zum nächsten Schritt, der urteilenden Einstellung oder ethischen Auseinandersetzung; diese scheint allgemeiner noch nicht verstanden zu werden.

> At the time Jung was experimenting with active imagination, first on himself and later with analysands, all such potentialities for psychotherapy via the inner way were still virtually unknown. Since that time, however, the situation has changed somewhat. Carl Happich's method, which is one of therapist-directed meditation, is being used, for example, and René Desoille has introduced the technique of waking dream … Contemporary psychotherapy, generally speaking, has found the way to the aesthetic stage of creativity, but not yet to the next stage of an ethical confrontation with its products, nor to a convinced standpoint of moral attitude; it appears that this stage is yet not generally understood.[32]

Although it seems that Jung and Happich developed their theories of active imagination and visualisation of images independently – Jung had not introduced his theory to a wider public in the 1920s – they certainly drew on some similar sources. Nevertheless, it must have come as a surprise to Jung when Happich published his article in the *Zentralblatt* and sent him a letter with a copy of the article on 10 January 1932, as this text contained thoughts similar to Jung's ideas about active imagination and the understanding of the symbol. Happich acknowledged the significance of Jung's psychology when he wrote that his research owed a great debt to Jung's groundbreaking studies about the images inside man.[33] Happich also sent Jung a copy of his book *Anleitung zur Meditation / Introduction to Meditation* on 18 March 1939, at a time when Jung was just about to finish his lectures on Eastern meditation, in order to provide an introduction to the psychological aspects of Christian meditation in the *Exercitia Spiritualia*.

In the first letter of his correspondence with Jung, dated January 1933, Happich referred to himself as 'seelsorgischer Berater vieler evangelischer Geistlicher in Deutschland … die in einer evangelischen (nach einem Gut in Berneuchen genannten) Bewegung zusmmengeschlossen sind, welche die Misstände in der evangelischen Kirche ganz ähnlich sehen wie Sie.' / 'pastoral advisor to many Protestant clergymen in Germany, who are united in a Protestant movement (named after the country estate Berneuchen) and who see the bad state of affairs in the Protestant Church much as you do.'[34] As he did not receive an acknowledgement from Jung, he sent another letter on 14 May 1933, in which he claimed to have worked with a large group of theologians for six years, meaning that he had already started to teach meditation to the Berneuchen group in 1927. Yet both Ritter and Stählin stated in their accounts that they were first introduced to Happich's meditation at Easter 1931. Happich also introduced himself to Jung as a trained psychiatrist and psychotherapist.[35] Jung and Happich shared an interest in alchemical literature and the Rosicrucians, which led to the exchange of some letters. Apparently Happich visited Jung in Küsnacht at the end of 1936 or beginning of 1937.

Walter Uhsadel, Pastoral Care Based on Jungian Psychology

Earlier, in the summer of 1936, Jung received another letter from a Michaelsbruder. The aforementioned Walther Uhsadel, at the time a pastor in Hamburg, sent Jung, along with a letter that is no longer in existence, a copy of the *Jahresbriefe des Berneuchener Kreises / Berneuchen Circle Annual Bulletin* of 1936, in which Uhsadel had written a review of the *Eranos Yearbook* 1934 and an article on 'Der Mensch in der Kirche' / 'On Man in the Church'. In that work, he argued for the significance of Jung's psychological insights for the renewal of the Protestant Church:

> Ist es ein Zufall, daß zur selben Zeit, da in der Theologie sich Ansätze zeigen, die Kirche aus dem intellektualistischen Mißverständnis zu befreien, auch eine neue Psychologie ein völlig neues Bild des Menschen vor uns hinstellt? Die Psychologie C.G. Jungs stellt Erkenntnisse vor uns hin, die vielfach in überraschender Weise dem begegnen, was uns als die biblische Lehre vom Menschen langsam wieder lebendig zu werden beginnt. Sie lehrt uns zunächst wieder sehen, daß der Mensch sehr viel mehr ist als das, was er sein Ich nennt, ja geradezu, daß das Ich nur *ein* Komplex unter anderen im *Bewusstsein* des Menschen ist, daß sich aber ein großer Teil unseres Lebens im *Unbewussten* abspielt.
>
> Is it a coincidence that just as theology is beginning to liberate the church from its intellectual misconception, a new psychology presents us with an entirely new image of man? The psychology of C.G. Jung presents us with insights that in many and surprising ways join hands with that which is slowly being revived for us as biblical teaching about mankind. Initially it teaches us to realise once more that the human being is much more than what he calls his I, indeed that the I is only *one* complex amongst many in the *consciousness* of man, yet that a great part of our life takes place in the *unconscious*.[36]

Uhsadel continued with his praise of Jung's psychology for opening up a realm of humanity that went beyond ego consciousness. The word of God would speak to all dimensions of human experience, including its unconscious layers, something the righteous could only fearfully intuit. The new psychological image of man would give renewed access to a knowledge that had been clear to the contemporaries of the New Testament or the first Christians. Thus Jung's psychological image of man based on the theory of archetypal symbolism would teach a new approach to the understanding of the message of the Bible.[37] According to Uhsadel, a new theology that could view man in his entirety as body, soul and spirit should not neglect what the Bible taught about the soul, a message that former generations of Christians had understood naturally.[38]

In his reply of 4 August 1936, Jung informed Uhsadel that by coincidence someone had already told him about the Berneuchen circle, and in particular its attempt to create a liturgical renewal,[39] and that he had gained a most positive impression of this movement:

> Soll eine Erneuerung oder, wie ich geneigt wäre zu sagen, eine Begründung der protestantischen Kirche überhaupt erfolgen, so kann dies nur schrittweise von einzelnen geschehen, die es nicht nur reden, sondern denen es auch eine Tatsache ist. Massenerfolg ist ein schlechtes Zeichen. Wenn die Kirche keine selbstverständliche Ewigkeit ist, so ist sie überhaupt nicht, deshalb halt ich auch die Continuität des Ritus für außerordentlich wichtig.
>
> Should there be renewal or, as I tend to say, a justification [foundation] of the Protestant church at all it can only happen gradually through single individuals, who do not only speak, but for whom it is also a fact. Success with the masses is a bad sign. If the church is not a self-evident eternity, it is nothing at all. That is why I deem the continuity of the ritual exceptionally important.[40]

Uhsadel had been a member of the Michaelsbruderschaft since 1934.[41] A generation younger than Ritter and Stählin, he studied theology, psychology, pedagogy and sociology after the war. He became a pastor in Hamburg, where he founded the north German section of the Stuttgart organisation Arzt und Seelsorger / Doctor and Pastor. From 1929 to 1933 Uhsadel was the editor of the *Evangelische Jugendführung / Guidance for Protestant Youth* and, between 1935 and 1942, the *Evangelische Jahresbriefe / Protestant Annual Bulletin*, both journals linked to the Berneuchen movement. At the time of his first contact with Jung in 1936 he was the elder of the Brotherhood for the convent of Hamburg-Schleswig-Holstein. Uhsadel's theological interest was mainly in practical theology, where he advocated the importance of Jungian psychology for pastoral care. In 1954 he published *Der Mensch und die Mächte des Unbewussten. Studien zur Begegnung von Psychotherapie und Seelsorge / Man and the Powers of the Unconscious. Studies on the Encounter of Psychotherapy and Pastoral Care*,[42] which he dedicated to Jung, and in 1966 *Evangelische Seelsorge / Protestant Pastoral Care* appeared, in which he gave an account of his first meeting with Jung on 29 May 1938:

> Als ich Jung im Jahr 1938 zum ersten Mal besuchte, drehte sich unsere Unterhaltung um die Frage, welche seelsorglichen Hilfen die alten, im Protestantismus so vernachlässigten geistlichen Lebensordnungen dem Menschen der Gegenwart bieten könnten, wenn er richtig angeleitet würde, von diesen Ordnungen Gebrauch zu Machen. Ich konnte Jung von manchen praktischen Erfahrungen in dieser Hinsicht berichten, die ich in einer Seelsorge gesammelt hatte, die – wenn auch in bescheidenem Maße – jene Ordnungen pflegte. Als ich mich verabschiedete, führte er mich in einen kleinen

Raum, in dem er seine Patienten behandelte. Er hatte für diesen Raum ein sehr schönes gotisches Kirchenfenster, das eine Kreuzigung darstellte, kopieren lassen. Der Raum hatte dadurch das Gepräge einer Sakristei bekommen. Indem Jung auf dieses Fenster wies, sagte er zu mir: 'Sehen Sie, dies ist doch das Entscheidende für uns.' Als ich ihn fragte, warum er das sage, antwortete er in seiner ruhigen, gesammelten Art: 'Ich komme gerade aus Indien, da ist mir dies von neuem aufgegangen. Der Mensch muss mit dem Problem des Leidens fertig werden. Der östliche Mensch will sich des Leidens entledigen, indem er das Leben abstreift. Der abendländische Mensch versucht, das Leiden durch Drogen zu unterdrücken. Aber das Leiden muss überwunden werden, und überwunden wird es nur, indem man es trägt. Das lernen wir allein von ihm.' Damit wies er auf den Gekreuzigten.

When I visited Jung for the first time in the year 1938, our conversation revolved around the question, which pastoral means of assistance the old but neglected Protestant form of spirituality and practice [*geistliche Lebensordnung*] could be offered to present-day man if he were correctly guided in how to make use of them. I was able to give Jung an account of many practical experiences in this respect, which I had collected during a period of pastoral care and which, even if to a modest degree, still sustained their use. As I took my leave, he led me into a small room in which he treated his patients. He had in this room a copy of a very lovely Gothic stained-glass window of the Crucifixion. Through this, the room had acquired the character of a spiritual place. While Jung was pointing to this window, he said to me: 'Just look, this is the crucial thing for us.' When I asked him why he said that, he replied in his calm, collected way: 'I have just returned from India, where this problem has arisen for me anew. Mankind has to cope with the problem of suffering. Eastern man wishes to free himself from the problem of suffering by stripping off life. Western man, on the other hand, attempts to supress suffering with drugs. However, suffering must be overcome insofar as one endures it. This we learn solely from him.' And with this he pointed to the Crucified One.[43]

Jung and Uhsadel agreed on the importance of ritual and experience of *cultus*. For modern, intellectually well-educated man, the church had lost its former attraction, and it was the task of the soul's educator to show the way to primordial experience, similar to Saint Paul's experiences on the road to Damascus.[44] Uhsadel introduced Jung to the way in which the Brotherhood tried to evoke such experience. According to Uhsadel, the human being in his or her contact with God needed to be understood as an entirety of body, soul and mind, and should not be reduced to his or her intellectual capacity alone.[45] A new emphasis on the liturgy and the sacraments, the revitalisation of the practice of confession and the importance of absolution were some of the thoughts that Uhsadel put forward, and Jung certainly agreed with them. Needless to say, such ideas about revitalising spirituality within German Protestantism were central to the Berneuchen circle and the Brotherhood of Saint Michael. In advance of their meeting, Uhsadel even sent Jung the liturgical order of worship and confession as developed by the Brotherhood,[46] to which Jung replied: 'Schon die bloße Lektüre der liturgischen Ordnung hat etwas sehr befriedigendes an sich, indem die unpersönliche Institution der Kirche und deren Handeln gegenüber dem rein Persönlichen des gewöhnlich-protestantischen Betriebes gebührend hervorgehoben wird.' / 'There is something utterly satisfying in the mere reading of the liturgical structure, for the impersonal institution of the Church and its actions are appropriately highlighted, in contrast to the purely personal level of everyday Protestant activity.'[47]

Meditative Practice in the Brotherhood of Saint Michael

Uhsadel's main interest was in the psychological understanding of the human soul as part of pastoral care. The topic of meditation did not play a vital part in his correspondence with Jung. In contrast, the Brotherhood was very much engaged with adapting Happich's form of meditation to Christian spiritual needs. Stählin, in his 1936 study *Vom göttlichen Geheimnis / On the Divine Secret* emphasised the importance of meditation alongside prayer as part of Christian spiritual life. He distinguished it from the common Christian understanding of meditation, seen as contemplation of a biblical text as part of sermon preparation, and described it in line with all Western and Eastern schools of meditative practice as follows:

> Es ist eine eigentümliche Art des Denkens, bei der wir nicht mehr über die Dinge uns Gedanken machen, einen Inhalt denkend durchdringen und uns um ein kritisches Urteil bemühen, sondern wo wir uns einer Sache völlig hingeben, in sie eindringen oder – was das Gleiche ist – sie in uns eindringen lassen. Es ist in der Tat eines und dasselbe, ob ich von meiner Versenkung in den Inhalt meiner Meditation rede oder davon, dass in meiner Meditation die Sache in mich eingeht, sich in mich versenkt. Immer verzichtet der Meditierende auf seine vorsichtig abwägende Zuschauerhaltung,

immer gibt er sich dem, worüber er meditiert, völlig hin, gewährt ihm Raum in seiner Seele und Macht über sein Denken und Sein.

> It is a peculiar kind of thinking in which we no longer think about things, push our way into the core of some matter and work towards a critical verdict, but rather one in which where we give ourselves fully over to a subject, penetrating into it, or – which is the same – letting it enter into us. In fact, it is one and the same, whether I speak of my sinking into the content of my meditation or say that in my meditation the thing enters into me, is submerged in me. The person meditating always renounces the cautious, weighing-up attitude of a spectator; he gives himself up entirely, always, to the subject of his meditation; he makes space for it in his soul and gives it authority over his thinking and being.[48]

The aim was to clear away the blockages produced by critical analysis and reason, which, like an impenetrable screen, bar one from the life of grace.[49] Stählin's argument that the over-intellectualism of the modern human being would prevent him or her from experiencing the mystery of God was similar to the ideas shared by Jung and Uhsadel in their correspondence. Jung had a copy of Stählin's book in his library. The two men even met at a seminar week in Königsfeld in the Black Forest in January 1937 organised by the Freundeskreis der kommenden Gemeinde, formerly Bund der Köngener, to discuss questions of teachings and guidance of the soul.[50] Jutta von Graevenitz took part in the conference and later recalled:

> Early in 1937 my husband and I participated in a conference of a group which had developed out of the Christian youth movement. C.G. Jung and the Lutheran bishop Stählin, well known in Germany, spoke on the relation between depth psychology and Christian religion. I thought Jung far superior to the forceful and lively bishop. It turned out that this conference at Königsfeld in the Black Forest was Jung's last sojourn in Nazi Germany. At that conference, under the impression of Jung's personality, the decision was made that I would myself become an analyst.[51]

As Stählin's article on 'Spiritual Exercises' from 1938 had indicated, the Brotherhood did not adhere to a purely psychological understanding of the human soul. Similarly to Uhsadel, Stählin put forward a diagnosis of humanity entangled in a crisis of the hitherto prevailing culture of consciousness. In Stählin's view, the human being was separated from the hidden psychological layers beneath his or her consciousness, where both healing and destructive forces lay dormant and where the fragmented psyche would find its expression in many different forms of illness.[52] According to Stählin, those diseases are not only individual, as in the case of neurotic conditions, but can also have a collective expression. When the human seeks to understand and dominate the universe through the limited scope of human consciousness, he or she is confronted with the reappearance of primal fears related to images of giants, elves, gnomes and trolls, 'in denen die Phantasie früherer Geschlechter die unheimliche andere Seite der Welt bildhaft erkannte und anerkannte.' / 'in which the fantasy of previous generations recognised and acknowledged the uncanny other side of the world.'[53] Aware of this dangerous situation, the human being might grasp what is needed for his or her rescue, but does not find a connection to his or her inner depths. The only result he or she gains from these attempts is a theory of the unconscious.[54]

By contrast, through spiritual exercises one can prepare oneself for an encounter with the reality of God, gain the ability to understand the divine word and be touched and penetrated by the power of the divine spirit. Here, the Brotherhood referred not to a knowledge of the East that is inaccessible to the Christian, but to the European tradition of meditation, which had been alive during the Reformation and was lost in the course of the Enlightenment. As Stählin reminded the Brothers at the feast of Saint Michael in 1961, the aim of meditation was to dive into the layer buried beneath consciousness, where human thinking is childlike and occurs in images. This practice was less concerned with teaching a particular type of meditation than with achieving a complete change in thinking through meditation, to enter a space that had been impossible for Protestants to reach because of their one-sided and over-intellectualised theology. Stählin noted: 'Wir können nicht hoch genug rühmen, welche Bedeutungen dieses meditative Denken für den Umgang mit Zeichen und Bildern hat.' / 'We cannot praise highly enough the significance of this meditative thinking for our treatment of signs and images.'[55]

In 1947, Ritter published a summary of the method, aim and practice of meditation in the Michaelsbruderschaft entitled *Über Meditation als Mittel der Menschenbildung / On Meditation as a Method of Human Education*.[56] In this work, he drew a clear demarcation line between these practices and Jung's analytical psychology: 'Für uns handelt es sich jedoch nicht darum, den Anschluss an die Erbmasse wieder zu gewinnen … Vielmehr sollen bestimmte und zwar religiöse Inhalte dem Zentrum des Menschen zugeführt werden.' / 'For us it is not about regaining the connection to the genotype … It is much more about feeding certain and specifically religious contents into the centre of man.'[57] He also emphasised that this meditation should have nothing in common with suggestive methods or hypnosis.[58] Ritter credited Happich's method of meditation as the origin of the meditative practice in the Brotherhood, which had been developed over the years into a unique sequence of exercises known as 'Der geistige Pfad' / 'The spiritual path'. But this new path was not only shaped by Happich, but also by Rouselle, from whom the brothers learned at Christmas in 1932 that 'die abendländische Kirche nicht nur eine Hierarchie des ausgegliederten Amtes, sondern zugleich eine sehr sinnvolle Stufenordnung geistlicher Grundfunktionen und Verhaltensweisen besitzt, in denen sich das Priestertum aller Gläubigen verwirklicht.' / 'the occidental church does not only have a hierarchy of the external office, but at the same time also a meaningful hierarchy of basic spiritual functions and behaviours, in which the priesthood of all believers is realised.'[59] The spiritual path was a meditation on the different offices within the early church.[60] The seven different offices represent the different stages of the spiritual path of life, which is a path of self-becoming and transformation into the figure of Christ:

> Der Weg wird vorgegeben durch die sieben altkirchlichen Ämter, die jeweils als Wegmarken auf dem eigenen geistlichen Lebensweg verstanden werden. Die Stufenfolge der Ämter steht für eine zunehmende Verknüpfung des eigenen Lebens mit dem Weg Christi: ein Weg der Selbstwerdung und ein Weg der Verwandlung in die Christusgestalt hinein. Jedes der sieben kirchlichen Ämter entspricht einem besonderen Aspekt des Weges mit Christus und auf Christus zu. Mit der Meditation der Ämter ist auch eine räumliche Imagination verbunden, denn jedes Amt hat auch einen besonderen Standort im Kirchenraum, der wiederum für das Ganze des eigenen Lebensraumes steht: vom Eintritt über die Schwelle in den geistlichen Lebensraum hinein (Türhüter als 1. Stufe), bis zur priesterlichen Hingabe des eigenen Lebens in den Tod (Amt des Priesters als 7. Stufe). Der 'Geistliche Pfad' verbindet so auf eine komplexe Weise unterschiedliche symbolische Ebenen: Meditation des Schriftwortes, Meditation des Weges Christi, Klärung des eigenen Lebensweges, Schule des Lebens und Sterbens, Aufmerken auf die jeweils eigenen Gaben und Aufgaben im Ganzen des Leibes Christi.
>
> The path is predetermined by the seven offices of the early church, which are to be understood as signposts on one's own spiritual path. The sequence of the offices represents the increasing connection between one's own life and the path of Christ: a path of self-becoming and a path of changing into the figure of Christ. Each of the seven

ecclesiastical offices corresponds to a particular aspect of the path with and towards Christ. Connected to the meditation of the offices is also a spatial imagination, because each office occupies a particular position in the church building, which in turn stands for the whole of the individual living space. From the entrance, over the threshold, into the spiritual living space (the gatekeeper is the first level), and all the way to the sacerdotal surrender of one's own life to death (the office of the priest is the seventh level). Thus the 'Spiritual Path' connects in a complex manner different symbolic levels: meditation on the biblical words, meditation on the path of Christ, clarification of one's personal way of life, a school of living and dying, attention to one's specific talents and tasks in the whole body of Christ.[61]

Parting of the Ways

Karl Bernhard Ritter was commissioned by the Brotherhood to give a written account of the path of meditation for each of these seven stages. The first four stages were published in 1952.[62] Similarities with Jung's process of individuation were still visible. In his lecture series on active imagination, Jung highlighted the stages of individuation in the symbolic representations in ancient texts on Eastern and Western meditation. On the highest level, the Buddha of the Eastern tradition is represented by the inner sun and finds its Christian equivalent in the idea of the inner Christ.[63] But when in 1962 the Brotherhood decided to replace the meditation on the different offices with a general meditation for every Brother,[64] the similarity with the stages of Jungian individuation became less obvious. The reason for this change was the increasing acknowledgement of Eastern meditative practices, which the Brotherhood encountered through the works of Karlfried Graf Dürckheim (1896–1988) and Hugo Enomiya-Lassalle (1898–1990).

Another mediator between Jung and the Berneuchen movement was the Hamburg medical doctor Felicia Froboese-Thiele (1890–1971). She was the translator into German of Jung's *Terry Lectures on Psychology and Religion* in 1938 and Jung wrote a Foreword to her monograph *Träume. Eine Quelle religiöser Erfahrung / Dreams. A Source of Religious Experience* (1957).[65] But Froboese-Thiele was also close to the Berneuchen Circle and a friend of Uhsadel's. In 1938, she published an article on Jung in the *Evangelische Jahresbriefe*, whose editor at the time was Uhsadel. In her article, she summarised the difference between Jung's understanding of meditation and the Christian practice of the Brotherhood:

> In der ärztlichen Seelenführung, wie Jung sie übt, gibt es keine geistlichen Übungen im strengen Sinne. Allerdings verlangt Jung von seinen Analysanden Alleinsein, Schweigen, Sich-Versenken, Einkehr, Besinnung. Er lässt sie meditieren – aber Inhalt der Meditation sind die aus dem Unbewussten – sei es nun in Träumen, Visionen oder sogenannten "unbewussten" Zeichnungen oder Malereien – autochthon aufgestiegenen Bilder und Worte. Und das ist der grundsätzliche Unterschied gegenüber allen religiösen Meditationsübungen des Westens und Ostens, in denen der Inhalt gegeben wird und streng begrenzt ist auf das, was die Weisheit und die Erfahrung der Kirche als Hort der religiösen Tradition als heilsam erkannt hat. Wenn und solange ein Mensch das Heil in der von der Kirche gebotenen Form ergreifen kann, darf und soll und braucht er den Jungschen Weg nicht gehen, er wird auch gar nicht auf die Idee kommen, es zu tun. Denn der Weg in die Tiefen ist gefährlich und ungesichert – und nur diejenigen werden und müssen ihn unter Umständen gehen, denen alle andern Wege verschlossen sind.

> According to Jung's medical pastoral care, there are no spiritual exercises in the strict sense of the word. Nevertheless, Jung demands of his analysands solitude, silence, contemplation, reflection, consideration. He lets them meditate – but the contents of the meditation are images and words, autochthonously emerging from the unconscious, from dreams, visions or so-called 'unconscious' drawings or paintings. This is the basic difference from all religious meditative exercises, where the content is prescribed and strictly restricted to what the wisdom and experience of the church as the repository of religious tradition acknowledges as salutary. If and as long as someone can grasp salvation as offered by the church, he or she will not, and does not need, to take the Jungian path; he or she would not even think of doing so. For the path into depths is dangerous and unsecured – and only those to whom all the other ways are closed, will and must take it if need be.[66]

Froboese-Thiele's argument about the differences between the content-guided character of Christian meditation and Jung's free-floating meditation on material from the unconscious encapsulates why the representatives of the Protestant spiritual renewal and Jung's Analytical Psychology did finally part, in spite of their parallel development and shared convictions.

The intellectual interchange between Jung and several members of the Berneuchen movement, especially the Brotherhood of Saint Michael, on matters of spiritual meditation was important for both parties. It was significant for Jung, as he saw in the Berneuchen movement a German Protestant revival of Christian spirituality, something he had previously denied was possible due to theological overemphasis on intellectual knowledge. Although he did not specifically refer to the Berneuchen circle or the Michaelsbruderschaft, one can hardly imagine that Jung, while drafting his lecture series on active imagination in 1938 and 1939, which dealt with the question of meditation in Eastern and Western traditions, did not have his intellectual exchange on meditation with brothers such as Happich, Uhsadel and Stählin in mind. Conversely, the Berneuchen movement found in Jung's psychology a model of individuation that was compatible with their idea of a spiritual regeneration of the German Protestant church. But although some Brothers such as Uhsadel and Stählin continued to emphasise the potential of Jungian psychology for the pastoral care of the soul, the Brotherhood finally turned away from Jung's psychological concept of active imagination, acknowledging the differences between a psychological and a Christian understanding of the soul.

Notes

1. Barth, *Der Römerbrief*, 451–2; Barth, *The Epistle to the Romans*, 330–1. Unless otherwise specified, all translations in this chapter are mine, with the help of Heather McCartney and Mererid Puw Davies.
2. Jaspers, *Der philosophische Glaube*, 18.
3. Jung, 'Das symbolische Leben (Diskussion)', *Gesammelte Werke* (in the following abbreviated as *GW*), 18/1, § 671; Jung, 'The Symbolic Life (Discussion)', *Collected Works* (in the following abbreviated as *CW*), 18, § 671.
4. This term is usually translated as 'pastoral care', though its literal meaning is 'care for souls'.
5. Jung and Jaffé, *Erinnerungen, Träume, Gedanken*, 17; Jung and Jaffé *Memories, Dreams, Reflections*, 11, abbreviated in the text as ETG/MDR: further references follow in the text.
6. Jung to White, 26 September 1945, in Lammers and Cunningham, *The Jung–White Letters*, 4–5.
7. Jacobi to Jung, 13 June 1949; Jung to Jacobi, 2 July 1946, unpublished correspondence, C.G. Jung Papers Collection, ETH-Bibliothek, ETH Zurich University Archives (abbreviated in the following as JA).
8. See Jehle-Wildberger, *C.G. Jung und Adolf Keller*. Compare Sonu Shamdasani's chapter in this volume.
9. See Lindt, 'C.F. Spittler und W.M.L. de Wette'.
10. Schleiermacher, *The Christian Faith*, 132.
11. Barth, *Der Römerbrief*, 451–2; Barth, *The Epistle to the Romans*, 330–1.
12. See Shamdasani's chapter in this volume.
13. Jung, *The Black Books 1913–1932*.
14. Jung, 'Psychologie und Alchemie', V; also in *GW* 12, § 11; English in: *CW* 12, § 11.
15. Jung, 'Psychology and Alchemy', § 11, n. 4.
16. Jung to Walter Uhsadel, 12 July 1947, unpublished correspondence, JA.
17. Berneuchener Konferenz, *Das Berneuchener Buch*.
18. Zimmermann, 'Vierzig Jahre Evangelische Michaelsbruderschaft', 40.
19. See Hederich, *Karl Bernhard Ritter*.

20. Ritter, 'Berneuchen 1923', 92.
21. Ritter, 'Mein Weg mit Wilhelm Stählin', 217.
22. Ritter, 'Mein Weg mit Wilhelm Stählin', 218.
23. Ritter, 'Die Entdeckung der Meditation', 96.
24. Ritter, 'Die Entdeckung der Meditation', 97.
25. Ritter, 'Die Entdeckung der Meditation', 98.
26. Ritter, 'Die Entdeckung der Meditation', 98.
27. Happich, *Anleitung zur Meditation*.
28. Happich, 'Das Bildbewußtsein als Ansatzstelle psychischer Behandlung'.
29. Happich, 'Das Bildbewußtsein als Ansatzstelle psychischer Behandlung', 668. In a letter to Jung of 10 January 1933 [JA] Happich distinguished between Jung's archetypes and his own notion of image consciousness: 'Der Kreis, den ich mit meinen Bildvorstellungen erfüllt denke, wird nur in der individuellen Existenz belebt. Ihre Archetypen liegen ja viel tiefer als das von mir gemeinte Bildbewusstsein.' / 'The circle, which I imagine to be fulfilled in my visualisations, only comes alive in individual existence. Your archetypes are located much deeper than the image consciousness of which I speak.'
30. Happich, 'Das Bildbewußtsein als Ansatzstelle psychischer Behandlung', 667.
31. Baier, 'Meditation im Schnittfeld', 59.
32. Von Franz, *C.G. Jung: Sein Mythos in unserer Zeit*, 145; Von Franz, *C.G. Jung: His Myth in our Time*, 118.
33. Happich to Jung, 10 January 1933, unpublished correspondence [JA].
34. Happich to Jung, 10 January 1933, unpublished correspondence [JA].
35. Happich to Jung, 14 May 1933, unpublished correspondence [JA]. Baier, 'Meditation im Schnittfeld', states that nothing in particular is known about Happich's psychotherapeutic training other than that he started his 'psychotherapeutic meditation' as part of his psychotherapeutic work in 1918 or 1920.
36. Uhsadel, 'Der Mensch in der Kirche', 134.
37. Uhsadel, 'Der Mensch in der Kirche'.
38. Uhsadel, 'Der Mensch in der Kirche', 135.
39. Sherry in *Carl Gustav Jung* assumes that Jung's interlocutor was Adolph von Weizsäcker. See Jung, *Letters*, 215. As shown above, Jung already knew of the movement from Happich's letter.
40. Jung to Uhsadel, 4 August 1936, in Jung, *Letters*, 276.
41. See Albrecht, 'Auf der Schwelle zur Erfahrungsoffenheit'.
42. Uhsadel, *Der Mensch und die Mächte des Unbewussten*.
43. Uhsadel, *Evangelische Seelsorge*, 120–1, trans. Oglesby in *Jung and Hans Urs von Balthasar*.
44. Jung to Uhsadel, 18 August 1936, unpublished correspondence [JA].
45. Uhsadel to Jung, 19 August 1936, unpublished correspondence [JA].
46. Uhsadel to Jung, 11 May 1938, unpublished correspondence [JA].
47. Jung to Uhsadel, 16 May 1938, unpublished correspondence [JA].
48. Stählin, *Vom göttlichen Geheimnis*, 73.
49. Stählin, *Vom göttlichen Geheimnis*, 117.
50. Daur, *An der Schwelle*.
51. Von Graevenitz, 'Memory of C.G. Jung', 28.
52. Stählin, 'Geistliche Übung', 9.
53. Stählin, 'Geistliche Übung'.
54. Stählin, 'Geistliche Übung', 10.
55. Stählin, 'Michaelsbruderschaft–Rückkehr und Rechenschaft', 33.
56. Ritter, *Über die Meditation als Mittel der Menschenbildung*.
57. Ritter, *Über die Meditation als Mittel der Menschenbildung*, 31.
58. Ritter, *Über die Meditation als Mittel der Menschenbildung*, 36.
59. Stählin, 'Michaelsbruderschaft–Rückkehr und Rechenschaft', 33.
60. For a detailed description of the 'Geistige Pfad' see Mielke, 'Der "Geistliche Pfad" als Erfahrungs-weg; Oeyen, 'Ein Weg zur Bildung christlicher Persönlichkeiten'.
61. Mielke, 'Der "Geistliche Pfad" als Erfahrungsweg'.
62. Ritter, 'Von den sieben Stufen der Erkenntnis und des Lebens'.
63. See Paul: 2 Cor. 13:5; Jung's lectures of 2 December 1939 and 8 November 1940.
64. Von Haebler, *Geschichte des Michaelsbruderschaft*, 214–7.
65. Jung, *CW* 18, 700–1. See Uhsadel, 'Zusammenarbeit von "Arzt und Seelsorger"'.
66. Froboese, 'Ärztliche Seelenführung', 134.

Bibliography

Albrecht, Christian. 'Auf der Schwelle zur Erfahrungsoffenheit: Zur Praktischen Theologie des Hamburger Pfarrers und Tübinger Professors Walter Uhsadel (1900–1985)'. In *Kirchliche Zeitgeschichte (20. Jahrhundert): Hamburgische Kirchengeschichte in Aufsätzen, Teil 5* (Arbeiten zur Kirchengeschichte Hamburgs 26), edited by Rainer Hering and Inge Mager, 355–74. Hamburg: Hamburg University Press, 2008.

Baier, Karl. 'Meditation im Schnittfeld von Psychotherapie, Hochgradfreimaurerei und Kirchenreform: Carl Happichs Innovationen und ihr soziokultureller Kontext', *Paragrana: Internationale Zeitschrift für Historische Anthropologie* 22, no. 2 (2013): 51–75.

Barth, Karl. *The Epistle to the Romans*, translated by Edwyn C. Hoskyns. London: Oxford University Press, 1968.

Barth, Karl. *Der Römerbrief (Zweite Fassung) 1922*, edited by Cornelis van der Kooi and Katja Tolstaja. Zürich: Theologischer Verlag Zürich, 2010.

Berneuchener Konferenz. *Das Berneuchener Buch: Vom Anspruch des Evangeliums auf die Kirchen der Reformation*. Hamburg: Hanseatische Verlagsanstalt, 1926.

Daur, Rudolf, ed. *An der Schwelle: Bericht über die Arbeitswoche des "Köngener Kreises" in Königsfeld, vom 1. bis 6. Januar 1937, über Grundfragen der Seelenkunde und Seelenführung*. Heilbronn: Salzer, 1937.

Froboese, Felicia. 'Ärztliche Seelenführung', *Evangelische Jahresbriefe* (1938): 133–36.

Happich, Carl. 'Das Bildbewußtsein als Ansatzstelle psychischer Behandlung', *Zentralblatt für Psychotherapie und ihre Grenzgebiete* 5 (1932): 663–77.

Happich, Carl. *Anleitung zur Meditation*. Darmstadt: Roether, 1938.

Hederich, Michael. *Karl Bernhard Ritter: Reformer, Kämpfer, Seelsorger: Ein Lebensbild*. Kassel: Evangelischer Medienverband, 2010.

Jaspers, Karl. *Der philosophische Glaube*. Frankfurt am Main: Fischer, 1958.

Jehle-Wildberger, Marianne, ed. *C.G. Jung und Adolf Keller: Über Theologie und Psychologie: Briefe und Gespräche*. Zürich: Theologischer Verlag Zürich, 2014.

Jung, C.G. 'Psychologie und Alchemie'. In *Gesammelte Werke*, vol. 12, edited by Lilly Jung-Merker and Elisabeth Rüf. Olten & Freiburg: Walter, 1972.

Jung, C.G. *Letters*, vol. 1, edited by Gerhard Adler and Aniela Jaffé; translated by R.F.C. Hull. Princeton: Princeton University Press, 1973.

Jung, C.G. 'Psychologie und Alchemie'. In *Collected Works* 12, edited by Herbert Read, Michael Fordham, Gerhard Adler and William McGuire; translated by R.F.C. Hull. Princeton and London: Princeton University Press and Routledge, 1977.

Jung, C.G. 'The Symbolic Life (Discussion)'. In *Collected Works* 18, edited by Herbert Read, Michael Fordham, Gerhard Adler and William McGuire; translated by R.F.C Hull, 281–90. Princeton and London: Princeton University Press and Routledge, 1977.

Jung, C.G. 'Das symbolische Leben (Diskussion)'. In *Gesammelte Werke* 18/1, edited by Lilly Jung-Merker and Elisabeth Rüf, 304–14. Olten & Freiburg: Walter, 1981.

Jung, C.G. *The Black Books 1913–1932: Notebooks of Transformation*, edited by Sonu Shamdasani; translated by Martin Liebscher, John Peck and Sonu Shamdasani. London and New York: W.W. Norton, 2020.

Jung, C.G. and Aniela Jaffé. *Memories, Dreams, Reflections*, edited by Aniela Jaffé; translated by Richard Winston and Clara Winston. New York: Pantheon Books, 1962.

Jung, C.G. and Aniela Jaffé. *Erinnerungen, Träume, Gedanken*, edited by Aniela Jaffé. Düsseldorf: Walter, 1985.

Lammers, Ann Conrad and Adrian Cunningham, eds. *The Jung–White Letters*. London: Routledge, 2007.

Lindt, Andreas. 'C.F. Spittler und W.M.L. de Wette: Zur Begegnung von Erweckungsfrömmigkeit und Universitätstheologie im Basel des 19. Jahrhunderts'. In *Gottesreich und Menschenreich: Ernst Staehelin zum 80. Geburtstag*, edited by Max Geiger, 361–84. Basel: Helbing und Lichtenhahn, 1969.

Mielke, Roger. 'Der "Geistliche Pfad" als Erfahrungsweg: Zum Meditationsweg der Evangelischen Michaelsbruderschaft', *Quatember* 72 (2008).

Oeyen, Christian. 'Ein Weg zur Bildung christlicher Persönlichkeiten', *Quatember* 72 (2008): 203–11.

Oglesby, Les. *C.G. Jung and Hans Urs von Balthasar: God and Evil – A Critical Comparison*. London: Routledge, 2014.

Ritter, Karl Bernhard. *Über die Meditation als Mittel der Menschenbildung*. Kassel: Stauda, 1947.

Ritter, Karl Bernhard. 'Von den sieben Stufen der Erkenntnis und des Lebens', 4 issues; 2nd revised ed. as *Der geistliche Pfad. Meditation über die siebenfache Gestalt des geistlichen Lebens*, edited by Evangelische Michaelsbruderschaft, 1952.

Ritter, Karl Bernhard. 'Berneuchen 1923 (Nach einem Menschenalter II)', *Quatember* (1953): 90–93.

Ritter, Karl Bernhard. 'Mein Weg mit Wilhelm Stählin (Nach einem Menschenalter IV)', *Quatember* (1952/53): 217–20.

Ritter, Karl Bernhard. 'Die Entdeckung der Meditation (Nach einem Menschenalter IX)', *Quatember* (1953): 96–98.

Schleiermacher, Friedrich. *The Christian Faith*, edited by H.R. Mackintosh and J.S. Stewart. London: T. and T. Clark, 1999.

Sherry, Jay. *Carl Gustav Jung: Avant-Garde Conservative*. New York: Palgrave Macmillan, 2010.

Stählin, Wilhelm. *Vom göttlichen Geheimnis*. Kassel: Stauda, 1936.

Stählin, Wilhelm. 'Geistliche Übung', *Das Gottesjahr* (1938): 8–16.

Stählin, Wilhelm. 'Michaelsbruderschaft–Rückkehr und Rechenschaft'. In *Freiheit und Ordnung: Symbolon*, by Wilhelm Stählin. Frankfurt am Main: Evangelisches Verlagswerk, 1980.

Uhsadel, Walter. 'Der Mensch in der Kirche', *Evangelische Jahresbriefe* (1936): 132–35.

Uhsadel, Walter. *Der Mensch und die Mächte des Unbewussten: Studien zur Begegnung von Psychotherapie und Seelsorge*. Kassel: Stauda, 1952.

Uhsadel, Walter. *Evangelische Seelsorge*. Heidelberg: Quell und Meyer, 1966.

Uhsadel, Walter. 'Zusammenarbeit von "Arzt und Seelsorger": Ein Erfahrungsbericht zum Gedenken an Frau Dr. med. Felicia Froboese-Thiele', *Zeitschrift für analytische Psychologie und ihre Grenzgebiete* 3 (1972): 111–21.

Von Franz, Marie-Louise. *C.G. Jung: Sein Mythos in unserer Zeit*. Frauenfeld: Huber, 1972.

Von Franz, Marie-Louise. *C.G. Jung: His Myth in Our Time*, translated by William H. Kennedy. Toronto: Inner City Books, 1998.

Von Graevenitz, Jutta. 'Memory of C.G. Jung'. In *C.G. Jung, Emma Jung and Toni Wolff: A Collection of Remembrances*, edited by Ferne Jensen and Sidney Mullen, 27–31. San Francisco: Analytical Psychology Club, 1982.

Von Haebler, Hans Carl. *Geschichte der Evangelischen Michaelsbruderschaft von ihren Anfängen bis zum Gesamtkonvent 1967*. Marburg: Evangelische Michaelsbruderschaft, 1975.

Zimmermann, Willi. 'Vierzig Jahre Evangelische Michaelsbruderschaft', *Quatember* (1972): 40–41.

6

Humane Horrors: The Dentist in Günter Grass's *örtlich betäubt / Local Anaesthetic* (1969)

Mererid Puw Davies

Preface

The Introduction to this volume argues that practices and theories of medicine in the German-speaking world have 'come to define the human'. It also shows, through the example of Birgit Pausch's novella *Die Verweigerungen der Johanna Glauflügel / Johanna Glauflügel's Refusals* (1977), how post-war West Germany shared that insight, and knew a critique of medical practice and its discourses according to which they fell short of humanist ideals. According to Pausch's eponymous protagonist, West Germany treats its patients in dehumanising ways, a deficit linked to wider injustices. This view is partly a legacy of the West German 'red decade' (1967–77), which saw the rise, fall and complex aftermath of protest movements that challenged society in its entirety. Indeed, the movements' discourses on medicine offer ways of understanding their thinking more broadly, and their wish for an alternative society in which people lead more humane, more fully human lives. For Glauflügel, by implication, to be human is a future aspiration for a more ideal society, rather than lived reality.

The novel discussed here, Günter Grass's *örtlich betäubt / Local Anaesthetic* (1969), about the relationship between a modern dentist and his patient, has its finger on that anti-authoritarian pulse. As Sebastian Coxon's chapter in this volume demonstrates, in the past, dental pain and its treatment were excruciating and drastic: perhaps the laughter in the works in question represents, among other things, collective defence against such horrors. By contrast, Grass's dentist, with his anaesthetics and technology, reduces dental suffering almost to nothing, and makes a palpable difference to patients' lives: he allows them to feel or become more fully human, if only temporarily.

But even as this astonishing improvement in medical care seems to enhance humanity, *örtlich betäubt* elucidates the argument, derived from Critical Theory, that precisely such advances are part of a reifying, dehumanising modernity. This bleak vision goes far further than that of Glauflügel, who believes that more equitable administration of medicine would render it more humane. By contrast, in the view of the patient in Grass's novel, treatment comes at the price of his very humanity, and that of his dentist too. *Örtlich betäubt* does not align itself with such argument, instead outlining it ironically and critically; yet it does so with great, troubling clarity. Thus, the work unfolds an acute paradox for the twentieth century and after, namely that modern medicine can be seen as inextricably bound up with the dark as well as the lucent sides of Enlightenment. The novel's focus on masculine conflicts and subjectivity, cast into stark relief by comparison with *Die Verweigerungen der Johanna Glauflügel*, suggests also that gendered aspects may be central to that paradox. Therefore, Grass's novel suggests with force (at least) three wider issues for the medical humanities. First, the ambiguous entanglements of the humane and inhumane in medical discourse continue to demand analysis; the medical humanities must involve, too, critical accounts of inhumanities. Second, those accounts are inseparable from considerations of gender. And third, in modernity, the question of what it is to be human remains agonisingly open.

Introduction

In *örtlich betäubt*, one of the protagonists, a dentist, laments the arts' neglect of his profession.[1] Implicitly comparing modern dentistry with its more painful, dramatic, and hence aesthetically exploitable antecedents, he remarks: '"Auch Zahnärzte kommen in der Literatur kaum ... vor.... Wir geben nichts her. Oder: Heute geben wir nichts mehr her. Allenfalls Nebenrollen. Wir arbeiten zu schmerzlos unauffällig. Die Lokalanästhesie hindert uns, Originale zu werden."' / '"There aren't very many dentists in literature ... not even in comedies.... We're not interesting. Or we've ceased to be interesting. Secondary roles at the most. We must work too painlessly and inconspicuously. Local anaesthesia prevents us from becoming weirdies."'[2] This unnamed dentist indeed seems shadowy, and at first sight merely a chorus commenting on other characters' engagements with the era's spectacular protest movements. He himself advocates less eye-catching '"Fleiß, Zweifel, Vernunft, Dazulernen, Zögern. Mehrmaliger Neubeginn, kaum merkliche Verbesserungen, einkalkulierte Fehlentwickungen, Evolution Schritt für Schritt"' (144) / '"hard work, doubt, reason, the acquisition of more knowledge, new beginnings, scarcely perceptible improvement, mistakes allowed for in the overall plan, step-by-step evolution"' (126) in everything, from healthcare to social policy. The dentist sees modern, humane medical practices and their development as a philosophical template for politics and society; and in this moderate outlook too, appears to offer little political or intellectual controversy that might play out excitingly in literature.

But of course the dentist's ostentatious complaint that he is uninteresting to the arts transparently invites challenge.[3] This chapter responds with a close reading of this figure and his practice, and a new interpretation of the novel itself and its complex relationship with the politics of the Federal Republic's 'red decade'.[4] In 1969, the committed Social Democrat Grass described anti-authoritarians as antagonists, offering 'Widerstand and Widerspruch' / 'resistance and contradiction'.[5]

He criticised them in the poetry volume *Ausgefragt / Questioned Out* (1967)), which had a controversial reception, and reprised that debate in *örtlich betäubt*.[6] Posterity upholds perceptions that Grass opposed anti-authoritarianism: in 2012, the 'Doyen der Grass-Forschung' / 'doyen of Grass scholarship' Volker Neuhaus called him '[der] konsequentest[e] Gegner der sich sozialistisch gebärdenden Außerparlamentarischen Opposition' / 'the most consistent opponent of the would-be socialist extraparliamentary opposition'.[7] Traditionally then, *örtlich betäubt* is often read, in line with perceptions of Grass's own politics in the 1960s, as an anti-protest novel, criticising a movement obsessed with the short-term anaesthetic effects of unreflecting action at the expense of deep, hard-won analysis or long-term strategy.

This essay challenges that view by presenting remarkable parallels between *örtlich betäubt* and anti-authoritarian thought. It does so, first, by outlining salient points of the novel's narrative and the generally optimistic ways in which scholarship has interpreted it to date. Second, this chapter shows how at first sight, the novel represents the dentist as a schematic yet superficially positive figure, a characterisation that seems to support such interpretations. Third, however, a more critical rereading highlights the dentist's more negative aspects; and fourth, the chapter shows how precisely those aspects tally with the ideas of the *maître à penser* of the protest movements, the philosopher Herbert Marcuse, on institutions and technological rationality. Fifth, it highlights intertextual connections in *örtlich betäubt* to the work of Sigmund Freud and E.T.A. Hoffmann, arguing that that textual hinterland resonates with the novel's Marcusean references, casting its scenes in the dental practice into a nightmarish chiaroscuro. Sixth, the chapter concludes by comparing and contrasting Grass's novel to a contemporary anti-authoritarian cartoon that mobilises the imagery and discourse of dentistry, and so shows how the novel is part of the complex, dialogical intertextuality of its time.

The objectives of this discussion are twofold. On the one hand, it demonstrates the extensive influence of a range of allusions in *örtlich betäubt*, from Marcuse to Hoffmann, and the ways in which awareness of this intertextuality changes our reading of the novel and hence of Grass's work. In this sense, the study suggests that Grass must have been very familiar with Marcusean argument. However, its aim is less to comment on Grass's own supposed intentions and views with regard to such thought than on ways his novel relates to the broader cultural history and poetics of the West German '1968'. On the other hand, the chapter elucidates anti-authoritarian analyses of medicine as violent and reifying.[8] In so doing, it embeds anti-authoritarian culture in wider and longer traditions of thinking about medicine, and shows how the later twentieth century, even as medicine reached new heights of humane potential, became alive to dark interpretations of those practices.

The Stories So Far

Örtlich betäubt is told only from the limited perspective of its first-person narrator, Eberhard Starusch, combining, among other things, apparent present-day experiences, fantasy, various genres, imagined film sequences, intertextual reference and flashbacks. Above all, Starusch privileges stories, saying: 'ich [kenne] nur Geschichten … Ich glaube nun mal an Geschichten.' / 'all I can do is tell stories … I happen to believe in stories.' (201/176). However, his challenging, fragmentary style simultaneously highlights their unreliability. Starusch (b.1927), is a West

Berlin secondary school teacher of German and history, with a jaw so prominent that it gives him persistent toothache and an odd appearance, and makes him tear his food like an animal. A colleague, Irmgard Seifert (also b.1927), recommends a local dentist for his painless, modern, technologically innovative methods, such as providing a television that patients watch during treatment. In early 1967, Starusch begins undergoing complex dental treatment to correct the effects of his jaw.

The novel is divided into three sections. The first records treatment of Starusch's lower jaw, and is mainly set in the dentist's surgery, where he and Starusch debate many issues, including Starusch's tales of his post-war past. In some, he perpetrates murderous violence on women, and in one case also on his young child. Not all these stories are mutually compatible, suggesting that they are at least in part fantasy, but the most consistent of them concern Starusch's claims of previous success as an engineer in a cement works, and his engagement with the owner's daughter, Linde Krings. Her father, a former Nazi general, returns from a prisoner of war camp in 1955, and engages her in miniature reconstructions of the Second World War, aiming this time for Germany to win. Linde starts a sexual relationship with her father's employee Schlottau, in exchange for information about these war games, and the engagement with the equally unfaithful Starusch collapses. She gives him money, which he invests in retraining as a teacher and in the dental treatment.

The second part takes place during a short scheduled break in treatment, and focuses on the plan of Starusch's student, Philipp Scherbaum, to burn his much-loved pet dog alive on West Berlin's premier shopping street, the Kudamm, in protest at the Vietnam War. This proposal is debated, heatedly and variously, by Starusch, the dentist, Seifert, Scherbaum and his girlfriend Vero Lewand, and complicated by the fraught relationships between them.[9] Lewand endorses anti-authoritarian action, and Seifert, anguished about her past in the Nazi League of German Girls / Bund Deutscher Mädel (BDM), is drawn to Scherbaum and his plan. While the dentist rejects it as a doomed acting-out of German complexes and ineffectual traditions of idealism and revolt, Starusch is torn between attraction and rejection. However, believing that Scherbaum's plan would be cruel, politically useless and personally damaging – even physically dangerous – for Scherbaum himself, he attempts unsuccessfully to dissuade him. Ultimately, the dentist convinces Scherbaum to give up and work on his school newspaper instead. Also in this section, brief details emerge of Starusch's teenage war years in Danzig, and his leadership, under the nickname

Störtebeker, of a gang that committed deadly arson.[10] Consequently, Starusch/Störtebeker was consigned to a dangerous penal battalion, and repeated brief references suggest its horrors.

The third section narrates the initially successful treatment of Starusch's upper jaw and its aftermath a little later in 1967. The treatment enables him for the first time to have a satisfactory sexual relationship with and become engaged to Seifert, while the dentist discovers in independent research that Starusch's stories about cement, Linde and Krings are inventions. But by 1969 and the end of the novel, Starusch remains unmarried and reverts to storytelling, in this case a sadistic narrative in which he inflicts extreme violence on Linde, her children, her husband and many bystanders. Toothache returns and the novel concludes: 'Und bei mir bildete sich unten links ein Herd. Die Degudentbrücke wurde durchgesägt. Minus sechs mußte gezogen werden. Der Herd wurde ausgekratzt. Mein Zahnarzt zeigte mir ein an der Wurzelspitze hängendes Säckchen: eitrig wäßriges Gewebe. Nichts hält vor. Immer neue Schmerzen.' (263–4) / 'And as for me, an abscess has formed on the lower left. The porcelain bridge was sawed through. The abscess was scraped out. My dentist showed me a small sac adhering to the root tip: tissue suffused with pus and water. Nothing lasts. There will always be pain.' (231) That is, Starusch's original treatment and sufferings are ineffectual in the medium term, and the dentist's expert work destroyed.

Worse, Starusch will always be prone to infection, and his congenital toothache is more than a physical complaint. Early on, the dentist remarks: '"Ihr Zahnstein ist versteinerter Haß. Nicht nur die Mikroflora in Ihrem Mundmilieu, auch Ihre krausen Gedanken, Ihr inständiges Rückwärtsschielen … das alles – die Summe aus Zahnbild und Psyche – verrät Sie: eingelagerte Gewalttätigkeiten, Mordanschläge auf Vorrat." (31) / '"Your tartar is your calcified hate. Not only the microflora in your oral cavity, but also your muddled thoughts, your obstinate squinting backward … all that – the sum of dental picture and psyche – betrays you: stored-up violence, murderous designs."' (28)

The dentist diagnoses the cause as '"ein längst verjährtes Versagen"' (69) / '"an old failure"' (61). While never spelled out, that failure seems linked to both Linde and Starusch's Nazi-era past, so his pain manifests Germany's guilt feelings in the present.[11] Theodore Ziolkowski writes: 'Starusch's agonies in the dentist's chair correspond to the agonies of an entire people trying to come to terms with its past.'[12] Thus, he argues that *örtlich betäubt* references a long cultural tradition in which teeth outwardly symbolise inner discontents, here, something rotten in the Federal Republic.[13]

Some readers see this ending as bleak.[14] However, Grass disputed the translation by Ralph Manheim of the novel's final sentence as 'There will always be pain'. A more literal rendering is 'There are always new pains', and Grass's criticism of the published translation draws attention to his view that at stake is not unchanging suffering, but a succession of new, different incidences of it.[15] While in this more dynamic vision there will be 'always new pains', there can also always be new ways, even if limited and temporary, of countering them, as Starusch and his dentist find, in both dentistry and politics. On this reading, the use of local anaesthetic to alleviate pain and effect incremental improvements appears humane, especially in comparison to dental 'Gewaltakte' (69) / 'acts of violence' (61) of the past, or general anaesthetic, which removes ability to consent; Starusch is at least able to live pain-free for two years after his treatment. Indeed, Julian Preece argues that '*Local Anaesthetic* is the most optimistic of all Grass's novels': since Scherbaum does not act, '[t]ragedy is averted, history does not repeat itself.'[16] Hence, the dentist's commitment to patient, liberally minded, if slow-moving, political (and clinical) process under judicious use of local anaesthetic is vindicated.

Critics debate the extent to which the dentist is part of Starusch's fantasy, relating this question to the novel's narrative technique.[17] Studies frequently assess, too, the dentist's politics in relation to Grass's. The dentist is often read positively, sometimes as a representative of the Enlightenment, indeed even as Grass's political mouthpiece.[18] Other readers simultaneously acknowledge the dentist's limitations or (productive) relativisation by other factors in the novel, and some highlight his deficits.[19] Michael Hollington notices that the term 'Betäubung' / 'anaesthetic', as practiced by the dentist, references the anti-authoritarian analysis of capitalism, which sees subjects as being anaesthetised by consumption.[20] Taking this view furthest, Hanspeter Brode calls the dentist a 'Technokrat von allerbeschränktestem Zuschnitt' / 'a technocrat of the most limited kind' and the treatments (and philosophy and politics) he offers 'pathogene Anpassungsvorgänge' / 'pathogenic processes of assimilation'.[21] Thus, the dentist's influence on Scherbaum leads to the student's 'Kapitulation vor schlechter und dumpfer Alltäglichkeit' / 'capitulation in the face of a bad and oppressive banality'.[22] Complementing Brode's unusual, perhaps unique critique, this study considers the dentist's darker side.

Representing the Dentist

Initially, and paradoxically, given the dentist's dominant presence and speech, his representation is limited, with no physical description beyond his synecdochal 'hoch geschlossene[s] Kittelchen und ... Segeltuchschuhe' (186) / 'high-buttoned smock and tennis shoes' (162), behind which the individual recedes. Otherwise, the dentist's philosophical, historical and political utterances, and comments on others, reveal nothing personal beyond his appreciation of Seneca. This schematic presentation is eloquent about Starusch himself, highlighting his self-absorption. Thus, the dentist is above all a catalyst, conduit and opponent to Starusch's and others' thoughts, for his chair recalls both confessional and analyst's couch. At the same time, he personifies important ideas and principles.[23]

However, intriguing glimpses suggest that the dentist is more than a non-individuated foil for the novel's more evidently realist characters. His tennis shoes, providing comfort as he stands to work, and soothing silence for the patient, may form part of his perfect clinical environment in conventional white. But they are mentioned several times, implying that they may be more than a minor detail; their informality in a professional context might suggest that the dentist is an individualist. Almost parenthetically, Starusch remarks: 'Mein Zahnarzt ist verheiratet, hat drei Kinder, steht mitten im Leben und übt einen Beruf aus, der zu Resultaten führt, die sich ablesen lassen. Allerlei Positives: ... und den Schmerz kann er beschwichtigen ...' (180) / 'My dentist is married, has three children, is in the prime of life and practices a profession that brings gaugeable results. So much that is positive: ... and he is able to appease pain' (157). Starusch observes too that the dentist interacts with colleagues, gives adult education lectures on tooth decay, and mentions his mother once with kindness. The only other biographical details briefly offered are that the dentist fought on the Eastern Front in 1944, becoming a prisoner of war, suggesting that he is likely to be at least a little older than Starusch. Thus, his portrayal acquires features of realist representation that prompt the reader's curiosity, yet frustrate it too, for they remain provocatively underdeveloped.

Power Tools

Starusch suggests that the dentist's mature, fulfilled personal life is of a piece with his meaningful profession. This continuity in turn underwrites the dentist's philosophical pronouncements and makes him consistent and effective at work and in debate, for he works against pain every day: '"Das ist nicht mein Beruf: Wehtun"' (186) / '"Hurting is not my profession"' (162). By contrast, Starusch and Scherbaum, despite calling for social justice, manifest physical violence against their partners and offer dehumanising, undifferentiated characterisations of women on the Kudamm. The dentist does not subscribe to such double standards, and speaks in a nuanced way of his relationship with his own mother, who liked to frequent Kudamm cafés. It may be this integrity that allows him to persuade Scherbaum, while Starusch, tormented by inner contradictions, cannot. By means of contrast, this characterisation highlights the protagonist's dysfunctional subjectivity and relationships, and professional crises.

The dentist and Starusch often seem to debate as equals, in line with the dentist's precept that dialogue is a productive political process, and that '"Gespräche verhindern Taten"' (143) / '"Dialogue prevents action"' (126) in a positive sense. Such a reading tallies with John Reddick's argument that the dentist represents 'enlightened and liberal tolerance that is essentially humanistic in nature'.[24] However, the dentist's moral positions are not simplistic. He considers napalm '"relativ harmlos"' (182) / '"relatively harmless"' (159) compared with nuclear weapons, and thus implicitly finds its use acceptable if it prevents nuclear war. To him, conditions in Persia, another touchstone of anti-authoritarian outrage, surpass those in some other countries, so relativising their significance. Moreover, the metal in Starusch's dental bridges is, as the dentist puts it: '"im übertragenen Sinne, nicht rein, weil es sich bei dieser Speziallegierung um ein Patent der Degussa handelt, die ziemlich suspekte Geschäftverbindungen zu Südafrika unterhält. Wo man auch hinblickt, ein Haar in der Suppe."' (151) / '"impure by implication; it is a special alloy patented by Degussa, which maintains rather shady business connections in South Africa. Wherever you look, there's a fly in the ointment."' (133) That is to say, the dentist accepts his work's ethically dubious aspects as the price of its overall contribution to alleviating suffering.

Starusch's bridges are fitted in the final appointment of the novel's first part, and this passage of some twenty pages lies at the very heart of his relationship with the dentist. The lengthy description of the appointment is interspersed with fantasy episodes, reflecting the way Starusch has become fearful and sensitive to pain. For example, towards the end, Linde appears and tells a violent fairy tale. Subsequently, the dentist and his assistant seem to morph into Schlottau and Linde respectively. With a white-hot 'Kombizange' (117) / 'combination pliers' (103), Schlottau brands Starusch's lip. The dentist quickly returns to his usual persona, apologising for the 'kleines Malheur' (118) / 'little accident' (105) that led him accidentally to cause a tiny L-shaped burn on Starusch's lip with a dental instrument. Starusch accepts his apology and the injury is treated with ointment. The appointment concludes with a double prescription of the painkiller Arantil, and Starusch's temporary discharge.

The session also involves political discussions. Starusch fantasises about bulldozers destroying the excessive consumer goods that repel him, but the dentist objects: '"Aufrufe zur Gewalt ... finden in mir einen unversönlichen Gegner"' (107) / '"I will not tolerate incitements to violence"' (95). Starusch eventually agrees with him. So just as this scene represents the key clinical moment of Starusch's treatment (fitting the bridges), its crisis (the burn) and resolution, his ideological conflict with the dentist both reaches, and apparently overcomes, crisis point too. Therefore, this episode could be seen as an instance of enlightenment and progress through debate, mirrored in the successful treatment.

Yet Starusch is aware that the dentist is more powerful than he, noting later, 'Er könnte auf mich verzichten; ich bin auf ihn angewiesen' (180) / 'He could manage without me; I am dependent on him' (158), an imbalance manifested physically in Starusch's helpless position in the chair. Moreover, part of the scene is presented by Starusch as a film or animated sequence in which the dentist controls the audio, and so is able to turn off Starusch's speech. Therefore, the dentist has the upper hand from the start, and exploits this advantage in order to make Starusch give up his arguments: 'der Zahnarzt besteht auf Gewaltverzicht und droht, bei ausbleibendem Widerruf, die Anästhesie des Unterkiefers zu unterlassen. Fürsorgeentzug. Das Zeigen der Folterwerkzeuge.' (102) / 'the dentist insists on my abjuring violence and threatens, if no retraction is forthcoming, to treat my lower jaw without anaesthesia. No more tender sick care. The instruments of torture are displayed' (90).

This language recalls pre-modern inquisition. In response, Starusch states: '"Ich widerrufe"' (102) / 'I retract' (90). However, he continues to nourish his fantasy of destruction, and the dentist threatens to send him to the waiting room unless he rethinks. Frightened, again Starusch announces his agreement with the dentist, but continues to think silently about the bulldozers. Consequently, the burn that follows appears as an escalation of the dentist's discipline of the recalcitrant subject. Acknowledging system and intent, and mistrusting the dentist's apologies, Starusch remarks to himself, 'Nichts tat ihm leid. Wer so schnell Brandsalbe sagt und sie auch griffbereit bei such führt, der kennt kein Mitleid, der will, was er tut' (118) / 'He wasn't the least bit sorry. Anyone who is so quick to say ointment-for-burns and has it at hand knows no pity; he's pleased with what he's done' (105). Thus, what brings Starusch into line with the dentist's views is not conviction, but the dentist's superior power and willingness to punish psychologically and physically.

Thus, the dynamic of threat and punishment is ongoing, and the workings of an abusive relationship are laid bare.

The Tolerance of Pain

In the appointment described at the end of the novel's first section, Starusch refers to Marcuse by name, and makes implicit allusions to his writings. Starusch's call for an 'Umwertung aller Werte' (38) / 'transvaluation of all values' (95) for example echoes Marcuse's for a 'radical transvaluation of values' in *An Essay on Liberation* (1969).[25] Starusch remarks, referring to the chair: 'An allen Orten, warum nicht in einem Rittergestühl, sollte die Große Weigerung beginnen' (108) / 'Every corner of the earth is ripe for the Great Refusal, so why not a dentist's chair?' (96), while Marcuse comments that 'The Great Refusal takes a variety of forms' (vii). Furthermore, *An Essay on Liberation*, like Starusch, criticises capitalism's 'obscene affluence and waste' (89), and Starusch's bulldozer fantasy recalls Marcuse's demand for an 'aesthetic morality' that 'insist[s] on cleaning the earth from the very material garbage produced by the spirit of capitalism' (28). It is from Marcuse too that Starusch may derive his interest in action, even violence, for in the essay 'Repressive Tolerance' (1965), Marcuse considers potential ethical differences between oppressive violence used by the state against the weak, and liberating violence practised by otherwise disenfranchised protesters.[26] The consequence of bulldozing, Starusch says to the dentist, could be the creation of an utopian space for something as yet unknown:

> 'Und jetzt läßt sich etwas aufbauen, etwas Grundneues ...'
> 'Und was, wenn ich fragen darf?' (119)
>
> '... and now something can be built, something radically new ...'
> 'What, may I ask?' (104)

This dialogue re-enacts the conversation with which *An Essay on Liberation* ends:

> And there is an answer to the question which troubles the minds of so many men of good will: what are the people in a free society going to do? The answer ... was given by a young black girl. She said: for the first time in our life, we shall be free to think about what we are going to do. (91)

Starusch fails to defend his Marcusean positions effectively in debate. But the events related in the passage dovetail with Marcuse's analysis of oppressive power and reason, thus explaining, *inter alia*, why the teacher cannot prevail against the dentist. When the dentist threatens to send Starusch to the waiting room, he allows him briefly to speak: 'der Zahnarzt strafte seinen Patienten mit Toleranz and gab ihm ... den Ton zurück' (108) / 'the dentist punished his patient with tolerance and ... gave him back his sound' (96). However, this permission is coerced compliance, so referencing the central argument of 'Repressive Tolerance' that capitalist democracies pervert tolerance. When the state claims to offer tolerance to its people, in forms such as freedom of speech, in reality this is a veneer further to enshrine its power, which far outweighs that of protesters. The state draws on this incommensurate power, its monopoly on violence, its control of the media and even of language to protect itself, and in any case withdraws tolerance in favour of direct oppression and violence whenever it matters. Such arguments proved significant to anti-authoritarians in the wake of the fatal shooting on 2 June 1967 by a plain-clothes police officer of a peaceful protester called Benno Ohnesorg, a student at West Berlin's Freie Universität. That tragedy was taken by many as confirmation of the thesis of repressive tolerance.

The dentist adopts just such strategies against Starusch, from the exploitation of a power imbalance, to manipulation of media and language, withdrawal of speech on equal terms and indeed, in this instance, all speech. At the same time, just as the state grants limited freedom of speech as a disingenuous strategy to legitimise itself, the dentist can restore 'Ton' / 'sound' to Starusch when he wants to, in order to give the illusion of consent. The dentist dominates language also in making it perform doublespeak (analogous to Marcuse's description of the state's 'Orwellian' (96) use of language), as in his insistence on 'Gewaltverzicht' (102) / 'abjuring violence' (90) while threatening to withdraw anaesthetic, and so to cause pain. Most strikingly, just as the state does in a covert way, the dentist relies on threats of psychological and physical punishment, even real injury, as well as dependence on or addiction to consumption (here, Arantil), to enforce compliance. So, while 'Repressive Tolerance' argues that society is unobtrusively governed by violence, most visible in institutions such as the police or asylums, Starusch's experience seems to confirm this analysis, by showing how it extends to the institution of medical practice.

On Marcuse's analysis, such institutions uphold the state. Similarly, the burn inflicted by Schlottau's pliers references the Christian martyrdom, outlined at the novel's start, of the patron saint of toothache and dentists, Apollonia.[27] This saint's teeth were violently extracted with 'Kneifzangen' (8) / 'blacksmith's tongs' (7) under the Roman Emperor Decius, and so this reference, like that to the torture of pre-modern European heretics, aligns the dentist's actions with persecutions sponsored by the authorities. Moreover, Starusch interprets his burn as a branding, a ritualised, socially legible injury indicating punishment and control. Thus, his capitulation to the dentist confirms Marcuse's observation that 'Non-violence is normally not only preached to but exacted from the weak' (102).

Marcuse writes in *Eros and Civilisation* (1955), in view of the totalising control achieved by the state:

> everyone, even at the very top, appears to be powerless before the movements and laws of the apparatus itself.... The masters no longer perform in an individual function. The sadistic principals, the capitalist exploiters, have been transformed into salaried members of a bureaucracy, whom their subjects meet as members of another bureaucracy. (98)

The effects on individual subjects are complex and painful, for while they still feel anger at their predicament, 'The aggressive impulse plunges into a void – or rather the hate encounters smiling colleagues, busy competitors, obedient officials, helpful social workers who are all doing their duty and are all innocent victims' (99). Consequently, aggression finds no focus, provoking diffuse states of guilt of indeterminate origin, which cannot be integrated productively into psychic life. This description fits both the dentist and Starusch. The former is a likeable professional of personal and philosophical integrity, yet accepts the need to deal with apartheid South Africa and discipline his patients; the latter, in part as a result, is driven by powerful aggression and guilt that he cannot even name.

Subjectivity and the Machine

While the novel's second part records a break in Starusch's treatment, the dentist remains a major figure within it, since he rings Starusch to discuss Scherbaum and they remain in touch throughout. Similarly, towards the end of the novel, after the end of Starusch's treatment, he and the dentist remain in contact. Read benignly, these contacts suggest Starusch's growing emotional as well as clinical dependence, recalling psychoanalytic transference, which is eventually superseded by a new kind of relationship between the two men that transcends that dynamic in a dialectical, positive way. Likewise, the dentist's interest in Scherbaum seems altruistic, and he even asks to meet and treat him gratis.

But read more critically, the dentist's calls to Starusch strengthen his control, and he actively draws the previously uninvolved Scherbaum into the same dependence. That action bears out Starusch's earlier fantasy in which the dentist leaves his practice to hunt down new patients, armed with a piece of technical equipment, which he 'geladen spazieren [führt]' (19) / 'can carry ... about with him in his pocket' (17).[28] According to Marcuse's *One-Dimensional Man* (1964), reason, once potentially subversive, is now a tool of domination, and 'scientific-technical rationality and manipulation are welded together into new forms of social control.'[29] This control proliferates, and '[t]he world tends to become the stuff of total administration, which absorbs even the administrators. The web of domination has become the web of Reason itself, and this society is fatally entangled in it' (169). In the context of anti-authoritarian, Marcusean discourse, the dentist, with his scientific training and modern reason, seems to embody just such technological rationality and its administration, especially when 'er rät, an Stelle aller staatlichen Administration seine weltweite Krankenfürsorge zu setzen' (101) / 'he recommends that all government be replaced by his worldwide Sickcare' (90). He justifies this idea as follows: '"Alle sind krank, waren krank, werden krank, sterben"' (83) / '"All people are sick, have been sick, get sick, die"' (74).[30] This global aspiration seems, like his attitude to Scherbaum, appropriative, even predatory.

The dentist enthusiastically consumes new technology, for example a Grundig '"sprechendes Notizbuch"' (182) / '"talking memorandum book"' (159), a recording device with which he captures a call with Starusch without his knowledge and consent. The gadget was recommended at a conference at chic St Moritz, underlining the privileges with which capitalism rewards the dentist as its administrator. This detail also betokens surveillance, and so anticipates the dentist's independent investigation of Starusch's fantasy about Linde. For this research, he calls on the knowledge of a colleague in a distant region of West Germany, implying that the institution of dentistry is omniscient, and that before it, nothing remains private.

The dentist's most prominent piece of hi-tech equipment is the chair with its 'halbautomatische Instrumatik, Ritter genannt, die ihm die Vielzahl der Instrumente ins kunstfertige Händchen lieferte' (18) / 'semi-automatic installation, bearing the name of Ritter, which played the multiple instruments into his skilful little hand' (15–6). It conducts tasks from refilling water glasses to replacing bodily functions; the dentist tells Starusch: '"Nicht schlucken, das macht der Absauger"' (19) / '"Don't swallow, the aspirator takes care of that"' (16). The tradename 'Ritter' happens also to mean 'knight' in German, and so evokes a rescuing hero, and protective, perhaps glamorous armour. Yet it is a cordless gadget from this chair that Starusch imagines the dentist taking outside the practice to hunt patients, so that like the Grundig recorder, it belongs in his ever-expanding arsenal of technological control. The Ritter equipment, with its 'Schnelllaufhandgelenken' (20) / 'high-speed wrist joints', replaces the human body and agency, for it appropriates and regulates formerly human actions such as swallowing and offering water, in machine-rationed quantities.[31] The practice thus becomes the habitation of robots and animate objects, like the chair and drill; or, in the terms of *One-Dimensional Man*, 'technological fetishism' (235). As Marcuse writes: 'technology has become the great vehicle of *reification* – reification in its most mature and effective form' (168–9). Correspondingly, Starusch associates the chair with powerlessness: 'Da saß ich mundtot im Rittergestühl und sah mich: mundtot im Rittergestühl' (110) / 'And so I sat silenced in the dentist's chair and saw myself: silenced in the dentist's chair' (97). That is, he imagines himself as an image on a screen, reduced and alienated to mere unmoving object as the automatic chair busies itself about him. Speechless, he is deprived of Immanuel Kant's key criterion of Enlightened subjectivity as he outlines it in his essay 'Beantwortung der Frage: Was ist Aufklärung?' / 'Answering the Question: What is Enlightenment?' (1784), namely maturity, or, in German, 'Mündigkeit', a term that suggests not only a state of subjective and intellectual autonomy, but a related ability to speak for oneself.

The Dentist and the Sandman

As Ziolkowski points out, Sigmund Freud 'interprets the pulling of teeth in dreams as castration.'[32] While this assertion may not make sense in all cases, here, Freud's argument works. In Kant's essay, the Enlightened subject is, by definition, adult and male. When the dentist extracts Starusch's teeth, he is 'mundtot' / 'silenced' not only because he cannot speak.[33] He is also, in a psychoanalytic reading, robbed of the mature masculinity needed to make him 'mündig'. This interpretation is supported by the novel's intertextual allusions to Gothic tales.

In the crucial appointment at the end of the novel's first part, the dentist's television reminds Starusch of the children's programme *Sandmännchen / Little Sandman*, versions of which played at bedtime in both East and West Germany in the 1960s, alluding to the traditional motif of the Sandman who makes children sleepy by throwing sand in their eyes. These programmes recall in turn E.T.A. Hoffman's horror story 'Der Sandmann' / 'The Sandman' (1816), in which the Sandman is said by a nanny to pluck out children's eyes to feed his offspring. The protagonist Nathanael, as a little boy, links this imaginary figure with an associate of his father, the lawyer Coppelius, who visits his home at night. Catching Nathanael spying on him and his father, Coppelius threatens to put out Nathanael's eyes and dismantles and reassembles his limbs like a doll's, so when, as an adult, Nathanael meets an eye-glass maker called Coppola who resembles Coppelius, he is terrified. Coppola makes eyes for a disturbingly lifelike doll called Olimpia, with which Nathanael deludedly falls in love. Nathanael painfully overcomes this crisis, but, even as he plans to marry his (human) childhood love, Clara, the story ends with his death amidst fire imagery. In his essay on 'Der Sandmann', 'Das Unheimliche' / 'The Uncanny' (1919), Freud interprets the loss of the eyes at the hands of a paternal figure (Coppelius as he appears in association with Nathanael's father) as an image for castration. This reading explains in part why Nathanael is so traumatised by the childhood assault by Coppelius that he cannot form a mature sexual relationship in adulthood and instead is drawn first to Olimpia, then to his death on the prospect of marriage.

Örtlich betäubt suggests remarkable parallels between the dentist and Hoffmann's Coppelius/Coppola. Both are father figures and professional pillars of the community, deal intimately with bodies and use technology around them. But respectability and technology have dark sides, and Grass's dentist with his extractions, read through Freud, aligns with Coppelius's proposed robbery of Nathanael's eyes. Thus, neither Nathanael nor Starusch can marry to prove their mature masculinity. The 'Ritter', with its humanoid articulations and activities, figures alongside the robotic Olimpia in this intertextuality. Likewise, Hoffmann's fire imagery re-emerges in the dentist's burn. Starusch interprets its L-shape as reference to Linde and the baneful influence of their (imaginary) failed relationship supposedly marked his later life. But simultaneously, 'L' evokes the French homonym 'elle' ('she'), and so the burn brands Starusch as a feminine third person, that is, neither a first person nor an agent in either grammatical or Kantian terms. And strikingly, in *örtlich betäubt*, one reference to the Sandman appears on the same page as a description of Starusch's tongue reduced by anaesthetic to a 'Kloß' (114) / 'dumpling' (101). This recurrent, alienated self-image as a foodstuff, first suggested much earlier to Starusch by the television's advertisements for frozen food, makes the dentist's chair seem a place of cannibalism, like that of Hoffmann's Sandman who feeds his children human eyes.

Linde's turn as a 'Märchentante' (114) / 'storyteller' (101) follows.[34] In her tale, a king (by implication, Krings) wishes to cut out his enemies' tongues to give to his daughter (Linde), who however persuades him to let her marry a teacher (Starusch) instead and live peacefully. Yet the story fails to console Starusch, not only because of the coda he adds, in which the teacher may murder the princess. It harks back to Starusch's fantasy of his own dismembered, edible tongue, and to Hoffmann's tale, for Nathanael's fears are first triggered by a nurse's story, like Linde's. Moreover, in her reappearance as the dentist's assistant, alongside Schlottau as an avatar of the dentist, further parallels with 'Der Sandmann' emerge. The doubled figures of the assistant/Linde and the dentist/Schlottau replicate Hoffmann's Clara/Olimpia and Coppelius/Coppola. Here, Starusch's victorious sexual rival Schlottau seems to him 'fremd und dennoch bekannt' (116) / 'strange and yet familiar' (102), precisely the condition that Freud foregrounds in the title of his essay on 'Der Sandmann', for the Uncanny derives from something both horrific and well-known, an effect of the return of the repressed that Freud associates with the motif of doubling.

The castrating, devouring father figure features in *Eros and Civilisation* too:

> The father, restrained in the family and in his individual biological authority, is resurrected, far more powerful, in the administration which preserves the life of society ... These final and most sublime incarnations of the father cannot be overcome 'symbolically' by emancipation: there is no freedom from administration and its laws because they appear as ... the wise order which secures the goods and services for the progressive satisfaction of human needs. (91–2)

This argument accounts not only for Starusch's aggressive relationship with his dentist, but for his acute dependence on him. In the dentist therefore, violence and care merge, just as they do in Starusch's final fantasy of violence at the end of the book. That story can be understood as a continuation of the mimetic rivalry that Starusch feels towards the dentist throughout. For example, the dentist betters Starusch as Scherbaum's mentor, likely a source of jealousy for the teacher who is, as

Chloe E.M. Paver puts it, 'infatuated' with his student.[35] Responding to Starusch's narrative about Krings on the Eastern Front, the dentist brings up his own service in the East, and Starusch cuts him off. Starusch may interrupt because the dentist's real experience threatens to undermine his fantasy, or because of rivalry with the dentist, aligned here with the father figure Krings, and his superior military experience. In context, it is unsurprising that in another of Starusch's fantasies, he is Scherbaum's older brother, for Scherbaum senior did not fight in the war and so seems not to offer such an aggressive, rivalrous father image.

In this last fantasy, Starusch is an instructor at a sports academy working as a lifeguard at a spa during a vacation, and when Linde and family are in his pool, he turns the wave machine up so high that the whole building is destroyed and swimmers drown. Starusch's self-image here in many ways recalls the dentist: his pedagogical profession evokes the dentist's adult education classes, and his lifeguard job, the dentist's aid to people in physical distress. The pool is a quasi-clinical environment, while the wave machine is driven by phallic 'Kolben' (261) / 'pistons' (229), recalling the dentist's instruments. Most obviously of all, Starusch here wears 'Segeltuchschuhe' (259) / 'tennis shoes' (227)] like the dentist's. These parallels on one level suggest that Starusch is seeking to trump the dentist in one final, extreme display of aggression. But on another level, the shoes suggest the two men are one another's doubles. Hence, this scene shows the uncanny, dual face of the dentist and his practice, a simultaneously health-giving, yet violent environment.

Anti-Authoritarian Ambiguities: Some Conclusions

On this reading, in Grass's representation, even accomplished medical practitioners such as the dentist are implicated in the ubiquitous violence of technological rationality, an argument that anti-authoritarians in the 1960s Federal Republic would have recognised. Thus, this study suggests that *örtlich betäubt* engages deeply with anti-authoritarian ideas.[36] This is not of course to claim that Grass meant *örtlich betäubt* straightforwardly to endorse protest discourse. Most evidently, the fact that everything in the novel is only seen through the unreliable narrative of Starusch means that such ideas cannot be taken as the novel's intended message. Rather, they form part of a highly complex, ironic work that foregrounds doubt and ambiguity. Nonetheless, once the novel is read in this way, it is difficult to see the dentist in a positive light.

In a student magazine of West Berlin's Freie Universität study is rewarded as an anticipation of *örtlich betäubt*.[37] This image was of human jaws, in which individual teeth are photographs of well-known student activists. The caption, 'Eine wirkliche Volksgesundung wird vor allem die Erreichung gesunder Gebisse erstreben müssen' / 'A true restoration of the people's health must strive above all to achieve healthy teeth' is said by the cartoon to be from a 1942 publication entitled *Deutsches Gold – Gesundes Leben – Frohes Schaffen / German Gold – Healthy Life – Healthy Work,* by Professor Ewald Harndt, a dentist, former NSDAP and SA member, and, from October 1967 *Rektor* of the Freie Universität, a key locus of protest.[38] The suggestion appears to be that if, in the view ascribed here to Harndt, uniform healthy teeth are representative of the health of a nation or organisation, dissenting activists might appear to be bad teeth requiring extraction. Therefore, the cartoon could suggest satirically that Harndt wants the student activists removed. That removal could be by means of exmatriculation or exclusion, a threat enacted on student activists and other dissidents at the time.[39] But in view of the very recent police shooting of Ohnesorg, the cartoon is likely to have been interpreted as suggesting more sinister forms of repression. That sense of threat is amplified by the way the cartoon, with its Nazi references, also calls to mind the robbery of teeth from victims' corpses in death camps, and the image therefore teeters between humour and terror.

Some of the cartoon's formal characteristics, such as montage, intertextual reference and double meaning, are not only characteristic of the dialogical styles of classic anti-authoritarian textuality. They tally with those of Grass's novel, thus relating it closely to that writing tradition.[40] In thematic terms, the cartoon, like the novel, fits with Ziolkowski's observation that cultural representations of toothache can stand for rot in the body politic, and the quotation ascribed to Harndt underlines Marcuse's argument that science, apparently neutral, is in reality in thrall to politics. It also anticipates the present interpretation of Grass's dentist as a monstrous agent who cloaks his violence in the language of care.

Just as Grass's dentist wants to eliminate dental decay and associated pain, the cartoon attributes the same wish to Harndt. By contrast, the cartoon's argument is about acceptance of bad teeth. On one reading, if those teeth (dissident students) cause Harndt pain, that thought may be represented with glee. On another, the cartoon seems to assert that a healthy organisation must include opponents, even if this acceptance means, too, acceptance of pain and the need to hear, rather than silence its symptoms. It therefore fits with the ambiguous, dialectical ending of Grass's novel with its emphasis on recurrent pain.

Thus, both novel and cartoon criticise a type of discourse that demands the elimination – or extraction – from society of that which is supposedly undesirable. In both texts, such discourse is rooted in the Nazi era, although the cartoon is more forthright than the novel in calling up and mocking the 1940s past of its dentist protagonist. By contrast, *örtlich betäubt* does not reflect extensively on the dentist's past and his service in the East. Instead, it ascribes eliminatory discourse more prominently to anti-authoritarian characters, especially former BDM member Seifert. The novel thus goes further than the cartoon in its diagnosis of Nazi-era influences in contemporary culture, for it is less interested in the Nazi past of the older generation than in the possibility of troubling links between past and present in anti-authoritarian thought. Nonetheless, both cartoon and novel share ironic resistance to monolithic interpretation and ideas and representations which tie *örtlich betäubt* in, closely, intertextually and startlingly, to anti-authoritarian thought and art, and their profound scepticism regarding the humanity of modern medicine.

Notes

1. Grass, *örtlich betäubt*, 128; *Local Anaesthetic*, 113. Further references to both works, first German, then English, follow in the text. Other translations are the author's.
2. Reference is to pre-modern treatments as described elsewhere by Grass's dentist (69, 61); compare Sebastian Coxon's chapter in this volume.
3. Grass's dentist is discussed in Enderstein, 'Zahnsymbolik und ihre Bedeutung'; Groß, 'Zwischen Liebespfand und Höllenqual'; Ziolkowski, 'The Telltale Teeth'; these are surveys of long literary traditions, not close readings. On the novel's reception, see Mews, *Günter Grass and His Critics*, 103–19; Eckel and Eichel, 'Zeit der Politik'. Mews notes more positive response in the US than West Germany. Consequently, *örtlich betäubt* has attracted less critical attention than Grass's better-known novels. References here to the Federal Republic of Germany (FRG) or West Germany include West Berlin.
4. See, for example, Arnold and Görtz, *Günter Grass*; Grass, *Essays und Reden I 1955–1969*; Koenen, *Das rote Jahrzehnt*.
5. Grass, 'Zu *örtlich betäubt*', 258.
6. Grass, *Ausgefragt*.
7. Neuhaus, *Günter Grass*, 224. 'Doyen' is from the work's note about Neuhaus, no page number.
8. For historical accounts, see Forsbach, *Die 68er und die Medizin*; *Luzifer-Amor*; for life-writing and literature e.g. Georg W. Alsheimer, *Vietnamesische Lehrjahre. Sechs Jahre als deutscher Arzt in Vietnam* (1968); Inga Buhmann, *Ich habe mir eine Geschichte geschrieben* (1980); Marianne Herzog, *Nicht den Hunger verlieren* (1980); Birgit Pausch, *Die Verweigerungen der Johanna Glauflügel* (1977); Peter Schneider, *Lenz* (1973); Verena Stefan, *häutungen* (1973); Bernward Vesper, *Die Reise* (1977).
9. Compare Bauer Pickar on Starusch's misogyny, 'Starusch im Felde mit den Frauen'; Paver, *Narrative and Fantasy*, 176–7.
10. In earlier works of Grass's, Störtebeker joins Oskar Matzerath in an arson attack. See Hall, *Günter Grass's 'Danzig Quintet'*.
11. Hall shows that Starusch's and Oskar's recollections of the arson differ, casting doubt on Starusch's account. Preece, *The Life and Work of Günter Grass*, 113 notes that Oskar claims that the attack killed over one hundred, and so identifies it as the core of Starusch's guilt, 'obsession, … prevarication and … failure to free himself from pain'.

12. Ziolkowski, 'The Telltale Teeth', 19.
13. This motif is interestingly varied in Helma Sanders-Brahms's film *Deutschland, bleiche Mutter* (1981).
14. For example, Graves, 'Günter Grass's *Die Blechtrommel* and *örtlich betäubt*'; others emphasise ambiguity, for example, Brode, 'Von Danzig zur Bundesrepublik'.
15. Neuhaus, *Günter Grass*, 134. Neuhaus gives his source as *Time*, 13 April 1970, 73.
16. Preece, *The Life and Work of Günter Grass,* 108.
17. There is evidence in the novel that at least some aspects of the dentist are Starusch's fantasy, although critics differ on the extent to which the dentist is an independent agent. For example, Neuhaus claims that the dentist is purely Starusch's imagination, *Günter Grass*, 131; Mews disagrees, *Günter Grass and His Critics*, 117. See, for example, Paver, *Narrative and Fantasy*; Bauer Pickar, 'Günter Grass's *örtlich betäubt*'.
18. For example, Groß, 'Zwischen Liebespfand und Höllenqual'; Hollington, *Günter Grass*; Neuhaus, *Günter Grass,* 132; Preece, *The Life and Work of Günter Grass*, 112; Reddick, 'Action and Impotence'.
19. Brode, 'Von Danzig zur Bundesrepublik', 76, argues that the dentist's blinkered Enlightenment opposes Grass's endorsement of a 'Tradition pragmatischen Vernunfthandelns' / 'tradition of pragmatically rationalist behaviour'; Ziolkowski, 'The Telltale Teeth', that the dentist's views fail because they demand too many compromises from idealists such as Scherbaum; Taberner reconsiders the apparent 'correspondence between Grass and the dentist', concluding that the latter lacks the imagination requisite in a politically effective intellectual, 'Feigning the Anaesthetisation of Literary Inventiveness', 69.
20. Hollington, *Günter Grass*, 138. Hollington's source is Gerd Bucerius, 'Wogegen sie kämpfen, das wissen sie: Impulse und Irrtümer bei den jungen Revolutionären in Berlin', *Die Zeit*, 15 March 1968, quoted (with no page references) in Arnold and Görtz, *Günter Grass*, 103.
21. Brode, 'Von Danzig zur Bundesrepublik', 78.
22. Brode, 'Von Danzig zur Bundesrepublik', 76.
23. See, for example, Reddick, 'Action and Impotence', 572–6.
24. Reddick, 'Action and Impotence', 574.
25. Marcuse, *An Essay on Liberation*, 6, 54. Further page references follow in the text. Starusch cross-references Friedrich Nietzsche here; interestingly, Marcuse does not.
26. Marcuse, 'Repressive Tolerance', 107–8. Further references follow in the text.
27. Compare Coxon, 'Pain and Laughter', in this volume.
28. The German expression suggests both a hunting dog and a loaded gun.
29. Marcuse, *One-Dimensional Man*, 146. Further references follow in the text.
30. In a way, this idea recalls the very different, militant politics of the contemporary Sozialistisches Patientenkollektiv (SPK) in Heidelberg. See, for example, Forsbach, *Die 68er und die Medizin*, 87–101.
31. The translation omits the compound noun 'Schnelllaufhandgelenke', possibly highlighting its strangeness.
32. Ziolkowski, 'The Telltale Teeth', 12; compare Enderstein, 'Zahnsymbolik und ihre Bedeutung'.
33. The German adjective suggests, literally, a state of being 'dead at the mouth'.
34. The term 'Märchentante' specifies that the teller is female and can be used pejoratively of an unreliable speaker, evoking old wives' tales and traditional ideas of sinister women narrators.
35. Paver, *Narrative and Fantasy*, 175. This constellation is complicated by Starusch's relationship with the dentist, at times sexualised and masochistic. Starusch's infatuation bodes ill, given parallels with Thomas Mann's *Der Tod in Venedig / Death in Venice* (1912), where middle-aged Gustav von Aschenbach is catastrophically obsessed with a teenager possessing bad teeth. Starusch has his teeth fixed partially for aesthetic reasons; Aschenbach's ambiguously drawn barber gives him cosmetic treatments.
36. See, for example, Preece, *The Life and Work of Günter Grass*, 93–9.
37. Anon, *FU Spiegel* 60.
38. Harndt is emblematic as a former Nazi who maintained a post-war academic career. See Thomas, *Protest Movements in 1960s West Germany*, 52; Forsbach, *Die 68er und die Medizin*, 69–74.
39. Compare Thomas, *Protest Movements in 1960s West Germany*, 56–7, 138–41.
40. Davies, *Writing and the West German Protest Movements*.

Bibliography

Anon. 'Eine wirkliche Volksgesundung wird vor allem die Erreichung gesunder Gebisse erstreben müssen', *FU Spiegel* 60 (November 1967): back cover.

Arnold, Heinz Ludwig and Franz Josef Görtz, eds. *Günter Grass: Dokumente zur politischen Wirkung*. Munich: Edition Text und Kritik, 1971.

Bauer Pickar, Gertrud. 'Günter Grass' *örtlich betäubt*: The Fiction of Fact and Fantasy', *The Germanic Review* 52, no. 4 (1977): 289–303.

Bauer Pickar, Gertrud. 'Starusch im Felde mit den Frauen: Zum Frauenbild in Grass' *örtlich betäubt*', *Colloquia Germanica* 22, no. 3/4 (1989): 260–82.

Brode, Hanspeter. 'Von Danzig zur Bundesrepublik'. In *Günter Grass*, edited by Heinz Ludwig Arnold, 1–39. 5th ed. Munich: Edition Text und Kritik, 1978.

Davies, Mererid Puw. *Writing and the West German Protest Movements: The Textual Revolution*. London: imlr books, 2016.

Eckel, Hermann and Rüdiger Eichel. 'Zeit der Politik'. In *Blech getrommelt: Günter Grass in der Kritik*, edited by Heinz Ludwig Arnold, 110–20. Göttingen: Steidl, 1997.

Enderstein, Carl O. 'Zahnsymbolik und ihre Bedeutung in Günter Grass' Werken', *Monatshefte* 66, no. 1 (1974): 5–18.

Forsbach, Ralf. *Die 68er und die Medizin: Gesundheitspolitik und Patientenverhalten in der Bundesrepublik Deutschland (1960–2010)*. Göttingen: V&R Unipress, 2011.

Grass, Günter. *Ausgefragt*. Neuwied: Luchterhand, 1967.

Grass, Günter. *Local Anaesthetic*, translated by Ralph Manheim. Harmondsworth: Penguin, 1973.

Grass, Günter. *örtlich betäubt*. Darmstadt: Luchterhand, 1978.

Grass, Günter. *Essays und Reden, I: 1955–1969*, edited by Daniela Hermes. Göttingen: Steidl, 1997.

Grass, Günter. 'Zu *örtlich betäubt*'. In *Essays und Reden, I: 1955–1969*, edited by Daniela Hermes, 258. Göttingen: Steidl, 1997.

Graves, Peter J. 'Günter Grass's *Die Blechtrommel* and *örtlich betäubt*: The Pain of Polarities', *Forum for Modern Language Studies* 9, no. 2 (1973): 132–42.

Groß, Dominik. 'Zwischen Liebespfand und Höllenqual: Zähne, Zahnschmerzen und Zahnbehandler im Spiegel der Literatur', *Jahrbuch Literatur und Medizin* 1 (2007): 31–49.

Hall, Katharina. *Günter Grass's "Danzig Quintet": Explorations in the Memory and History of the Nazi Era from Die Blechtrommel to Im Krebsgang*. Oxford: Peter Lang, 2007.

Hollington, Michael. *Günter Grass: The Writer in a Pluralist Society*. London: Marion Boyars, 1980.

Koenen, Gerd. *Das rote Jahrzehnt: Unsere kleine deutsche Kulturrevolution 1967–1977*. Cologne: Kiepenheuer & Witsch, 2001.

Luzifer-Amor: Zeitschrift zur Geschichte der Psychoanalyse 14, no. 28 (2001).

Marcuse, Herbert. *Eros and Civilisation*. Boston, Beacon Press, 1955.

Marcuse, Herbert. *An Essay on Liberation*. London: Allen Lane, 1969.

Marcuse, Herbert. 'Repressive Tolerance'. In *A Critique of Pure Tolerance*, by Robert Paul Wolff, Barrington Moore and Herbert Marcuse, 81–123. Boston: Beacon Press, 1969.

Marcuse, Herbert. *One-Dimensional Man: Studies in the Ideology of Advanced Industrial Society*. 2nd ed. London: Routledge, 1991.

Mews, Siegfried. *Günter Grass and His Critics: From The Tin Drum to Crabwalk*. Rochester, NY: Camden House, 2008.

Neuhaus, Volker. *Günter Grass*. 3rd ed. Stuttgart: Metzler, 2010.

Neuhaus, Volker. *Günter Grass: Schriftsteller – Künstler – Zeitgenosse: Eine Biographie*. Göttingen: Steidl, 2012.

Paver, Chloe E.M. *Narrative and Fantasy in the Post-War German Novel: A Study of Novels by Johnson, Frisch, Wolf, Becker, and Grass*. Oxford: Clarendon Press, 1999.

Preece, Julian. *The Life and Work of Günter Grass: Literature, History, Politics*. Basingstoke: Palgrave Macmillan, 2001.

Reddick, John. 'Action and Impotence: Günter Grass's *örtlich betäubt*', *Modern Language Review* 67, no. 3 (1972): 563–78.

Taberner, Stuart. 'Feigning the Anaesthetisation of Literary Inventiveness: Günter Grass's *örtlich betäubt* and the Public Responsibility of the Politically Engaged Author', *Forum for Modern Language Studies* 34, no. 1 (1998): 69–81.

Thomas, Nick. *Protest Movements in 1960s West Germany: A Social History of Dissent and Democracy*. Oxford: Berg, 2003.

Ziolkowski, Theodore. 'The Telltale Teeth: Psychodontia to Sociodontia', *PMLA* 91, no. 1(1976): 9–22.

7

Inhumane Institutions: Wilhelm Genazino's Clinical Treatments

Thomas Wilks

Preface

This chapter foregrounds the unanticipated experiences of patienthood for incurably introspective individuals whose self-sustaining strategies are compromised by putatively curative treatment at provincial German clinics. The case studies used are novels by Wilhelm Genazino, acclaimed on his death in December 2018 as 'the psychohistorian of the old West Germany'.[1] This chapter reveals evidence of that epithet's psychological and cultural implications for inhumanity in German medicine, by applying theories of anti-psychiatry from the decade prior to the first trilogy of source texts from the 1970s, as well as sociological frameworks of authority in industrialised societies.

By the new millennium, health insurance reforms had curtailed 'cures' to ease ostensibly career-related malaise, stigmatising a middle-aged figure such as Genazino's fictional character Gerhard Warlich (2009), born and educated in the 'old West Germany'. The contemporary iteration of the clinic is no more equipped to help Warlich than the working world. He has been rejected for his post-'68 anti-authoritarian and communitarian tendencies, which he had only been able to express pathetically at work and in love, rather than as rousingly (if fleetingly and ambivalently) as some characters in Günter Grass's novel from the era of protest, *örtlich betäubt / Local Anaesthetic* (1969), discussed in Mererid Puw Davies's chapter in this volume.

The fact that the focal points of the present discussion are fictions, distinguished in the artfulness of their nomenclature, humour and irony, sharpens the reader's awareness of communication difficulties and failures in response to physical and psychiatric therapies. The patient's and the reader's challenges in negotiating intralingual translations, verbal and non-verbal, from medical institutions, are reflected in the English translations offered here. Simultaneously, this chapter explains gaps between meanings intended and received in presentation, in both the clinical sense when the patient discloses symptoms to the analyst and in the performative sense of how patients and medics appear to each other. Literary sources of humour are also 'translated' into serious social targets: like Ernest Schonfield's discussion in this volume of Kerstin Hensel's novel *Lärchenau* (2008), this chapter too probes beneath satirical and grotesque elements to argue that narration potentialises severe criticism of medical infrastructures. Absurdities where patients are incapacitated, rather than recovering the health they lost in inhumane workplaces, are highlighted. Thus, translation of examples from Genazino, barely known to Anglophone readers, together with the close readings that Davies, Schonfield and this chapter offer, allows peculiarities of German-language medicine to reach non-German-speaking audiences.

Furthermore, the narratives in question illustrate tensions between what Sonu Shamdasani's contribution to this collection identifies as the pre-Jungian cure of pathology – no less false an assumption for Genazino's physically uninjured civilians than for the soldiers surveyed in Mark Hewitson's chapter – and higher psychological and spiritual development. Such development becomes self-activated when the patient confronts inadequate pathology through narration transcribed on the page rather than in talking cures. Misdiagnosis through confusion between somatic and psychosomatic presentation, ambiguously medicalised discourses and unhelpfully de-medicalised language impose on the patient's negotiation of the world around him. These confusions and discourses are no match for the creative inner worlds into which literature sustains insight.

Introduction

The novels of Wilhelm Genazino (1943–2018) consistently portray protagonists in socially restricted or compromised lifestyles, who incorporate the observant and articulate mode of *flânerie* into peculiar existences complicated by precarious careers and intimate relationships. They thrive on contemplating the slightest visual and lexical distractions beyond their fleeting everyday occurrences in a manner consistent with their author's philosophy of 'der gedehnte Blick' / 'the protracted gaze'. This mode of interpreting fixed images beyond their beholder's immediate perception of their visible content, which Genazino has frequently applied to photographs, prompts narration that breaks boundaries between visual and verbal mediation.[2] The narrative strategy of conveying these perceptions holds Genazino's novels and their protagonists' lives together even in their most adverse circumstances, such as when clinical intervention disrupts settled routines. This chapter will compare the ineffectiveness of medical milieux and practitioners towards Abschaffel, the heterodiegetically presented subject of Genazino's first successful novel trilogy (1977–9), with those experienced by the autodiegetic Gerhard Warlich more than a dozen novels later, in *Das Glück in glücksfernen Zeiten / Fortune In Times Far From Fortunate* (2009).[3] I discern a consistent authorial critique of modern German medicine through the experiences of these two protagonists from far-apart stages in Genazino's career. His narratives enhance our understanding of confrontations that patients face in a social organisation of medicine that is not sufficiently humane for them.

Interpretations of the trilogy have been dominated by the career status of 31-year-old bachelor Abschaffel as a 1970s office worker, including in the two monographs comparing Genazino's novels published prior to *GgZ*.[4] In that novel, 41-year-old Warlich's coinciding relationship, career and psychological breakdowns render him a more experienced character confronting multiple failures. His prolonged clinical situation has not yet been afforded the scrutiny this chapter will provide in comparing his treatment with Abschaffel's. Both men are oversensitive to deteriorations in their working lives. These impact on their health, culminating in their admission to in-patient clinics in which therapy worsens their symptoms and compromises their employability. We become more aware than their therapists of the patients' idiosyncratic and unreliable presentations in their analytical sessions. These therapists' minimal interventions are at the forefront of the clinics' inhumanity in failing to respond to the patients' needs.

Genazino's case studies of patienthood within his protagonists' problematical professional and biographical trajectories expand on the convictions of sociological and anti-psychiatric theorists about practice and infrastructure in the treatment of mental illness. Yet, neither Genazino in his essays and interviews nor his protagonists explicitly acknowledge these discourses. I seek in this article to accommodate the convictions of Erich Fromm (1955), Erving Goffman (1959, 1961), R.D.

Laing (1960), David Cooper (1967) and Thomas S. Szasz (1961, 2008) in a treatment setting that none of them have explored: the German 'Kur' / 'cure', that is, a therapeutic stay at a residential resort or clinic.

Furthermore, I will expose Genazino's hitherto unexplored intertextualities with canonical figures and scenes from Thomas Mann, which are of varying social and medical comparability, as well as varying shades of subtlety. Through Abschaffel and Warlich, Genazino disperses a remarkable series of cues for a wider intertextual analysis of the institutionalisation, exploitation and perpetuation of patienthood, which all link his two protagonists' predicaments with Mann's well-known hypotexts within literary studies. Nevertheless, my highlighting of Mann's intermediary role in underlining distinctions of German medicine through novelistic treatment will be gradual. Genazino's references are widely dispersed and succinct, keeping in check the fundamental contrasts between Mann's bourgeoisie and Genazino's precariously classable protagonists. My concern in presenting these literary comparisons is to facilitate assessment of how inadequacies in therapy prompt patients to respond presciently to their conditions.

Working Towards Patienthood: Abschaffel's and Warlich's Conditions

> In the 19th century inhumanity meant cruelty; in the 20th century it means schizoid self-alienation.[5]

Abschaffel and Warlich both fall victim to the inhumanity of industrialised labour that Fromm pinpoints. They both become increasingly inefficient in performing lacklustre employment roles that entrap their eccentricities. Abschaffel experiences psychosomatic paralysis, while Warlich is dismissed from his job and disinclined to find another one. Abschaffel's voluntary six-week curative treatment (*VS*, 394) of psychotherapy and, to a lesser extent than prescribed for him, group therapy and gymnastics differs from Warlich's indefinite psychiatric treatment accompanied by a drug regimen. The two men share a need before they enter the clinics for compassionate companionship to counter their excessive introspection. Socially isolated, they have neglected to communicate the significant deteriorations they sense in their health.[6] Abschaffel, who 'hielt einfach alles aus und blieb allein' / 'simply endured everything and remained alone' (*A*, 46), cannot sustain an intimate relationship, and he limits his visits to his parents. Warlich's parents are dead, and his long-term relationship with Traudel is strained by her wishes for marriage and a child, and eventually by Warlich's unemployment. She finds his preoccupation with founding a 'Schule der Besänftigung' / 'School of Soothing' unusual and unbearable, to the extent that she admits him to a clinic. Warlich defines his project as 'eine Abendschule, die endlich das lehrt, was viele Menschen wissen wollen' / 'an evening school that at long last teaches what many people desire to know' (*GgZ*, 57);[7] contrastingly, the clinic placates him through drugs rather than through the humane mediation of knowledge.

Abschaffel's 'cure' marks his only extended break from his administrative position in the open-plan office of a haulage firm on an industrial estate on the outskirts of Frankfurt. He has worked there for 13 years, retaining his status as 'ein abgebrochener Gymnasiast' / 'a grammar school drop-out' (*VS*, 182). The opening sentence of the trilogy remains as defining for him when he leaves the clinic as it had been before his symptoms took hold: 'Weil seine Lage unabänderlich war, mußte Abschaffel arbeiten' / 'Because his situation was unalterable, Abschaffel had to work' (*A*, 8).[8] As nobody attends to his welfare, Abschaffel resorts to his own remedy of habitually wandering through the streets, both in Frankfurt and in the clinic village of Sattlach,[9] to combat his anxiety and boredom. He blends observations of banalities with profound thoughts: 'Ich muß mich soweit bringen, sagte er, bis mein Kopf wieder wirklich mir gehört, und das gelingt mir am besten dadurch, wenn ich mich zerstreue' / 'I need to reach a point at which my mind really belongs to me again, and that's best achieved if I distract myself' (*VS*, 264). However, neither Abschaffel nor Warlich can extend this coping mechanism to their work, which they perform erratically. A pattern emerges, which is emphasised in the clinics: when the men are not engaged in interaction, they become constrained by their thought patterns, which they are not prompted to reveal to those around them. After the death of an especially unhealthy colleague, Gersthoff, who had returned from a 'cure', Abschaffel attempts to avoid thinking, remaining motionless at his desk: 'Mit geschlossenem Gehirn verrichtete er seine Arbeit.... Einmal glaubte er, ein hohles Gebirge zu sein, wenig später war er überzeugt, sein Körper sei nur eine Plastiktüte mit altem Blut' / 'His brain closed, he did his work.... He once thought he was a concave mountain, but a little later he was convinced his body was only a plastic bag containing old blood' (*VS*, 345). Even after Abschaffel's psychosomatic symptoms become physical, his painfully stiff back impairing his movement, it is only when a concerned colleague persuades him to accompany her on a visit to her brother-in-law, a general practitioner, that convoluted medical intervention is triggered. The absence of a comprehensive or holistic treatment of Abschaffel's condition beyond the most immediate manifest symptoms becomes conspicuous.

Abschaffel asserts his self-determination towards his health in a moment of speechless rumination as he is wandering into town on his first day of sick leave from work, belittling the unnamed likes of Gustav von Aschenbach in Mann's *Der Tod in Venedig / Death in Venice* (1912). He is distracted by children cycling on the pavement, but they do not prompt him to deviate from his route. Instead, Abschaffel acknowledges that his medical and temperamental circumstances render him liable to develop a figurative variety of Aschenbach's fatal cholera. Furthermore, this deterioration would conceivably occur within the next 15 years, thus only in moderate middle age, but far beyond either Genazino's or Mann's narrative timespans: 'Er war grundsätzlich nicht dagegen gefeit, ein cholerischer alter Mann zu werden'/ 'He was fundamentally not immune to becoming a choleric old man'. Moreover, encountering these cyclists induces Abschaffel to recognise that 'es [war] vielleicht nur eine Frage der Zeit … bis er wirklich Kinder anpöbelte' / 'it would perhaps only be a matter of time … before he really harassed children' (*VS*, 374). Far from developing Aschenbach's fatal attraction, Abschaffel could dismiss children verbally in order to pursue more characteristic diversions, but he is stalled by his first medical diagnosis.

Abschaffel is initially referred to an orthopaedist, Dr Schmücker, who likens his patient's spine to those of elderly ladies, diagnosing severe osteoporosis: 'Was bei Männern los ist, wenn sie das haben, weiß man bis heute nicht genau' / 'What's wrong with men who have this isn't yet exactly known' (*VS*, 380). This verdict ironically reflects Abschaffel's inability to describe his symptoms in sufficient detail. Abschaffel is sent on to Dr Troogenbuck, a psychotherapist. This separation of attention to his physical and mental conditions raises the patient's anxious anticipation of 'a kind of examination', having been passed between doctors 'wie eine Veröffentlichung des Gefühls, daß niemand wußte, was wirklich mit ihm los war' / 'like an announcement of the feeling that nobody knew what was really wrong with him' (*VS*, 385). The prevalence in these initial transactions within a supposedly caring profession of impersonal language of transfers and commissions, which also circulates in the freight logistics office where he works, heightens for Abschaffel what Goffman terms 'the participant's dramaturgical problems of presenting … before others' in an appropriate role.[10] Abschaffel's anxiety about performing his incapacity for work to this doctor is emblematic of a need that is not met throughout his treatment, for support in negotiating a different performance space from his usual workplace.

Abschaffel's exchange with Dr Troogenbuck, predicated on psychobabble, proceeds unhelpfully as both doctor and patient are insensitive to language cues, taking each other's words too literally: 'Sie somatisieren, sagte Dr. Troogenbuck leise. Wie? fragte Abschaffel zurück. Sie haben eine schwere Osteoporose, sagte Dr. Troogenbuck, und das ist ein bißchen früh für Sie' / 'You're somatising, said Dr Troogenbuck softly. What? asked Abschaffel. You have severe osteoporosis, said Dr Troogenbuck, and that's a bit premature for you' (*VS*, 389). The ambivalence of Abschaffel's question is evident. Troogenbuck is prompted to respond by positing osteoporosis as an unlikely somatic symptom, rather than clarifying what somatising *means*, compounding misunderstanding between doctor and patient. Abschaffel does not acknowledge that his earlier diagnosis is being rejected. Abschaffel's manoeuvring of the swivel chair in which he sits, not quite facing Dr Troogenbuck, 'um sich mit der Lage abzufinden' / 'to come to terms with the situation' (*VS*, 389) sets the scene for persistently unmet gazes and distorted spatialisation throughout his and Warlich's treatments. The ruptures between Abschaffel's gestures and his language, and between both of these and his underlying thoughts are his most enduring but undiagnosed psychosomatic affliction. These ruptures result in inappropriate performance as a patient within his treatment space: in Goffman's words, Abschaffel's behaviour in the 'region' of the clinic, a 'place which is bounded to some degree by barriers to perception',[11] is either unbounded, or the barriers Abschaffel senses between doctor and patient roles are set too high.

In a clinical regime that separates therapies for physical and mental complaints, too little of the patient's overall incapacity to sustain a 'working consensus' – an agreement of the scope and limitations of his role in relation to his therapist's – is treated.[12] The fault for this shortcoming lies socially rather than medically. Far from being drawn to the 'lively' atmosphere and to 'skilled service' in the dining hall in Mann's Berghof sanatorium in *The Magic Mountain* (1924),[13] Abschaffel is reminded every mealtime of the euphemistic status of the 'KURKLINIK SATTLACH' / 'SATTLACH HEALTH CLINIC', as it is inscribed on all of the crockery in the dining hall, 'häusliches Entgegenkommen an die Patienten' / 'a homely concession to the patients' (*FJ*, 417). Yet, when he sharpens his gaze on the entrance to the institution from outside, a small metal sign informs him that he is officially resident in the 'PSYCHOSOMATISCHE KLINIK SATTLACH' / 'SATTLACH PSYCHOSOMATIC CLINIC'. He thus externalises the dining experience he shares with the patient community as a commercially sensitive exercise, carried out under this name. He finds this description inappropriate for those it accommodates, but not necessarily for himself: 'Das klang ernst, krank, sachlich und wirklich und war deshalb für die Patienten wahrscheinlich eine Zumutung' / 'That sounded severe, morbid, matter-of-fact and concrete and was thus likely to be an imposition on the patients' (*FJ*, 417). Just as when he avoids walking through the foyer, where patients sit with visitors and talk about other patients – 'Im Foyer herrschte gewöhnlich die Atmosphäre eines Krankenzimmers am Sonntag' / 'The atmosphere of a sick bay on Sunday usually prevailed in the foyer' (*FJ*, 436) – Abschaffel casts doubt on the circumscription of clinical practice.

Abschaffel's and Warlich's loss of motivation in the workplace, which they are not prompted to explore with their clinicians, 'can only be read as the atrophy of the entire Western institution of work and puritanical achievement'.[14] In Warlich's case, where no physical injury is sustained, the administration of his drug regimen reroutes atrophy to his own body, engendering long-term detachment from the working world and from partnership with Traudel. Following her failure to reinvigorate their sex life on a visit to the clinic, he recounts her only subsequent communication with him. Her 'herzergreifenden Brief' / 'heartrending letter' / 'rührt' / 'stirs' him, not by engendering a firm response to her but prompting the remark that 'Ich darf sagen, daß mir eine solche Ruhe, wie ich sie hier gefunden habe, nie zuvor zuteil geworden ist' / 'I might say that such tranquillity as I've found here has never been bestowed on me before' (*GgZ*, 148–9). Warlich finds no resolution to his status anxiety. His career in a laundry since he gained his doctorate on Heidegger, despite (or because of) becoming operations manager, has not animated him. Traudel does not reassure him. Above all, he is hampered by the artificial imposition of mental balance through ingesting tablets and by his concomitant habituation to hospitalisation.[15] Warlich conveys no understanding of the purposes of his prescribed drugs, fluoxetine, Zoloft, mirtazapine, Cipralex and modafinil, for symptoms he has not explicitly acknowledged (*GgZ*, 149). Although not yet finalised, his drug regimen is likely to define his condition beyond the institution.

Warlich reveals early in the novel that the 'core of his misfortune' is the absence of a confirmed vocation: 'Bin ich ein Philosoph, ein Ästhet, ein stiller Kommunikator, ein Konzeptkünstler? Und wie kann es mir gelingen, aus einer dieser Tätigkeiten einen Beruf zu machen, der mich hinreichend ernährt und mir endlich die Gewißheit verschafft, daß ich mich in einem sinnvollen Leben befinde?' / 'Am I a philosopher, an aesthete, a tacit communicator, a conceptual artist? And how can I succeed in making out of one of those occupations a career that nourishes me sufficiently and provides me ultimately with the certainty that I am in a meaningful life?' (*GgZ*, 13). Warlich does not present this dilemma to his therapist. He will not allow himself to be outperformed rhetorically. Yet, his admission to the clinic resulted from his increasing failure to make himself understood, which culminated in a loss of language.

An evident prefiguration of Warlich's breakdown occurs in his discomfort at having to observe his colleagues neglecting their work off-site, not long before he is dismissed for unprofessional conduct during his own working hours. He characterises himself as 'ein Mann, der ein kommendes Unglück zwar spürt, aber nicht aussprechen kann' / 'a man who senses an impending misfortune but cannot express it' (*GgZ*, 42). In what initially appears a ludicrous fantasy to allay his boredom, he hypothesises the purchase of a snack: 'Die Scheibe Brot würde ich nicht essen, sondern in meine Brieftasche stecken und mir vorstellen, ich würde die Scheibe Brot bei nächster Gelegenheit anstelle meiner Brieftasche aus der Tasche ziehen und sie jemandem anstelle eines Geldscheins hinhalten' / 'I wouldn't eat the slice of bread, I'd stick it in my wallet and imagine taking it out of my pocket instead of my wallet and handing it over to someone instead of a banknote' (*GgZ*, 42). On the subsequent occasion when he succeeds in purchasing a sausage and a less appetising slice of rye bread (as the usual rolls have sold out), he has lost his grip on financial and emotional security. He deposits the bread in his pocket, and replaces his fantasy of an impersonal monetary transaction with an intensifying 'Verlockung' / 'enticement' to take the hand of a 'bedürftiger Bekannter' / 'needy acquaintance' and donate the bread by surprise, which would restore his 'liebenswerter und vorbildhafter' / 'loveable and exemplary' humanity. He soon encounters his 'Jugendliebe' / 'childhood sweetheart' Annette, with whom his relationship had been compromised, and wrongly assumes that she will understand this gesture, which he enacts speechlessly (*GgZ*, 123–8). Her returning of the bread, which reduces him to tears, is the climax of a series of misunderstandings of his motives. This rejection becomes unbearable following the refusal of Warlich's 'Schule der Besänftigung' / 'School of Soothing' project by the culture officer Dr Heilmeier[16] for its incompatibility with the civic mission to institute a 'Pop-Akademie' / 'Pop Academy' (*GgZ*, 77), his dismissal from the laundry and his inability to contemplate an inferior job for which he had been interviewed a few hours earlier (*GgZ*, 120).

Abschaffel prepares for Sattlach by filling out copious paperwork (*VS*, 394–5), supplied with a colour brochure depicting the site but not, it would appear, anybody located there. By contrast, Warlich's admission to his unnamed clinic is tragicomic. When Traudel arrives at the scene of his confrontation with Annette, he anticipates that she will drive him home. Instead, he is transported unexpectedly to a psychiatric clinic (*GgZ*, 139–49).[17] In the clinic, Warlich attempts to think of 'ein paar schlichte Sätze' / 'a few simple sentences' in advance of Traudel's first visit, to annul his resentment at the change enforced in their relationship by their new separate living arrangements, and at her status as his guest. For want of better distraction from his rumination, he visits the television room, and is struck by the 'Unbesorgtheit' / 'carefree state' of African gnus surrounded by predators in the wildlife film that happens to be showing. He irritates himself 'vier Sekunden lang' / 'for all of four seconds' by likening a lion's attack to the 'erschöpften Niedersinken des männlichen Kopfes nach einem Orgasmus' / 'exhausted post-orgasmal sinking of the male head' (*GgZ*, 135).[18] Interrupted by Traudel's arrival, he suspends any rational explanation of what he has seen and its juxtaposition with his thoughts. He will not even clarify whether his comparison and irritation were prompted by filmed or imagined animals, let alone what species of male head or instance of its movement had entered his thoughts.

During her visit, Traudel belatedly explains that she had responded to the disintegration of Warlich's performance management: 'als du einen Bekannten als Mitarbeiter deiner Schule vorgestellt hast; dann die Scheibe Brot! Ich war fix und fertig' / 'when you introduced a friend as being on your School's staff; then the slice of bread! I was done in' (*GgZ*, 137). She assumes, in Goffman's terms, 'expressive responsibility',[19] by communicating her conscious shift from performing the role of Warlich's domestic partner to that of the judge of his malady. The clinic now obstructs their reconciliation by displacing the already fragile intimacy in their communications, and engenders ironic affronts to their sensitivities. At home, Warlich had remonstrated with Traudel for pressurising him into marriage for no better reason than that if he were injured in a derailment, she would only be permitted to visit him in 'irgendeinem Provinzkrankenhaus' / 'some provincial hospital' if she could prove her relationship to him. Warlich's retort, 'Muß man sich verheiraten, weil man nur so die Bürokratie von Krankenhäusern überlisten kann?' / 'Is it necessary to get married just to be able to outwit hospital bureaucracy?' (*GgZ*, 22), becomes all the more insensitive when he considers permanent certification of his sickness without being examined in person (*GgZ*, 146). Moreover, one of Warlich's last duties at work, before being abruptly dismissed for becoming caught up in a demonstration by anarchists while on an extended lunch break, had been to drive to a remote location to ensure that the laundrymen were performing their deliveries (*GgZ*, 39).

At the clinic, Traudel insists on taking Warlich's laundry, despite there being an in-house service (*GgZ*, 137). Nevertheless, they fleetingly regain harmony in their relationship, albeit in the self-service dining hall, known characteristically as the 'Casino', where they 'spintisieren' / 'ruminate' ludically about the consequences of throwing their unappetising, unfinished lunch against the wall (*GgZ*, 139). Their game remains unplayed, as Warlich has a therapy session that afternoon; as Szasz points out, 'if the patient and the persons with whom he interacts were to play the same game by the same rules – that is, if they had a reciprocal or symmetrical relationship to one another – the mental illness game could not come into being and could not flourish'.[20] Warlich's medicated volatility is a game-changer. He implicates Traudel in an extended clinical infrastructure that now governs his most intimate existence: 'Als [Traudel] den Schlüssel meines Zimmers umdreht, ist klar, daß sie mir einen quasi-ehemäßigen Samariterdienst erweisen will. Aber meine Verletztheit sträubt sich dagegen, sich so schnell niederlieben zu lassen, schon gar nicht zum Sonderpreis einer fixen Besuchssexualität' / 'When [Traudel] turns the key to my room, it's clear that she wants to prove herself a quasi-matrimonial good Samaritan to me. But my woundedness resists being loved down so swiftly, especially not at the bargain price of a quick visiting sexuality' (*GgZ*, 140). Once he has buttoned her blouse again, she leaves, 'sichtbar gekränkt' / 'visibly offended', ending their tangible partnership, and confirming Warlich's self-determined phase of patienthood. He now even ceases to resist the banal catering, taking a book to accompany 'immer dieser Jugendherbergstee und zu oft die scheußliche Gelbwurst!' / 'youth hostel tea always and horrible pork-and-veal sausage too often!' (*GgZ*, 155). The manners of Mann's *Magic Mountain* habitués, who 'considered it beginners' awkwardness to glue yourself to a book' (270) and for whom 'it was customary to grumble about the food' (14) are subjected to simultaneous subversions by Warlich, who also fails to be socially reconstructed in the clinic.

Warlich, despite being unemployed, is convinced by a fellow patient to apply to be certified for long-term incapacity for work. Dr Adrian, a meteorologist, presents early retirement as 'einen großen Erfolg seines Lebens' / 'a great success of his life', achieved by means of a paper trail instigated unquestioningly by his therapist (*GgZ*, 147). In finding sickness in name to be easier to live with than any health assumed by release from treatment, Dr Adrian personifies the titular 'Glück' / 'fortune' which has evaded Warlich, who is persuaded that staying in the clinic could bring about a decisive turning point in his life (*GgZ*, 146). Mann's Adrian Leverkühn, the protagonist of *Doktor Faustus / Doctor*

Faustus (1947), provides an illuminating hypotext for this character. Dr Adrian's certified unfitness is equivalent to selling his soul to a consuming clinical regime when he might otherwise be providing for his family. Warlich, the tranquillised narrator and self-styled scholar, is comparable to Serenus Zeitblom, narrator of *Doctor Faustus*, as they both attempt to understand Adrians who have attained an intriguing state of knowledge. In his discussion of the *Abschaffel* trilogy during a colloquium at Paderborn University (7 January 1998), Genazino alludes to moments of 'Modernitätsmehrwert' / 'overvalued modernity' in Mann's narrative situations, in which a narrator is abandoned by his characters, accentuating the disposability or dissolution of the subject.[21] Warlich's self-interest, no less than Dr Adrian's, underscores a nexus of abandonment during their 'Obdachlosennacht' / 'Homeless Night' (*GgZ*, 151). They abandon conventional therapy; their analysts support this abandonment; they abandon their residence, having long since abandoned employment; and they abandon patienthood. However, no solidarity ensues for Warlich when Dr Adrian reveals an ulterior motive of depravity during an unscheduled peep-show visit.

Dr Adrian does not disclose why he was hospitalised. Warlich reiterates this omission by perceiving the clinical confirmation required 'von Zeit zu Zeit' / 'occasionally' by the insurers as mere rubber-stamping (*GgZ*, 151). Warlich adds fuel to Szasz's castigation of clinical practice since its institutionalisation by Jean-Martin Charcot in 1882 for facilitating malingering, narcotisation and tranquillisation in the 'socially self-enhancing' name of mental illness, 'which pulls the suffering person back into the same sort of disrepute from which this semantic and social reclassification was intended to rescue him'.[22] Genazino's juxtaposition of Warlich's unresolved health problem with an enumeration of Dr Adrian's prescribed pills signals the two men's current existential comparability and is a damning indictment of the patient regime. Moreover, Dr Adrian's pharmaceutical side effects remain untreated clinically and narratively: 'Es ist gleichgültig, ob wir unser Problem eine unipolare Depression, eine mittelschwere Melancholie, eine bipolare Störung, ein autistisches Syndrom, eine akute Angstneurose oder sonstwie nennen. Dr. Adrian nimmt Remergil, Serotonin, Noradrenalin und, wie ich, Cipralex. Er klagt über Hemmungen, Antriebsschwäche und Weinerlichkeit.' / 'It makes no odds whether we name our problem unipolar depression, moderate melancholy, bipolar disorder, autistic syndrome, acute anxiety neurosis or otherwise. Dr Adrian is taking Remergil, serotonin, noradrenaline and, like me, Cipralex. He complains about inhibitions, lack of motivation and tearfulness' (*GgZ*, 153–4).[23]

Here, Warlich, whose own outburst of lachrymosity precipitated his admission to the clinic, becomes entangled in the in-patient discourse he hitherto sought to avoid and, unsuspectingly, in Dr Adrian's self-administered rainy night's therapy.

Ambiguities of narrative time and reported speech ironise Warlich's remark about this venture: 'Die Erlaubnis [Dr Adrians] Therapeuten bedeutet, daß die Unternehmung als hilfreich gilt' / [Dr Adrian's] 'therapist's permission means that this venture counts as beneficial' (*GgZ*, 151). It is unsurprising that Warlich participates, as both his perceptions about sights outside the clinic and his narrative strategy for presenting these underline the psychotherapist Kathy Zarnegin's contention about this novel: 'Um in der Metaphorik des Buches zu bleiben: Der beobachtende intellektuelle Erzähler dechiffriert die soziale Realität als den eigentlichen Ort des Wahns' / 'Keeping to the book's use of metaphor, the observant intellectual narrator deciphers social reality as the actual site of delusion'.[24] As he and Dr Adrian are leaving the clinic grounds, Warlich observes the seemingly homeless waste-bin scavengers, whose activity is 'aussichtsreich' / 'promising', as their poverty contrasts with the 'begüterte' / 'well-off' situation of the patient community. Enlivening the understated juxtapositions of his narration, he intimates a further instance of medical neglect in his next observation, immediately before, or perhaps during, his attempt to prompt Dr Adrian to advise him about early retirement: 'es gibt (das weiß ich seit ich in der Klinik bin) Menschen mit krankhaften Suchzwängen, die an keinem Behälter vorübergehen können' / 'there are (I've known this since being in the clinic) people with unhealthy compulsions, who can't walk past any bins' (*GgZ*, 152). The telling ambivalence of the parentheses underlines Warlich's increased understanding of sickness rather than health. Dr Adrian's venture fails: Warlich returns to the clinic when he realises that he has been enticed into a single peep-show cabin by his companion not in the interests of economy but for the only mutual experience that Dr Adrian is willing to activate. Needless to say, Warlich does not discuss this incident during his psychotherapy.

Talking Cures or Silencing Resolutions?

Abschaffel's and Warlich's therapists do not recognise the depersonalised patient's demands, extending to the consulting room, and fundamental for Laing, 'for constant confirmation from others of [his] own existence as a person'.[25] Abschaffel reports consecutively to two medics on commencing his treatment. The first, Dr Haak, has no named role, but his managerial approach to Abschaffel's physical treatment predominates as he condenses it into compound nouns. Abschaffel's 'Bewegungstherapie' / 'physiotherapy' consists initially of 'Entspannungsbehandlung' / 'relaxation treatment' before progression to 'Terraintraining', a neologistic Anglicism (*FJ*, 406). Neither the medical specificity of these treatments nor their social and spatial configurations are explained. Moreover, the terminological ambiguity of the 'Diätgruppe' / 'diet group' Haak advises the overweight Abschaffel to join merely denotes that he will be among those who are served 'kaloriengemäße Mahlzeiten' / 'meals of appropriate calories'. Abschaffel accepts the regime unquestioningly, buoyed by Dr Haak's optimism. The doctor's clichéd, colloquial prognosis, 'In ein paar Wochen sind sie wieder auf dem Damm' / 'In a few weeks you'll be back on track' (*FJ*, 406), ignores the patient's complex individual needs for developing either longer-term physical resilience or mental robustness. Abschaffel becomes merely the charge of a second clinician for the mechanical reconditioning of a body disengaged from its mind. The 'Damm' idiom is especially resonant. A five-page-long paragraph towards the end of Abschaffel's stay presents him walking along a snowy village street, the Dammweg, where he internalises the sight of a mother initially pushing a small boy on a sledge but then instructing him, against his wishes, to propel himself. Abschaffel becomes preoccupied by unanswered questions about his own parents, in line with the route on which his psychotherapy leads him (*FJ*, 525–30). In his frozen moment of introspection, evocative of Hans Castorp's more skilled performance on skis in the central 'Snow' chapter of *The Magic Mountain* (468–97), Abschaffel does not appreciate the significance of self-propulsion for progressing on his path through life.

Abschaffel's ward physician Dr Buddenberg, 'ein verschlossener, ein wenig mühsam sprechender Psychotherapeut' / 'an uncommunicative psychotherapist who spoke a little laboriously', is less forthcoming than Haak. Having been distracted by the peripheral apparatus of Dr Haak's clinical performance, such as the screw-fitted lid of his expensive fountain pen and a white towel, fresh to the point of appearing frozen, by the handbasin, Abschaffel is instantly struck by Dr Buddenberg's everyday apparel, identical to his own father's: 'Am liebsten hätte er nun Dr Buddenberg gefragt, ob nun auch er solche Westen von seiner Mutter geschenkt bekam' / 'He would have most liked to ask Dr Buddenberg whether he also got given cardigans like that by his mother' (*FJ*, 407). Such unspoken concern about the compatibility of Dr Buddenberg's non-professional life with his own sets the tone for Abschaffel's entire course of psychotherapy. Abschaffel's perceptions regularly punctuate the near-monologous vacuum in which the doctor provides no verbal prompts for the patient to focus his concerns more appropriately, and in which we are made aware of Abschaffel's need for a more sympathetic communicative exchange. Buddenberg prescribes three weekly group therapy sessions, in which Abschaffel feels unable to participate, as Buddenberg and some co-patients remain as silent as he does. Abschaffel likens this experience to the profound awkwardness of his lunch breaks among colleagues in his workplace. Abschaffel's eschewal of the social contact mediated by these sessions after attending only three, believing he would never be able to speak there (*FJ*, 408), together with his habit of meandering alone around the village in the hours he has kept free, continues the patterns of behaviour he had exhibited in Frankfurt.

Communication failure dominates Abschaffel's individual sessions with Dr Buddenberg. Abschaffel resists an instinct to tell 'lächerlichen Bürogeschichten oder … Einzelheiten darüber, wie er normalerweise lebte' / 'ridiculous office tales or … details about how he usually lived'. He thus gives his therapist hardly any indication of his recent difficulties, believing instead that 'etwas Gehaltvolles' / 'something meaty' is required (*FJ*, 418). This assumption, unchallenged by Dr Buddenberg, leads Abschaffel on a narrow path of recounting sensitivities from his childhood towards his parents, bringing to light unresolved tensions from an era and a confined working-class milieu from which his long-standing white-collar existence in Frankfurt has detached him. Abschaffel deploys a healthy repertoire of social cues, interspersing question tags ('So war es, glauben Sie nicht auch?' / 'That's how it was, don't you think so too?', *FJ*, 433) with pauses. The therapist does not maintain eye contact with his patient; we are told twice that Buddenberg mostly remained silent for the entire session.[26] Abschaffel regularly considers whether to share thoughts that have consumed him since each previous session, blending his banal experiences around Sattlach with recollections of his youth, which he formulates to himself during many hours alone. However, he pursues the childhood angle relentlessly and emotively with Buddenberg, and fails to notice on at least one occasion that the analyst was tired too. Nevertheless, Abschaffel returns to his own room feeling anxious (*FJ*, 425). His unease is exacerbated while he is walking across the car park one afternoon, having failed to find sufficient distractions in the village. He witnesses Dr Buddenberg emerging from his car, inside which a child seat is fitted. Abschaffel's firm assumptions that his analyst shared 'weitgehend dieselbe Wohn- und Lebensausrüstung' / 'largely the same domestic and existential apparatus' as his own, including even the amount of clothing he possessed, have become 'eine Menge falscher Gedanken' / 'a mass of false thoughts'.

The doctor's name brings to mind the intergenerational dissolution of power and vigour of a family, as chronicled in Mann's novel *Buddenbrooks* (1901). It is no coincidence that Abschaffel, estranged from his parents, is disconcerted to discover that his analyst, to whom he performs as a troubled son in therapy, is likely to fulfil the role of a protective father outside the clinic.[27] As a consequence, Abschaffel's presentation to Dr Buddenberg becomes less reliable. At the next session, he decides to tell lies (*FJ*, 460). In his fourth week of treatment, the listlessness that constitutes the only reciprocal characteristic of their contact prevents Abschaffel from making 'a friendly offer' to his therapist to become a fully-fledged 'Geschichtenerzähler' / 'storyteller' (*FJ*, 485), such is his loss of ability to believe that fellow humans can comprehend each other.

The final meeting reverses the direction of the communicative impasse of the previous sessions. Buddenberg now expounds at length, conveying imperfect information in an unsympathetic manner, thereby distorting its interpretation by his overwhelmed patient. Abschaffel is silenced by the verdict passed on him, and leaves 'angenehm verwirrt' / 'pleasantly confused' (*FJ*, 546–9). Buddenberg twice reminds Abschaffel to follow Dr Haak's advice about imprecise 'Bewegungstraining' / 'physical training', using an idiom that is insensitive on the one hand to the patient's unresolved psychosomatic troubles and, on the other, to Abschaffel's tendency to take figures of speech too literally: Buddenberg 'ermahnte ihn eindringlich, diesen Rat nicht auf die leichte Schulter zu nehmen' / 'warned him emphatically not to shrug his shoulders about this advice' (*FJ*, 546). Abschaffel is tempted to retort that he 'noch niemals leichte Schultern gehabt hatte' / 'had always shouldered his responsibilities' (*FJ*, 548), thus trivialising the psychosomatic complaints that had led him to the clinic in the first place. Dr Buddenberg belatedly admonishes Abschaffel for attending only one-to-one sessions and having 'damit Ihren Therapieplan selbständig eingeschränkt, was eigentlich unzulässig ist' / 'thereby restricted your therapy plan independently, which is technically impermissible'; 'die wenigen Bruchstücke einer Analyse' / 'the few fragments of analysis' have led to 'die Möglichkeit des Irrtums' / 'the possibility of error' in Buddenberg's concluding verdict (*FJ*, 547).[28] He prescribes further analysis back home,[29] as Abschaffel 'dazu begabt' / 'has a talent for it'. Buddenberg distinguishes in his patient a 'strukturelle Störung' / 'structural disorder', parentally induced: 'eine Art Beeinträchtigungswahn' / 'a kind of paranoia' (*FJ*, 547–8). This overtly clinical crystallisation of six weeks of Abschaffel's barely interrupted presentation, although semantically imprecise, condenses Goffman's model of the mental patient in a non-custodial hospital being told:

> that his past has been a failure, that the cause of this has been within himself, that his attitude to life is wrong, and that if he wants to be a person he will have to change his way of dealing with people and his conceptions of himself. Often the moral value of these verbal assaults will be brought home to him by requiring him to practise taking this psychiatric view of himself in arranged confessional periods.[30]

The conclusion of Abschaffel's in-patient career is merely a contingent diagnosis.

Dr Buddenberg proceeds to de-medicalise his discourse even less sensitively. He likens psychotherapy to the short-lived exhilaration of a fairground chairoplane ride. Its participant temporarily gains a lofty view until the deflating end of each session, which needs to be followed up with perpetual return rides in order to capture an elusive viewpoint:

> Die Psychoanalyse müssen Sie sich ungefähr wie ein Kettenkarussell vorstellen.... Schön, nicht? ... Da setzt man sich unten rein in eine Sitzgondel, und wenn es losgeht, fliegt man in seinem Sitz immer höher, mit jeder Runde. Es ist wunderschön, den Rummelplatz und womöglich die halbe Stadt von oben zu sehen. Aber man kann nicht oben bleiben... . Man muß noch mal fahren und noch mal fahren und noch mal fahren, um immer mehr zu sehen.

> You have to imagine psychoanalysis as being somewhat like a chairoplane.... Nice, isn't it? ... You sit down in a gondola, and when it starts, you're flying higher and higher in your seat every circuit. It's wonderful to see the fairground and maybe half the town from the top. But you can't stay up there.... You need to go round and round and round again to see more and more. (*FJ*, 549)

This euphemism for a deceptively Sisyphean task is at odds with Abschaffel's intractable indulgence in flights of fantasy about elevating himself above the groundings of social intercourse: 'Er war der einzige Gast in seinem Privatflugzeug, und niemand begegnete ihm bei seinem weiten, unangefochtenen Flug' / 'He was the sole passenger on his private aeroplane, and nobody encountered him on his long, unchallenged flight' (*VS*, 246). The carousel chains of a chairoplane would enchain him to psychoanalysis. Given no indication that the analyst occupying the opposite seat would meet his gaze, let alone facilitate appropriate adjustments to seating levels, Abschaffel is offered a weak link in the chain of his Frankfurt existence. Buddenberg merely provides a list of practitioners, rather than securing a course of therapy in any defined proximity to the damaged positions on Abschaffel's damaged existential sprocket of work, home and spare time.

To the reader familiar with Genazino's autobiographical treatment of fairgrounds in two later essays, Buddenberg provocatively trivialises a symbolic meeting point not so much of Bakhtinian allure but of social leisure and private introspection. Introspection is inevitable for the sensitive individual of modest means, unable to penetrate the collective spectacle in the pleasurable, harmonious terms in which its designers conceived it. The fairground is the opening setting of Genazino's Büchner Prize speech (2004). Here, he traces the foundations of his social conscience in his childhood experience of waiting with his parents to watch free firework displays that closed civic fairs at which they had been unable to afford rides or refreshments, but that were crowned by large sums of public money ceremonially going up in smoke. This intertextuality prompts more earnest questioning about the financial efficacy of a German 'cure' such as Abschaffel's, funded by health insurance contributions. Treatment fails to meet fundamental human needs, to paraphrase Szasz, of close interpersonal compatibility or of games worth playing with rules worth following.[31]

A further resonance with the essay 'Der Kampf gegen die eigene Biografie' / 'Struggling Against your Own Biography' (2006), in which Genazino justifies perpetuating his tendency to lie about disappointments, also deflates Dr Buddenberg's advice. Genazino recounts: 'Als Kind hatte ich mir einen Rummelplatz als etwas ganz Wunderbares vorgestellt. Ein zweistöckiges Karussell würde ich dort sehen, mit schaukelnden Pferden und großäugigen Drachen, von Hunderten Glühbirnen erleuchtet und von schöner Musik in Schwung gehalten' / 'As a child I'd imagined a fairground to be something just wonderful. I'd see a two-level merry-go-round there, with rocking horses and round-eyed dragons, illuminated by hundreds of lightbulbs and kept going by beautiful music'. However, on his first visit to a 'richtigen Rummelplatz' / 'proper funfair', he 'war enttäuscht und desillusioniert' / 'was disappointed and disillusioned'. He lied 'flott' / 'vigorously' to his mother when he returned home about non-existent attractions, 'weil mir die Darstellung der Wahrheit zu kompliziert, zu langweilig, zu unergiebig oder gar nicht verfügbar war' / 'because telling the truth was too complicated, too boring, too unrewarding or not even at my disposal'.[32] Abschaffel has no need to imagine himself at the fair to ease himself into telling unsettling lies.[33]

No longer upset by the fixed and unoccupied child seat in Dr Buddenberg's car, Abschaffel repeats selected pronouncements from the final session to himself as he prepares to leave the clinic, revealing a need for assistance as much as a wish for company in his preparation for any future chairoplane rides:

> Begabt für eine Behandlung! ... Er mußte dieses merkwürdige Lob zerstreuen. Obwohl er sich zugab, daß es für ihn schön wäre, wenn Dr. Buddenberg sein Kollege werden könnte ... Dann könnten sie stundenlang über den Beeinträchtigungswahn sprechen und nebenher ein paar Waggons nach Augsburg, Hannover und Stuttgart fertig machen
>
> A talent for therapy! ... He had to dispel that curious thought. Although he admitted that it would be nice for him if Dr Buddenberg could be his colleague ... They could then talk for hours about paranoia while preparing a few goods waggons for Augsburg, Hanover and Stuttgart (*FJ*, 549–50).

Abschaffel negates any sense of persecution by desiring such collegiality, but embeds delusion into his image of improved relations at work. He conforms to Goffman's patient type, whereby the image he presents of his life (albeit only to himself, rather than in the usual patient-to-doctor mode) 'selects, abstracts, and distorts in such a way as to provide him with a view of himself that he can usefully expound in current situations'.[34] Goffman's euphemistic reference to 'situations' highlights the contiguity for characters such as Genazino's of performing as patients and in their vocational roles.

Warlich exploits Goffman's typology by structuring his narrative to undermine his therapist's status. He describes 'das langsame Eindringen der Tablettensubstanzen in mein Blut' / 'the slow penetration of the tablet substances into my blood' before recounting a refined selection of his exchanges, including an articulate self-diagnosis, with his therapist. Warlich only names Dr Treukirch later, in reference to his responsibility for changing the patient's drug cocktail every three days and thereby justifying hospitalisation: 'Vermutlich bin ich nur hier, damit die richtige Medikation herausgefunden werden kann' / 'Presumably I'm only here so that the right medication can be found' (*GgZ*, 130–3).[35] Encapsulating his untreated condition in ten words: 'Ich leide an einer verlarvten Depression mit einer akuten

Schamproblematik' / 'I'm suffering from disguised depression with an acute shame problem'; then perceiving his presentation 'als Fachmann seines Leidens' / 'as a specialist in suffering', Warlich leaves the therapist '(presumably) dumbfounded' (*GgZ*, 131–2). Warlich thus renegotiates his autodiegetic performance by narrating this succinct self-diagnosis as though to antagonise his therapist by limiting him to a minor role in the narrative. Warlich understates his condition by foregrounding only two of its now diminished components: 'Ich glaube nicht, sagte ich, daß Sie es schwer mit mir haben werden. Meine Innenwelt ist nicht sehr geräumig. Man kann mich schnell durcheilen und dann feststellen: Außer ein paar Schuldgefühlen und ein bißchen Scham ist nicht viel da' / 'I don't think, I said, that you'll have a hard time with me. My inner world isn't very spacious. You can hurry through me and then establish that except for a few guilt feelings and a bit of shame, there's not much there' (*GgZ*, 132). Warlich's dismissively reductive anticipation of his therapy's conclusion before he allows his analyst to commence, like his habit of taking reading matter with him, signals his unspoken desire for the self-sustaining flow of stimuli for a poetic narrative that he cannot release. This incapacity is compounded by the long intervals between therapy sessions.

Dr Treukirch's failure to question Warlich's introductory self-diagnosis is comparable to Dr Buddenberg's delayed and ill-founded (d)evaluation of Abschaffel's complaint. In both cases, no resolution or advice for managing the condition is dispensed. Diagnosis becomes an open wound. Nevertheless, Treukirch exercises appropriate restraint by retracting his initially cryptic labelling as 'Selbstaussetzungen' / 'self-abandonments' of two anecdotes that Warlich has presented – 'Daraufhin erzählte ich ihm, wahrscheinlich zu ausführlich, die Sache mit der Bockwurst und der Brotscheibe, die er noch nicht kannte' / 'At that point I told him, probably too elaborately, about the matter of the sausage and the slice of bread, which he hadn't known about' (*GgZ*, 132). Treukirch advises his patient that 'Wichtig ist, was wir noch nicht wissen; wichtig ist, was die beiden Handlungen bedeuten, was Sie mit ihnen eigentlich sagen wollen' / 'What's important is what we still don't know; what's important is what both these stories mean, what you're really wanting to say with them' (*GgZ*, 142). This is the therapist's only substantial intervention in the last session that Warlich recounts. Delivered at the nadir of the now drugged philosophical patient's postdoctoral career, Treukirch's remark is insensitive. Nevertheless, the distillation Warlich foregrounds contrasts with the detailed narration of Abschaffel's uncontrolled monological therapy sessions. Yet, Warlich's inability, even in one-to-one analysis, to signal his need for more appreciative receptiveness to his over-refined utterances, which conceal more of his thoughts than they reveal, remains untreated.

In ostensibly bringing to an end a mere 10 minutes of wondering which of his recent 'Erlebnisse' / '(unusual) experiences' he will later report to Dr Treukirch, as well as in concluding his narrative, 'eine Art Glück durchzittert' / 'a kind of fortune trembles through' Warlich. He asserts that 'offenbar kann ich, trotz allem, immer noch wählen, wie ich in Zukunft leben will' / 'Evidently, despite everything, I can still choose how I want to live in the future' (*GgZ*, 158). Abschaffel experiences a comparably fleeting sensation only before hospitalisation. In the toilet at work, ruminating protractedly on his lack of success as a child in competitions, 'er glaubte plötzlich, ein Meister des Lebens zu sein, weil er, zum Beispiel, das Glück schon ganz früh als Gespenst leerer Kindernachmittage entlarvt hatte' / 'he suddenly believed he was a Master of Life because, for example, he had very early on unmasked fortune as the phantom of empty children's afternoons' (*VS*, 252). A sequence of self-reproaches in the subjunctive swiftly prompts him to recognise that he had deliberately *evaded* 'fortune' by not even entering these competitions, despite having just recalled in ambiguous terms his 'involvement' in them, hoping to win a prize.

Abschaffel's consequent admission to himself that he had just been lying to himself more than he had done for a long time (*VS*, 253), through his combined verbal dexterity and excessive introspection, distinguishes his preparedness for therapy from Warlich's. Abschaffel does not return to these troubling thoughts with Dr Buddenberg, although they have provoked him to assert to himself 'Ich habe keinen Mut zum Leben' / 'I don't have the courage to live' twice in succession, and even 'Ich will alle Schmerzen schon gehabt haben, ich will tot sein' / 'I want to have had all my pain, I want to be dead' (*VS*, 253). This recognition of a feeling 'daß niemand leben konnte, ohne daß ihm etwas geschah' / 'that nobody was able to live without something happening to him', which he internalises to the extent of not seeking help when physical pain overcomes him, is not captured by separated physical and psychological treatment during his 'cure'. Instead, Abschaffel dwells on his relationship with his parents beyond this enduring oversensitivity to his mother's frequent call to 'Paß auf, damit dir nichts geschieht' / 'Take care nothing happens to you' (*VS*, 253).[36] He prompts Buddenberg to surmise 'Sie gehen also ins Bordell, weil sie nur dort ihre Mutter hassen können' / 'So you go to brothels because it's only there that you can hate your mother' (*FJ*, 533), synthesising the recurring strands of the analysis, which is not informed by our privileged insight into Abschaffel's cognitive behavioural needs. Buddenberg's rare response is caustically described as 'etwas Unerhörtes' / 'something unheard of' for Abschaffel (*FJ*, 534). However, we cannot reduce such poor two-way communication to satire, as the patient leaves the consulting room so emotionally disturbed by new thoughts of hatred towards his mother that he senses he 'mußte … mit dem würgendsten Schmerz bezahlen, der jemals aus seinem Körper hoch in die Kehle gestiegen war' / 'was having to … pay with the most choking pain that had ever climbed up his body into his throat' (*FJ*, 535). This return to the pain and paralysis that prompted his first medical examination is ignored in the concluding session two days later.

Warlich invents 'eine törichte Geschichte' / 'a daft tale' about his childhood during his analysis, building on the self-diagnosis with which he commences. He bridges insensitive silences from Dr Treukirch, who has invited him to talk about melancholy (*GgZ*, 140–1). Yet, Warlich expresses no anguish to himself about his mendacity. In formulating the conclusion of his narrative, he affirms a will to live, which Abschaffel does not demonstrably regain. Warlich's habitual, irremediable self-determination has sustained him through adversities instigated by others who have been bound to performances that have impacted on him less than humanely. As long as Warlich and Abschaffel negotiate everyday realities on their own terms, they remain able to value their lives. Nevertheless, they risk not developing interpersonal aptitudes or resilience beyond their own physical or narrative confines. Delimiting these spaces requires more insight than either man has been granted or is prepared to offer in clinical, social or workplace performances. Abschaffel displays new-found pragmatic pessimism as he contemplates his return to an office 'voller heimlicher Kränkungen' / 'full of covert woundings' (*FJ*, 571). Psychological wounds replace the unacknowledged physical illnesses that afflicted him and, previously, his late colleague Gersthoff, who had been dismissed after hospitalisation following a stroke and a heart attack (*A*, 95) but was reinstated when the shop steward intervened. Abschaffel resolves to exhibit stronger self-discipline at work, having been sensitive before his own departure to the impact of Gersthoff's lengthy absence. Moreover, cure-related gossip had artificially animated a visibly dying Gersthoff on his eventual return after his four-week recuperation, during which he and his fellow patients disregarded the dietary regime by frequently taking the bus to nearby restaurants to dine heartily (*VS*, 224). Distancing himself from office politics, Abschaffel aims 'jeden Tag den Eindruck erwecken [zu] können, der Herr seines Geschicks zu sein' / to 'kindle the impression every day of being the master of his fate' (*FJ*, 571), and thus to disassociate himself from the role performances of his colleagues.

Genazino once described Abschaffel as 'durch und durch psychotisch' / 'psychotic through and through'.[37] Both patients present psychosis without the term being used, in line with Laing's definition: as 'a social or biological *failure* of adjustment, or *mal*-adaptation of a particularly radical kind, of *loss* of contact with reality of *lack* of contact with reality, of *lack* of insight'.[38] They confirm David Cooper's view that the clinic is a site of 'social invalidation', but their dysfunctional performances in therapy enable them to challenge the clinical regime that Cooper condemns, where 'a person is progressively made to conform to the inert, passive identity of invalid or patient'.[39] They do not produce 'the illusion of activity' that Cooper ascribes to institutionalised social activities,[40] or even participate fully in analysis. Abschaffel abandons the group component of his tripartite regime, whereas Warlich presents himself as a clear-cut case for Dr Treukirch, who does not instigate sufficiently precise or personalised therapy.

Conclusion

Both Abschaffel in the 1970s and Warlich, who has made no apparent concessions to the twenty-first century,[41] have lost their health through the agency of managerial society that prompted Fromm's redefinition of inhumanity. In the clinic, as in employment, they are confronted with role-restricted activities that appear meaningless, from communal dining to compartmentalised therapies. These do not promote holistic recovery but impose constraints on self-identity and socialisation, which their therapists fail to help them regain. Their experiences are literary portrayals of Szasz's conclusion that 'psychiatric theories have more often functioned as obscurantist teachers misleading the student than as genuine clarifiers helping him to help himself. Bad teachers are, of course, worse than no teachers at all. Against them, scepticism is our sole weapon'.[42] Only Abschaffel, who has lost his faith in fortune, is armed with this weapon, whereas Warlich steadfastly pursues the solace of 'fortune' in the most apposite of surroundings. Reclaiming his status as the centre of action at the end of the novel, throughout which he has narrated his own coming-to-terms with his life, Warlich assumes control over his precarious existence. Abschaffel, requiring a narrator to record his inconclusive perceptions of his condition, retains a transitive relationship to his condition.[43]

While Abschaffel's and Warlich's increasing isolation within their clinics signals the absence of the communitarian basis for recovery that

Fromm anticipated only in the long-term,[44] both protagonists develop self-absorbed narratorial skills. They manifest to themselves and us, more than to their therapists, latent tendencies to seek autobiographical meaning through acute and extended observations of life around them in addressing their interpersonal and professional challenges.[45] Their art of applying Genazino's characteristic 'gedehnte Blick' / 'protracted gaze' to render the benign banalities of everyday life outside the clinical treatment spaces malignant is not symptomatic of illness.[46] Prior to entering the clinic, Warlich has hinted that literature is the most appropriate medium for what he manifestly sustains as his patient belief, in both senses of the adjective: 'Wenn ich ein Buch schreiben könnte, wäre seine Hauptthese: Der Mensch kann Katastrophen immer nur betrachten, nicht verstehen' / 'If I could write a book, its main thesis would be: man can only contemplate catastrophes, not understand them' (*GgZ*, 18–9). Abschaffel, meanwhile, has not developed the critical vocabulary of an analyst and cannot enunciate the full extent of his own condition.[47] Although he elaborates selected episodes all too plausibly for his analyst, his unresolved case is presented to us through an unidentified narrator. By contrast, Warlich's absence of explanation for narrating his story to us predominantly in the present tense, and thereby becoming the author of his own fate of indeterminate hospitalisation, is a discernible undercurrent of his medical and novelistic treatment.

In both cases, medical professionals and institutions fail to validate the centrality of narration to the diagnosis and treatment of the patient. Both Abschaffel's and Warlich's uses of their treatment sessions and spaces are ineffective in modifying their behaviour and its underlying thoughts. However, the insensitivities of the clinic underline the significance of the introspective character function the patients share for their self-sustaining performances in the different narrative forms created equally enduringly by Genazino three decades apart.

Notes

1. Böttiger, 'Der Psychohistoriker der alten Bundesrepublik'.
2. Genazino, *Der gedehnte Blick*, 38–61: his 'Ästhetik der Nachhaltigkeit' / 'aesthetic of sustainability' (55) elucidates commentaries on photographs in *Aus der Ferne* (1993) and *Auf der Kippe* (2000).
3. I will refer to each component of the trilogy separately: *Abschaffel* (1977) as *A*; *Die Vernichtung der Sorgen* (1978; 'Eliminating Preoccupations') as *VS*; and *Falsche Jahre* (1979; 'False Years') as *FJ*. They are collected in Genazino, *Abschaffel*. *Das Glück in glücksfernen Zeiten* will be re-

ferred to as *GgZ*. I propose 'Fortune In Times Far From Fortunate' as a translation of that title. Neologisms characterise Genazino's presentations of his protagonists' mindsets. Translation compromises such connotative richness. The invented surname Abschaffel is derived from a verb conveying abolition: its connotations are rendered neatly by the English 'Dunaway'. In the absence of publications, all English translations here are mine.

4. Hirsch, *'Schwebeglück der Literatur'*; Fansa, *Unterwegs im Monolog*. Brief consideration of Abschaffel's melancholy alongside Warlich's in exemplifying sociological concerns about attentional and time-marking strategies is provided by Fuchs in 'After the Flâneur'; reference to Warlich's psychiatric treatment is fleeting, and none is made to Abschaffel's.
5. Fromm, *The Sane Society*, 352.
6. Marx remarks on Abschaffel: 'ihm wie fast allen späteren Romanfiguren Wilhelm Genazinos ist das Gefühl vertraut, verrückt zu werden'/ 'Like almost all of Wilhelm Genazino's later novel characters, he is familiar with the sense of going mad', Marx, 'Erzählfiguren der Verrückung im Werk Wilhelm Genazinos', 62. According to Genazino, in an interview to mark the publication of *GgZ*, Warlich's case is an extreme variant: 'er hat Verwandte in älteren Romanen. Aber diesmal steigert sich das Problem. Neu ist das markante Scheitern der Figur' / 'He has relations in older novels. However, this time the problem has increased. What's new is the character's pronounced failure'. Schacherreiter, 'Vom Scheitern eines Verantwortungsfreien'.
7. Genazino had called for recognition that literature accommodates such a 'School' in his Büchner Prize acceptance speech in 2004. Genazino, 'Der Trost und die Untröstlichkeit der Literatur', in *Der gedehnte Blick*, 196–205.
8. Gómez-Montero builds on Abschaffel's 'hopelessness': 'Abschaffel kehrt in den Büroalltag zurück und wird bis auf weiteres der Langeweile und damit der Sinnlosigkeit seiner Existenz überlassen' / 'Abschaffel returns to office life and is resigned indefinitely to boredom and the concomitant futility of his existence'. Gómez-Montero, *Sinnverlust und Sinnsuche*, 188.
9. The invented location connotes satiation (*satt*, adj.) and aptly incongruous humour (*lach* being an imperative form of the verb meaning 'to laugh').
10. Goffman, *Presentation*, 26.
11. Goffman, *Presentation*, 109.
12. Goffman's 'working consensus' is the 'interactional *modus vivendi*' in which participants in a project 'contribute to a single over-all definition of the situation which involves not so much a real agreement as to what exists but rather a real agreement as to whose claims concerning what issues will temporarily be honoured' (Goffman, *Presentation*, 21).
13. Mann, *The Magic Mountain*, 44, 77. Further Mann references appear within the text.
14. Hoffmeister (on the *Abschaffel* trilogy), 'The Novel of the Everyday', 135.
15. Genazino revealed in an interview that he had not predetermined that Warlich would enter the clinic. He indicates that Warlich's stay is half the length of Abschaffel's: 'Er hat eine normale psychische Störung.... Das geht dann oft nach zwei, drei Wochen wieder vorbei. Auch der Held der Geschichte wird ja nach drei Wochen wieder entlassen und kommt zurück nach Hause. Wahrscheinlich wird er dauerhaft Arzneimittel nehmen müssen, als prophylaktische Maßnahme, dass so etwas nicht wieder auftritt' / 'He has a normal psychological disorder.... That often passes after two or three weeks. This story's protagonist is one of those who's discharged after three weeks and goes home. He'll probably have to be on long-term medication as a preventive measure so that the disorder doesn't reoccur.' Herdegen, 'Genazino und das Glück'.
16. Literally 'salvation officer'.
17. Warlich uses the verb 'einliefern', conveying transport or delivery of the kind he oversaw at the laundry as well as admission. Its speechless manner supports Szasz's contention that 'individuals become categorized as insane when they become troublesome to, and unwanted by, the people around them, and lack the power to resist being incarcerated in a madhouse'. Szasz, *Psychiatry*, 68.
18. Compare Abschaffel when his pain is most intense: 'Er ließ den Kopf auf die zusammengedrückte rechte Schulter sinken' / 'He dropped his head onto his compressed right shoulder', *VS*, 369.
19. Goffman, *Presentation*, 203.
20. Szasz, *The Myth of Mental Illness*, 263–4.
21. Transcribed in Hirsch, *'Schwebeglück der Literatur'*, 292.
22. Szasz, *The Myth of Mental Illness*, 43.

23. The similarity of Warlich's cocktail of two antidepressants and drugs to treat anxiety, social phobia and narcolepsy to Dr Adrian's prescriptions highlights for Christian Goldammer the 'seemingly unfathomable' nature of any illness from which either patient may be suffering: 'Neither the doctors nor the patients are in a position to delineate an ultimate, concrete pathology'. Goldammer, 'Infantil, adoleszent oder emanzipiert?', 11–2.
24. Zarnegin, 'Wilhelm Meisters Trauerjahre', 240.
25. Laing, *The Divided Self*, 46.
26. The narrator does not cease to reiterate that Dr Buddenberg 'schwieg' / 'remained silent': compare *FJ*, 424, 433, 460. As well as assuming the patient's irritation at a standard clinical non-interruption for which he might not have been prepared, we may allow for an unreliable narrator ignoring responses from Dr Buddenberg that Abschaffel does not take in, or which silence him, just as Dr Buddenberg may *be silenced* by his patient, rather than *remain silent*.
27. The slight renaming renders the Mann connection less blatant than Dr Adrian's. Indeed, the prominence of real West German Budden*bergs* merits exploration: not least Wolfgang Buddenberg, a prosecuting judge during the 1962 'Spiegel Affair' and the 1970s RAF terrorism investigations, whose wife was killed by an explosive device in the family Volkswagen.
28. Buddenberg's verdict is provocatively anti-Freudian. The fragments of analysis are too 'few' to sustain any parallel with Freud's substantial *Bruchstücke einer Hysterie-Analyse / Fragments of an Analysis of a Case of Hysteria* (1905).
29. This assumption that Abschaffel feels at home in Frankfurt is challenged by his listless, aimless perambulations through the streets to delay his return home. On his first night back, he has a nightmare (*FJ*, 550–67).
30. Goffman, *Asylums*, 139.
31. Szasz, *The Myth of Mental Illness*, 257.
32. Genazino, 'Der Kampf gegen die eigene Biografie', 227–8.
33. Buddenberg's chairoplane analogy is rendered even more inappropriate in Louis MacNeice's poem 'Variation on Heraclitus', where this type of seat unsettles its occupier: 'Nor can this now be the chair – the chairoplane of a chair – / That I sat in the day that I thought I had made up my mind'. MacNeice, *Solstices*, 60.
34. Goffman, *Asylums*, 139.
35. Treukirch's name is emblematic of two absences in Warlich's life, with which he is not enabled to come to terms during therapy. These were manifested conflatedly in his confrontation with Annette. Warlich first encountered her at church (*Kirche*), where they sat together 'wie ein früh gealtertes Kinderehepaar'/ 'like a prematurely aged child married couple', and he gifted her not a sacramental loaf but three religious icons he had kept in his hymnal. When they became sacrilegiously intimate in a vestry toilet after confirmation lessons, their mothers separated them; they resumed their relationship nearly a decade later, when Annette abandoned her marital fidelity (*Treue*). The presence of Annette's baby complicated their liaison and distracted Warlich (*GgZ*, 124–5). Subsequently, he does not grant Traudel wedlock or offspring to confirm the fidelity she ultimately jeopardises by depositing him in the clinic. Religion is not necessarily absent from the equation once Dr Treukirch engenders a discourse of sickness: Szasz, in a late polemic, avers that 'belief in mental illness is like belief in God, mediated through language' (Szasz, *Psychiatry*, 16).
36. The verb 'nachgerufen' is used punningly, signifying how an unreceptive Abschaffel's mother shouted out: obituarisation is also connoted.
37. During a colloquium at Paderborn University (7 January 1998), noted by Hirsch, '*Schwebeglück der Literatur*', 292.
38. Laing, *The Divided Self*, 27.
39. Cooper, *Psychiatry and Anti-Psychiatry*, 10.
40. Cooper, *Psychiatry and Anti-Psychiatry*, 10.
41. The trilogy is untypical of Genazino's work in its narrator's attentiveness to technology, from IBM electric typewriters in the office to a microwave oven in a delicatessen. Computers and mobile communication devices are not presented in Warlich's lifeworld.
42. Szasz, *The Myth of Mental Illness*, 272–3.
43. Compare Barthes, 'To Write: An Intransitive Verb?', 18: 'to write is today to make oneself the centre of the action of speech, … to make action and affection coincide'.
44. Fromm, *The Sane Society*, 451.

45. Compare Szasz, *The Myth of Mental Illness*, 130: 'in the symbolism of his symptom, the patient could be said to present his own complaint and – albeit in a highly condensed form – even his autobiography'.
46. Although Genazino discusses 'der gedehnte Blick' / 'the protracted gaze' as a hermeneutic problem that emerges when viewing photographs, he gradually defines a combination of capacities for 'Einbildungskraft' / 'imaginativeness', exercised through the eyes, and mental 'Nachhaltigkeit' / 'persistence', which are highly developed in his protagonists. He observes that we retain significantly more of our observations than we can utter (*Der gedehnte Blick*, 60). Abschaffel and Warlich find no communicative situations to process their retinues of acute observations.
47. As Marx notes, a psychoanalyst in Oldenburg used Genazino's novel *Ein Regenschirm für diesen Tag / The Shoe Tester of Frankfurt* in treating a schizoid patient, and diagnosed the narrating protagonist with five syndromes (Marx, 63 n. 63); compare Hoffmann, 'Die Bedeutung einer Romanfigur als unsichtbarer Begleiter'.

Bibliography

Barthes, Roland. 'To Write: An Intransitive Verb?'. In *The Rustle of Language*, translated by Richard Howard, 11–21. Berkeley: University of California Press, 1989.

Böttiger, Helmut. 'Der Psychohistoriker der alten Bundesrepublik: Zum Tod von Wilhelm Genazino', *Süddeutsche Zeitung*, 14 December 2018. Accessed 11 April 2019. https://www.sueddeutsche.de/kultur/wilhelm-genazino-nachruf-schriftsteller-1.4253310.

Cooper, David. *Psychiatry and Anti-Psychiatry*. London: Tavistock Publications, 1967.

Fansa, Jonas. *Unterwegs im Monolog: Poetologische Konzeptionen in der Prosa Wilhelm Genazinos*. Würzburg: Königshausen und Neumann, 2008.

Fromm, Erich. *The Sane Society*. 2nd ed. London: Routledge, 1991.

Fuchs, Anne. 'After the Flâneur: Temporality and Connectivity in Wilhelm Genazino's *Belebung der toten Winkel* and *Das Glück in glücksfernen Zeiten*', *Modern Language Review* 109, no. 2 (2014): 431–46.

Genazino, Wilhelm. *Abschaffel; Die Vernichtung der Sorgen; Falsche Jahre: Roman-Trilogie*. Munich: Deutscher Taschenbuch Verlag, 2002.

Genazino, Wilhelm. *Der gedehnte Blick*. Munich: Hanser, 2004.

Genazino, Wilhelm. *Das Glück in glücksfernen Zeiten*. Munich: Hanser, 2009.

Genazino, Wilhelm. 'Der Kampf gegen die eigene Biografie'. In *Idyllen in der Halbnatur*, by Wilhelm Genazino, 227–33. Munich: Hanser, 2012.

Goffman, Erving. *Asylums: Essays on the Social Situation of Mental Patients and Other Inmates*. Harmondsworth: Penguin, 1968.

Goffman, Erving. *The Presentation of Self in Everyday Life*. London: Penguin, 1990.

Goldammer, Christian. 'Infantil, adoleszent oder emanzipiert? Männer und ihre Emotionen in der deutschen Gegenwartsliteratur'. Paper presented at the 7th Conference of the Interdisciplinary Working Group – Männer- und Geschlechterforschung, Akademie der Diözese Rottenburg-Stuttgart, 10 December 2010. Accessed 22 October 2019. https://www.fk12.tu-dortmund.de/cms/ISO/Medienpool/Archiv-Alte-Dateien/arbeitsbereiche/soziologie_der_geschlechterverhaeltnisse/Medienpool/AIM_Beitraege_siebte_Tagung/Goldammer_infantil_adolezent_oder_emanzipiert.pdf.

Gómez-Montero, Karina. *Sinnverlust und Sinnsuche: Literarischer Nihilismus im deutschsprachigen Roman nach 1945*. Cologne: Böhlau, 1998.

Herdegen, Andrea. 'Genazino und das Glück', *Frankenpost*, 30 June 2009. Accessed 29 September 2019. http://www.frankenpost.de/dossiers/art3294,1039889.

Hirsch, Anja. *"Schwebeglück der Literatur": Der Erzähler Wilhelm Genazino*. Heidelberg: Synchron, 2006.

Hoffmann, Christa. 'Die Bedeutung einer Romanfigur als unsichtbarer Begleiter einer psychoanalytischen Behandlung', *Psyche* 63, no. 5 (2009): 429–54.

Hoffmeister, Donna L. 'The Novel of the Everyday'. In *After the "Death of Literature": West German Writing of the 1970s*, edited by Keith Bullivant, 125–38. Oxford: Berg, 1989.

Laing, R.D. *The Divided Self: An Existential Study in Sanity and Madness*. Harmondsworth: Penguin, 1967.

MacNeice, Louis. 'Variation on Heraclitus'. In *Solstices*, by Louis MacNeice. London: Faber and Faber, 1961.
Mann, Thomas. *The Magic Mountain*, translated by H.T. Lowe-Porter. London: Vintage, 1999.
Marx, Friedhelm. 'Erzählfiguren der Verrückung im Werk Wilhelm Genazinos'. In *Verstehensanfänge: Das literarische Werk Wilhelm Genazinos*, edited by Andrea Bartl and Friedhelm Marx, 57–68. Göttingen: Wallstein, 2011.
Schacherreiter, Christian. 'Vom Scheitern eines Verantwortungsfreien', *Oberösterreichische Nachrichten*, 24 March 2009. Accessed 10 April 2019. http://www.nachrichten.at/nachrichten/kultur/Vom-Scheitern-eines-Verantwortungsfreien;art16,131789.
Szasz, Thomas S. *The Myth of Mental Illness: Foundations of a Theory of Personal Conduct*. London: Paladin, 1981.
Szasz, Thomas. *Psychiatry: The Science of Lies*. Syracuse, NY: Syracuse University Press, 2008.
Zarnegin, Kathy. 'Wilhelm Meisters Trauerjahre: Die Melancholie der Glückssuche in W. Genazinos Roman "Das Glück in glücksfernen Zeiten"'. In *Die Wissenschaft des Unbewussten*, edited by Kathy Zarnegin, 235–53. Würzburg: Königshausen und Neumann, 2010.

8

Medical Experiments on Humans in Kerstin Hensel's *Lärchenau* (2008)

Ernest Schonfield

Preface

Medical humanities in a German-speaking context are obliged to reflect upon the active participation of the medical profession in the euthanasia and genocide of the Third Reich. This chapter examines the legacy of Nazi medical crimes in Kerstin Hensel's *Lärchenau,* a novel set in East Germany before and after German reunification in 1990.[1] Its fictional character Dr Konarske cannot be described as a Nazi, since he is born in 1944 and has no obvious political affiliation. Yet he conducts medical experiments on women that bear a certain resemblance with the medical crimes, sterilisation and fertility programmes of the Nazi regime. Drawing on the work of Alexander and Margarete Mitscherlich, this chapter argues that the characters in the novel repeat sadomasochistic behaviour patterns because they have repressed their own childhood traumas and those of their parents: the work of mourning has yet to be done.

In so doing, this chapter forms connections with other contributions in this volume. First, Mark Hewitson's contribution investigates post-traumatic stress disorder in the context of the wars of the 1870s. This chapter, by contrast, explores trauma among civilian populations, arguing that Hensel's fiction offers insights into long-term behavioural problems caused by intergenerational domestic violence. Second, the focus in the following on the Mitscherlichs also offers an alternative psychoanalytical approach to that of C.G. Jung. While Martin Liebscher and Sonu Shamdasani examine how Jung fosters personal development by engaging with religion and myth, this chapter is informed instead by the Mitscherlichs' psychoanalytic study of the residual libidinal attachment to authority figures in West Germany of the 1950s and 1960s, an approach that resonates with the social psychology of the Frankfurt School. A similar critique of authoritarianism can also be applied to the GDR, as Margarete Mitscherlich and Brigitte Burmeister have argued in *Wir haben ein Berührungstabu / We Have a Fear of Touching*.[2] Third, Hensel's novel has affinities with Katharina Pethke's documentary film *In dir muss Brennen / Burning Within (2009)*, analysed in Annie Ring's chapter, since both works represent 'inhuman' medical practices, whereby human beings become subordinated to so-called 'objective' concerns (whether these are economic, as in Pethke's film, or scientific/eugenic, as in *Lärchenau*).

Fourth, and finally, this chapter complements Mererid Puw Davies's analysis of Günter Grass's post-war West German novel *örtlich betäubt*. Davies shows that the legacy of National Socialism was a key term in political debates around 1968 in West Germany, whereby each side (the government, the student activists) sought to undermine the other by associating them with National Socialism. The West German political establishment denounced activists by asserting their connections with totalitarianism and extremism, while the activists pointed out that many members of the West German establishment had little claim to moral authority because of their actions during the so-called Third Reich. Davies notes that the dental profession had brought itself into disrepute by the collaboration of some of its members with the Nazi regime (this connection is exemplified also by the character of Dr Szell in the Hollywood film *Marathon Man*, 1967). Taken together therefore, Davies's chapter and this one reassess the uncomfortable implications of the Nazi legacy for the medical professions in both post-war German states.

Introduction

> Sie fing zu murmeln an. Über die Versuche an weiblichen Häftlingen. Über die Spätschäden.[3]
>
> She started to mumble. About the experiments performed on female prisoners. About post-traumatic disorders.[4]

During the so-called Third Reich, the German medical profession was implicated in genocide, mass murder and euthanasia programmes. The Nuremberg Doctors' Trial – 9 December 1946 to 20 August 1947 – was documented by Alexander Mitscherlich and Fred Mielke as early as 1947, with a revised edition appearing in 1960.[5] Until the early 1960s, however, discussion of National Socialist crimes focused mainly on Hitler and senior Nazi officers. After the trial of Adolf Eichmann in Jerusalem in 1961, the definition of a Nazi perpetrator was expanded to include administrators.[6] This trial, and the subsequent Frankfurt Auschwitz trials (1963–5), encouraged historians to turn their attention to the middle managers of the genocide. Major studies of Nazi medical crimes appeared in the following decades.[7] Henry Friedlander considers the Nazi sterilisation programmes and euthanasia of the handicapped as a preliminary step towards genocide.[8] More recently, Paul Weindling has studied the archival testimonies of the victims of medical crimes, many of whom were Polish, Sinti and Roma, in addition to Jews.[9]

The legacy of Nazi medical crimes is explored in Ingeborg Bachmann's unfinished novel *Das Buch Franza / The Book of Franza* (written 1965–6, first published as *Der Fall Franza* in 1978, published as *Das Buch Franza* in 1995). The protagonist, Franza Ranner, marries the psychologist Leopold Jordan, a specialist in treating Holocaust victims. He encourages her to research the Nuremberg Medical Trials and engineers her mental breakdown. While the opening of *Franza* adopts the perspective of Franza's brother, Martin Ranner, much of the book is also narrated by Franza herself. She is an unreliable narrator, but she clearly identifies as an animal-like test subject:

> Wie habe ich mich benommen, wie ein Tier, das in seinem Käfig auf- und niederrennt, und wenn ich die Stäbe hätte durchrennen können mit meinem Schädel, wäre ich noch im Käfig gewesen, in den Käfig seiner Notizen, die mich verfolgten…[10]

> I felt like an animal that runs back and forth in its cage, and even if I'd been able to crash through the bars with my head, I would have still been in a cage, in the cage of his notes which followed me …[11]

Franza is convinced that abuse is still widespread in post-war Austrian society. She claims that sadists and criminals are 'among us', working within the law, under the cover of professional ethos:

> die Sadisten [sind] nicht nur auf psychiatrischen Abteilungen und in den Gerichtssälen zu finden, sondern unter uns … mit blütenweißen Hemden und Professorentiteln, mit den Folterwerkzeugen der Intelligenz.[12]

> sadists are found not only in the psychiatric hospitals and in the courts, but also here among us with snow-white lab coats and titled professorships, armed with the intelligentsia's tools of torture.[13]

Such comments are relativised by Franza's post-traumatic disorder and her unreliability as a narrator. Nevertheless, there are clear textual parallels between her experience and Nazi medical crimes, for example, her husband's sadism and his lack of remorse.[14] Ironically, according to Franza, in the Nuremberg medical transcripts, the words 'forgive me' only ever occur when one of the victims apologises for crying in court.[15] Later, Franza escapes to Egypt, where she encounters an actual perpetrator, the former SS doctor Kurt Körner. Stephanie Bird argues that Franza's submissiveness and self-deception make her complicit in her own destruction.[16] *Das Buch Franza* reveals 'the mechanisms through which individuals, in this case a woman, willingly become subservient to power, and comply with it by mistaking it for or choosing to see in it a moral authority.'[17] In this way, Bachmann's approach to the problem of complicity with fascism subverts the crude dichotomy of victims and perpetrators.

This approach resembles the psychological perspective adopted by Alexander and Margarete Mitscherlich in *Die Unfähigkeit zu trauern* (1967) / *The Inability to Mourn* (1975).[18] The Mitscherlichs examined the extent to which the general population had invested themselves psychologically in the Nazi regime. They concluded that much 'Trauerarbeit' / 'work of mourning' was still required before Germans could overcome recurrent authoritarian patterns in their interpersonal relationships. The Mitscherlichs' work inspired some West German feminists to reflect on women's collusion with patriarchy; for example, the Hamburg women's collective around Frigga Haug argued that collective 'Erinnerungsarbeit' / 'memory work' should inform the social sciences.[19]

These authors pointed the way beyond categorical oppositions between women and patriarchy, and raised the controversial possibility that many 'ordinary' Germans were complicit with National Socialism. However, it was not until the late 1980s that studies appeared on women's participation in the so-called Third Reich. Whereas Gisela Bock considered that forced sterilisation programmes had presented women primarily as victims of Nazism, Claudia Koonz's *Mothers in the Fatherland* (1987) studied middle-class women who played an active part in the formation of the Third Reich.[20] The ensuing debate between Bock and Koonz hinged on the question of whether women were victims of Nazism or its supporters. The debate exemplified the transition from Bock's essentialist model of feminist history, which considered women's history in categorical opposition to patriarchy, to Koonz's more nuanced gender studies approach, implying that certain aspects of National Socialist family policy could be seen as responding to the conservative wing of the German women's movement.[21] Some campaigners had regarded the recognition of motherhood as 'woman's highest calling' as a precondition for social improvement, a discourse also adopted by the Nazis.[22] These findings indicate the importance of sustained memory work for the humanities, and literary fiction, with its irony, ambiguity and reflectivity, offers a highly nuanced approach to National Socialism and its after-effects.

This chapter focuses on the representation of medical experiments on humans in Kerstin Hensel's *Lärchenau* (2008). Hensel previously addressed the theme of the 'fascist doctor' in her unpublished work *Karzinom / Carcinoma* (1981), an absurd drama recalling the plays of Friedrich Dürrenmatt, set in an East German clinic.[23] *Lärchenau* develops this preoccupation in a much more subtle way, by exploring the childhood development of the main protagonists. At the centre of *Lärchenau* is the East German doctor, Gunter Konarske, and his wife, Adele, née Möbius. Konarske conducts a series of medical experiments on women without their knowledge: on nurse Angela, wife of the local physician Dr Krause, and then on Adele. The novel's title, *Lärchenau,* refers to a fictional village in Brandenburg, near Storkow in the Oder-Spree district. The protagonists' childhood experiences set up behavioural patterns that are repeated in later life. Adele and Gunter are born in 1944 and never meet their fathers, and are thus in search of ideal father figures, as described by Alexander Mitscherlich in *Auf dem Weg zur vaterlosen Gesellschaft / Society Without A Father* (1963), which describes difficulties faced by Germans after 1945 in adapting to a world in which paternal authority was either absent or diminished.[24] Gunter constructs an ideal image of his deceased father, who was acclaimed by the villagers as a 'Zauberer' / 'magician' (*L*, 71), while Adele regards Adolf Hitler as a father figure. The long time span of *Lärchenau* – it begins in 1944 and ends in the year 2007 – enables Hensel to suggest that there are enduring continuities in German history, and even that some things get worse after the reunification of Germany, which occurs two thirds of the way through the novel.

On one level, *Lärchenau* is a tribute to Bachmann's *Das Buch Franza*. In both novels, the female protagonist is subjected to unethical medical experiments by her husband. In both cases, the female character's susceptibility to authoritarian dominance is traced back to her early childhood. Both girls fantasise about mythical princes and king-like figures, and this prepares them to play a subservient role in adult life. In both texts, the women flee to the Middle East in order to escape their sadistic husbands – Adele travels to Amman, the capital of Jordan, a discreet allusion to Leopold Jordan in *Franza* (*L*, 406–12). Both novels are set mainly after 1945: they do not explore Nazi medical crimes themselves; instead, they consider the long-term repercussions of these crimes and the repetition of patterns of violence in recent German and Austrian history. The novels are also linked by the view that violence (particularly sexual violence) is an inescapable aspect of human existence. Bachmann describes society as a 'Mordschauplatz' / 'murder scene',[25] and Birgit Dahlke argues that in Hensel's fiction, sexual violence is an instance of an omnipresent violence in human relationships.[26] Thus for both Bachmann and Hensel, violence is not limited to the crimes of dictatorships (whether the 'Third Reich' or the GDR); it is a pervasive feature of human existence.

Despite these similarities, there are major differences between *Lärchenau* and *Das Buch Franza*. Whereas Bachmann's text focuses on psychiatric abuses in Vienna, Hensel's novel focuses on abuses in fertility treatment and genetic research in East Germany. In *Das Buch Franza*, the subjective experiences of the main protagonist are foregrounded, and Franza herself is the unreliable narrator of the latter half of the book. In *Lärchenau*, the impersonal third person narrator grants only limited access to the characters' thoughts. Furthermore, while *Das Buch Franza* addresses the Holocaust explicitly, in *Lärchenau* the Holocaust is only referred to in passing. There is something shockingly casual about the references to the Holocaust, for instance when the Jewish tailor Simson Blumgebind returns home from a concentration camp and dies in the arms of Rosie Konarske (*L*, 59), or when someone notices that the elderly Roma woman Mitschka Prohaska[27] has a number tattooed on her arm (*L*, 353), and wonders if it is a telephone number. In *Lärchenau*, the typical response to the Holocaust is either indifference or incomprehension.

Perhaps the most striking difference between the two texts, however, is that *Lärchenau* covers a much greater time span. While *Das Buch Franza* covers the period from the early 1940s to 1965, *Lärchenau* begins in 1944, before jumping back to Adele's mother's childhood at the beginning of the twentieth century, and the winter of 1915, when Adele's grandfather Benno Möbius died while serving in Wallachia (*L*, 22). *Lärchenau* then follows the lives of its characters all the way through to August 2007, covering a time span of nearly a century. Hensel's critical engagement with the past is thus exemplary in terms of its *longue durée.* Like Michael Haneke's film *Das weiße Band / The White Ribbon* (2009), Hensel takes the period around the First World War as a starting point in order to suggest the existence of long-term structural violence in German history and culture.

This chapter offers an interpretation of *Lärchenau* drawing on the historical record of Nazi medical atrocities and their literary reception by

Bachmann and Hensel. This approach is intended to act as a corrective to the tendency to label Hensel's work as a form of 'grotesque satire'.[28] Typically, reviews of *Lärchenau* stress its humorous, 'baroque' or 'mythological' qualities.[29] Satire, legend and fairy tale are popular literary genres. Reading Hensel's prose in these generic terms risks reducing it to an amusing, eccentric curiosity, an example of lowbrow fiction. This chapter seeks to counter this existing critical trend, reading *Lärchenau* as a complex, serious and challenging text and an important instance of critical *Vergangenheitsbewältigung* / 'coming to terms with the past'. It will argue that, far from being an exaggeration, *Lärchenau* is actually rather restrained in its depiction of the endemic acts of violence of German history. We will first address narrative technique and genre, before turning to a brief examination of the historical record. This will lead to a discussion of moral complicity and the wider implications of the novel's representation of fertility experiments and cell rejuvenation.

Narrative Technique and Genre

The narrative technique of *Lärchenau* is varied: much of the dialogue is in regional dialect, and the narrative switches frequently between the large cast of characters. The narrative speeds up during German reunification, focusing in particular on the events of one month, August 1990 (*L*, 272–7). There is a preference for lists of three elements, conveying a sing-song quality, for example when Gunter goes away and leaves Adele alone, it could be: 'Für Tage. Oder Wochen. Oder Monate. Nie war es vorauszusehen' / 'For days, or weeks, or months. It could never be predicted' (*L*, 292). Despite some formal experimentation, however, much of *Lärchenau* is narrated in a fairly straightforward manner. The timeline is mostly linear, focusing mainly on the period from 1944 to 2007, although the text also depicts the childhood of the Möbius sisters in the first decades of the twentieth century, and the courtship of Gunter's parents in the early 1940s. The detached third-person narrator reels off the events rapidly as they occur, without emphatic commentary. The opening adheres to realist conventions, offering a precise description of Lärchenau's geographical location and its lack of tourist attractions (*L*, 7). However, despite these traditional narrative conventions, Hensel's texts are notable for their graphic imagery and depictions of sex, violence and sexual violence. In Hensel's works, everyday life in Eastern Germany, before and after the turning points of 1945 and 1989, is characterised by violent, oppressive behaviour.

Hensel's work is often interpreted in terms of the grotesque. Lyn Marven focuses on the grotesque as a manifestation of trauma, also observing that the grotesque body has the potential to transgress the confines of totalitarian ideologies.[30] Jill E. Twark also emphasises Hensel's use of the grotesque, pointing out that *Gipshut / Plaster Cap* (1999) features a character with an abnormally large body due to a hormone imbalance – an inversion of the dwarf Oskar Matzerath in Günter Grass's *Die Blechtrommel / The Tin Drum* (1959).[31] Indeed, Hensel's texts, with their anarchic and subversive imagery, have often been compared to those of Günter Grass[32] and Irmtraud Morgner.[33] Even so, in 2007 Twark observed that Hensel's more recent texts have become less grotesque, bucking the grotesque trend of the 1990s.[34] However, Twark does not develop this point, and her interpretation of *Gipshut* focuses almost entirely on the grotesque. Furthermore, in an essay of 2015, Twark characterizes *Lärchenau* as an instance of 'grotesque satire'.[35] Hensel, like Grass, does use satire, for instance while Grass's novel *Hundejahre / Dog Years* (1963) uses dog breeding to satirise Nazi aspirations to breed a Nietzschean *Übermensch*, Hensel's *Lärchenau* adopts a similar procedure, using pig farming to poke fun at the socialist ideal of 'der neue Mensch' / 'the new human'.[36] Like the work of Grass, Hensel's work does contain a vein of robust, earthy satire. But nobody would pigeonhole Grass as a mere 'satirist'. To read Hensel in this way is reductive.

Categorising Hensel's work as satire risks trivialising it. Heinrich Mann's reputation as a satirist has not translated into canonical status. When Hensel's *Falscher Hase / Meat Loaf* (2005) is compared to Heinrich Mann's *Der Untertan / The Loyal Subject*, this only reminds us that he lacks the canonical status of Thomas Mann.[37] Indeed, categorising *Der Untertan* as a satire is a means to dismiss it as a 'low' form of art, making it easier for critics who disagree with its political analysis to write it off as a mere curiosity.[38] Kurt Tucholsky argued that *Der Untertan* is not a satire or a caricature, but 'modest photography'.[39] The purpose of this chapter is to mount a similar defence of *Lärchenau*. What happens if we read the grotesque imagery of *Lärchenau* not as an exaggeration or a distortion, but as an accurate depiction of 'real existing' violence? This chapter argues that the obscenity in *Lärchenau* is justified by the obscenity of the historical record.

Eugenics Experiments on Humans – The Historical Record

There is a long history of medical experimentation on humans, particularly in the modern period.[40] Today, medical trials on human beings comprise a global industry, with many of the most dangerous trials carried out on subjects in developing countries.[41] For our purposes, however, a brief historical sketch will suffice. The first eugenic organisation in the world was the Gesellschaft für Rassenhygiene / Society for Racial Hygiene, founded in Berlin in 1905. The term 'racial hygiene', coined by Alfred Ploetz, was understood in terms of racial purity, and the improvement of public health.[42] During the Weimar Republic, eugenics informed the development of the welfare state. This trajectory was informed by a new national centre for eugenics, the Kaiser-Wilhelm-Institut für Anthropologie / Kaiser Wilhelm Institute for Anthropology, founded in 1927, also in Berlin. These eugenicists tended to be 'unrepentantly meritocratic' and elitist, attempting to replace universal social welfare with selective welfare benefits for social elites.[43] When the National Socialists came to power, they embraced eugenics, passing a sterilisation law in July 1933 under the supervision of the psychiatric geneticist Ernst Rüdin.[44] The Kaiser-Wilhelm-Institut für Anthropologie ran training courses for SS doctors in 1935–6 in the implementation of racial policy.[45] Sex hormone research and fertility control were central to this policy. Two notable war criminals were Karl Gebhardt (1897–1948) and Carl Clauberg (1898–1957), who conducted medical experiments on prisoners in Ravensbrück and Auschwitz respectively. Karl Gebhardt, for example, extracted foetuses from 350 forced labourers.[46]

However, Clauberg is particularly relevant for our discussion. The flip side of Nazi extermination, euthanasia and sterilisation programmes was research into fertility. His early research on female hormones in the late 1920s led to the development of infertility treatments Progynon and Proluton.[47] In the 1930s, he regularly checked the wives of SS officers for their fertility. In the same decade, he worked at the women's clinic in Königsberg, where he sterilised large numbers of women.[48] On 22 March 1940 he met with Himmler and advocated his hormone research to advance the reproductive potential of the SS. Himmler is said to have asked Clauberg if he could also reverse fertility by chemical means.[49] Clauberg promised to try, and began animal experiments. In May 1942, Himmler offered Clauberg facilities at Ravensbrück, but Clauberg persuaded him that Auschwitz would be more practical because of its proximity to his clinic in Königshutte.[50] And so in 1942, Clauberg was given control over an entire block at Auschwitz: Block 10. There, Clauberg directed the mass sterilisation programme, which included forced abortions on Eastern European workers, Jews, Roma and Sinti. At the height of the programme, he had around three hundred women under his control. His method was 'to inject a caustic substance into the cervix in order to obstruct the fallopian tubes'; this was formalin, sometimes injected together with novocaine.[51] The total number of women estimated to have been sterilised ranges from seven hundred to 'several thousand'; many of the injections were fatal.[52] According to the nurse Sylvia Friedman, when a woman died after an injection, Clauberg 'showed absolutely no interest, no reaction, as through the matter didn't concern him at all.'[53] He worked simultaneously on fertilisation and sterilisation programmes, in 1944 becoming director of a new institution known as the 'City of Mothers'.[54] In 1945 he was captured by the Soviets and spent 10 years in prison in the USSR. Repatriated with other Germans in 1955, he lived another 2 years to boast about his scientific achievements to the press.[55] After 1945, 'racial hygiene' was rebranded 'human genetics', and rehabilitated, with a focus on genetic malformations.[56]

The case of Clauberg, with his two-pronged approach towards fertilisation and sterilisation, shows the extent to which high-ranking Nazis regarded their own wives as breeding animals similarly to the way that they regarded female prisoners in the camps. The crucial difference was that the wives were considered to belong to the correct breed and therefore their fertility was to be maximised, whereas the Eastern European, Jewish, Roma and Sinti women in the camps were considered to belong to undesirable breeds and were therefore to be made infertile by means of forced sterilisation. The sterilisation victims were not told, and did not know, that they were the subjects of a medical experiment. The plot of *Lärchenau* conforms to this procedure: the female protagonist Adele does not know that her husband is using her as an experimental subject – first for his fertility treatments and, later on, for his experimental anti-aging serum. Konarske, however, differs from Clauberg in that he does not subscribe to the racial ideology of the Nazis. He remains detached from ideology as well as from his victims' suffering. His primary motivation is not ideology, but the narcissistic quest for scientific glory.

Victimisation and Complicity

The sexual objectification of women by the Nazis effectively turned the female body into an instrument for the expression of the male will. Konarske is a sadist in a similar vein to Jordan in *Das Buch Franza*. He embarks on his medical career at the age of 13, treating the local farmers and their livestock, and seeing little difference between them. When the local farmer Helmar Eden – the surname is ironic – asks Konarske if he can cure Beate, his invalid wife, he replies: 'Klar … Ich krieg jedes Schwein wieder hin' / 'Of course, I can fix any pig' (*L*, 115).[57] Konarske gets a nasty surprise when Beate grabs his hand and forces him to feel her breasts (*L*, 116). In revenge, he prescribes a bath in the lake. He pushes Beate in a tarpaulin-covered wheelbarrow towards the lake, but then he changes course and takes her to a cattle barn instead, where the two of them are completely alone. As Konarske lifts the tarpaulin, there is blood in Beate's mouth, and he enjoys seeing the fear in her eyes (*L*, 117). Within hours, Beate is dead, never having reached the lake. Although the cause of death is not explicitly stated, it seems likely that Konarske murders her in the cattle barn. Konarske's comment on Beate's death certainly supports this interpretation: 'Sie hat es so gewollt' / 'She wanted it that way' (*L*, 118), as does the fact that he spends the whole afternoon thinking about the terror in her eyes. Later, when he becomes a doctor, Konarske amuses himself by referring to each patient metonymically, according to his or her medical condition: 'Darmkrebs ... Phlegmone ... Platzwunde ... Beinbruch' / 'bowel cancer ... phlegmon ... laceration ... fractured leg' (*L*, 183). He has no desire to understand or ameliorate his patients' psychic distress: 'Konarske verachtete die Seele' / 'Konarske scorned the soul' (*L*, 391).

Konarske is an active sadist. He gets a sexual thrill from scaring his wife (*L*, 192); his nickname for her is 'Mauseprinzessin' / 'mouse princess' (*L*, 193, 198, 199). Ominously, this associates her with a laboratory mouse: 'Es ergehe Adele nämlich ähnlich jener Labormaus, welcher Konarske kürzlich mit einem gentechnologischen Eingriff bestimmte Riechzellen aus der Nasenschleimhaut entfernt habe.' / 'Adele's situation resembles that of the mouse from which Konarske recently extracted olfactory cells from the nasal mucous membrane, with the intervention of gene technology' (*L*, 202). The sensory deprivation of the mouse is analogous to the way in which Konarske deprives Adele of specific information about the research he is conducting on her, infringing her capacity for informed consent.

Given the unsympathetic character of Konarske, readers may be entitled to ask what attracts Adele to him in the first place. The answer seems to lie in the depiction of their troubled, fatherless childhoods. It is significant that Adolf Hitler is symbolically present at the birth of both of the main protagonists. When Gunter is born, Hitler's voice is heard on the radio and, as the midwife presents the baby to the mother, she says: 'Sie haben dem Führer ein schönes Kind geschenkt' / 'You have given the Führer a fine baby' (*L*, 20). Gunter never meets his father, Doctor Rochus Lingott, an expert in homeopathy who uses herbs from the nearby lake (*L*, 10). Lingott is arrested by the SA for having failed to display a picture of the Führer in his office; he is never seen again.[58] The only father figure Gunter knows in his childhood is his maternal grandfather, Otto

Konarske, an abusive bully. Gunter spends the early years of his life playing with his absent father's medical instruments. Gunter loves to dissect things and when he is only 3 years old his mother Rosie asks him to cut her arm with her nail scissors in a bid to relieve her from her numbness (*L*, 66). Because of Rosie's silent depression, he learns very little about his father, except what his schoolmates tell him: 'dein Vata is 'n jroßer Zaubara jewesen' / 'your dad was a great magician' (*L*, 70). This gives him a feeling of superiority over the other children: 'Seit diesem Tag bemerkte Rosie das feine Lächeln um den Mund ihres Sohnes' / 'Ever since that day, Rosie noticed that her son's mouth had acquired a sophisticated smile' (*L*, 71). Gunter resolves to emulate his father; unfortunately, he lacks his father's kindness.

For Adele, Hitler functions not only as a symbolic godfather, but as an actual father. Her mother Liese tells her that her father is a kind of 'king', and promises to reveal his true identity when her daughter is old enough to understand (*L*, 89). Over the Christmas of 1954, Adele eavesdrops on her mother and hears her say: 'Mei Madl is doch'n Fiehror sein Kind' / 'My girl is the daughter of the Führer' (*L*, 106). In the winter of 1943, Hitler visited the town, and she had the honour of preparing potato soup for him (*L*, 25). When his limousine drove off, Liese chased after it, and she enjoyed a moment of passion in the woods – but was it really with the Führer, or was it with one of the local peasant boys (*L*, 27)? Whatever the facts may be, Liese is convinced that her daughter is the child of the Führer, who, after 1945, is still with her in spirit (*L*, 80). Having revealed Adele's 'noble' lineage, Liese dies and Adele is sent to a children's home.[59] At the children's home, in 1954, Adele sees a picture of the Führer, and she realises that her father must be the 'Führer' himself (*L*, 146). Now she understands 'Das Große ihrer Abstammung' / 'the greatness of her ancestry' (*L*, 146). From this day on, Adele refuses to believe the bad things people say about Hitler – she has at last identified her consoling 'Märchen' / 'fairy tale' (*L*, 147), which compensates for her isolation and abandonment. Her fantasy is the embodiment of the fascist logic that defines the leader as a powerful father figure.

In *Die Unfähigkeit zu trauern* (1967), Alexander and Margarete Mitscherlich argued that West Germans had repressed their previous attachment to the authoritarian figure of the Führer, when the Führer had replaced their own ego-ideal. Before 1945, subordination to the Führer and his grand plans had enabled individual Germans to compensate for their feelings of inferiority. The subject's self-sacrifice and abandonment to the authority of the leader was experienced as the realisation of a cherished ideal:

> Indem ich dem Führer folge, ihm Verehrung zolle, verwirkliche ich ein Stück dieses phantasierten Ich-Ideals. Ich nehme an diesem bedeutungsvollen Leben des Führers, an dessen historisch einmaligen Plänen unmittelbar teil, der Führer und seine Bedeutung werden zu einem Teil von mir.[60]

> By following the leader and worshipping him, each person realizes something of this fantasied ego-ideal. Each thus shares directly in the highly significant life of the leader and in his historically unique plans; the leader and his importance become part of oneself.[61]

The Mitscherlichs drew on Freud's essay 'Massenpsychologie und Ich-Analyse' / 'Group Psychology and the Analysis of the Ego' (1921), which argues that an authoritarian leader occupies the place of the ego-ideal in each of his followers.[62] According to the Mitscherlichs, Germans experienced their loyalty to the Führer as a form of liberation, although it was in fact the reverse, namely, a form of masochistic bondage: 'Im Zustand ihrer Hörigkeit erniedrigen sich die Massen vor Führerfiguren, um neues Selbstgefühl zu erlangen … Die akute Verliebtheit in den Führer steigert die masochistische Lustbereitschaft' / 'In this state of bondage, the masses humble themselves before the leader figure more and more, in order to gain self-esteem … The acute infatuation with the Führer increases the pleasurable masochistic tendency'.[63] The Mitscherlichs identify this form of love as characteristically German, 'eine deutsche Art zu lieben' / 'a German way of loving' (as Chapter I of their book is titled), and argue that this structural pattern repeated itself in personal attachments even after 1945. Although their analysis focuses on West Germany, it also has implications for East Germans. As Margarete Mitscherlich put it in 1991, the traditional German faith in authority was never seriously called into question during the four decades in which the GDR existed.[64]

The plot of *Lärchenau* confirms the Mitscherlichs' theory that the traditional 'Autoritätsglaube' / 'faith in authority' continued after 1945. Significantly, both protagonists, Adele Möbius and Gunter Konarske, bear their mother's surname since their fathers were absent. Both are born in 1944 and, as children, both experience neglect. While still a toddler, Adele loves playing at being a housewife, watching over her 'Wohnreich' / 'domestic kingdom' (*L*, 82) with her dustpan and brush. Liese and her friend Traudel have great expectations for Adele. When Traudel comments that Adele will go far in life, the mother responds: 'Bis zum Führer?' / 'As far as the Führer?' (*L*, 82). The mother thinks that her daughter will be a bride fit for a Führer. While Adele is raised to believe that she is an alpha female, Gunter is raised as an alpha male. Even as a toddler, he is effectively the man of the house. In time, he decides to emulate his father, the 'Zauberer' / 'magician' (*L*, 71) he never knew. In the absence of their real fathers, these children become fixated on idealised patriarchal figures: Gunter's ego ideal is his deceased father, whereas Adele's ego ideal is Hitler himself. Later, when Adele meets Gunter, he becomes her new idol and she keeps a photograph of him under her mattress, right next to her photo of Hitler (*L*, 170). Unlike Hitler, however, Gunter's mission is not racial supremacy, but scientific glory.

Adele's relationship with her husband Gunter follows the pattern described by the Mitscherlichs, in which the attachment to an authoritarian leader predisposes the individual to masochistic enjoyment. Adele enjoys the humiliating treatment inflicted on her, or at least, she tries to enjoy it, because it confirms her sense of her own higher calling:

> Nach jeder Demütigung, die Konarske seiner Frau verabreichte, fühlte sich diese erweckt. Jede Herablassung, jede Beleidigung verschaffte ihr gleichsam Widerwillen als auch Lust. Nach jedem Kampf gab es nur einen Sieger: Konarske. Aber Adele nannte es Glück.... Doch ... die Menschen waren unfähig zum Staunen über Adeles hohe Zunft.
>
> After every humiliation that Konarske subjected his wife to, she felt aroused. Every condescension, every insult caused her both repulsion and pleasure. After every battle there was only one winner: Konarske. But Adele called it happiness.... And yet, people were unable to marvel at her high calling. (*L*, 193)

In this way, Adele's private humiliation is offset by her sense of devotion to a higher purpose – and by the satisfaction she gets when the villagers address her as 'Frau Doktor' (*L*, 186). No one else can understand her, because they belong to an inferior species, they have no higher purpose. The characters' sense of superiority over their peers is also reflected in their attempts to lose their dialect and speak only standard German. This process begins when Adele's mother Liese dreams of learning *Hochdeutsch* / High (or standard) German in order to experience a symbolic connection with the Führer: 'denn im Hauptquartier von Adeles Erzeuger ... würde die reine Sprache der Heiligen gesprochen' / 'In the headquarters of Adele's progenitor, the pure language of the saints was spoken' (*L*, 40). Linguistic register thus functions here as an instrument of domination.

Gunter Konarske's narcissism takes precedence over everything else. He has no interest in his son, Timm, because the baby displays no genetic irregularities of any kind: 'Keine Zelle, die dem Gewöhnlichen entwuchs!' / 'No cell which outgrew the ordinary!' (*L*, 200). This shows once again how Konarske differs ideologically from the Nazis: he has no racial pride, only pride in his own scientific genius. Nevertheless, the underlying attitude is similar: like the Nazis, he regards other people, even members of his own family, as raw material. Because Timm has no scientific interest, for Konarske he is of no interest. Konarske does not seek to control fertility for racial purposes, but only in order to affirm his own scientific superiority. Timm later develops a tendency towards self-harm as a consequence of his neglect by his parents. He falls in with a group of neo-Nazis led by the 'Admiral', Kai. This portrayal of the restrictive, repressive nature of the nuclear family accords with 1970s feminist critiques of patriarchal family structures.[65]

As Sonja Klocke points out, leading medics in the GDR enjoyed special privileges, and this, combined with traditional gender structures, cements Konarske's 'dominant position in the household',[66] allowing the couple to enjoy the luxuries of a bourgeois lifestyle. The exceptional status of the Konarskes is highlighted when the loyal SED (Socialist Unity Party of Germany) member Elsbeth Giersch comments that the Konarskes are a bourgeois relic:

> Die Konarskes, obwohl von denen keiner in der Partei sei, hätten … eine Riesenküche…. Die Konarskes sind asozial, ein bürgerliches Relikt, das die schwierige Übergangsphase des Sozialismus zum Kommunismus kennzeichne.
>
> Doktor Konarske sah sich veranlaßt, im Frühjahr eine übermannshöhe Hecke um sein Anwesen zu pflanzen.
>
> The Konarskes, although none of them are in the Party, have got an enormous kitchen. The Konarskes are anti-social, a bourgeois relic, characteristic of the difficult phase of transition from socialism to communism. In the spring, Dr Konarske found it necessary to plant a hedge above head height around his estate. (*L*, 228)

This passage emphasises that the Konarskes are exempted from the usual mechanisms of socialisation and participation in the GDR; they live a cloistered existence in a fortress-like house. Despite the egalitarian rhetoric of the GDR, elite members of society still enjoyed a life of privilege; one character even comments 'daß es bei Konarskes inzwischen wie bei Fürstens zuginge' / 'the Konarskes live like princes' (*L*, 201). Despite their extreme wealth, however, their family life appears devoid of warmth and even speech, as the Konarskes barely talk to each other. Their home life resembles the emptiness of Franza's life in Vienna: 'Wir spielten ein königliches Spiel. Schweigen, tun als ob, schweigen, tun als ob' / 'We played a princely game. Silence, pretence, silence, then more pretence'.[67] Referring to Hensel's early work, Marven has commented that trauma disrupts the use of language, rendering a person mute.[68] This evaluation certainly seems to apply to Adele, who tries to fill the monotony of her married life by listening to Strauss's opera *Der Rosenkavalier / The Knight of the Rose*. In this way, we can see how Adele is predisposed towards her own subjugation by the stories she heard from her mother when she was only a small child.

Fertility Experiments and German History as *Schweinerei*

Lärchenau spans the entire period of history from around 1930 to the first decade of the twenty-first century. It suggests that the legacy of National Socialism had consequences for the development of the GDR. It also implies that there were limitations to medical ethics in the GDR. In response to crimes committed by medical professionals during the 'Third Reich', the GDR expected doctors to be politically engaged for the 'humane und gerechte Sache' / 'humane and just cause', extending the Hippocratic oath to emphasise a physician's obligation to socialist society in general.[69] In particular, *Lärchenau* makes a mockery of the GDR's ambition to breed a new form of socialist human being, likening it to pig breeding on a collectivised farm. The section on pig farming alludes ironically to Christa Wolf's *Nachdenken über Christa T.* (1968) / *The Quest for Christa T.* (1979), which features a country vet, Justus, who wants to achieve 'world-class' levels of pork and milk production.[70] Konarske, although he is not a vet, also wants to use his medical knowledge to boost agricultural production. He tests a new fertility treatment on the swine of the local farmer, Eden, who is now the chairman of the local *Landwirtschaftliche Produktionsgenossenschaft* (LPG) / Agricultural Production Cooperative (*L*, 207–9). The pigs become sex-mad; they breed faster and even win prizes. Unfortunately, they die more quickly as well. This episode culminates in a rebellion of the pigs recalling George Orwell's *Animal Farm* (1945). The pigs are slaughtered, their eyes full of hate (*L*, 252). The GDR agricultural ministry responds to this disaster by summoning the 'Agraringenieurin' / 'agrarian engineer' Olga Poljuchowa from Moscow, who is tasked with introducing the latest Soviet method of artificial insemination (*L*, 253). This method is tested out on Helmar Eden's prize sow, named 'Liebauge PS 444'/ 'Bright Eyes 444 Horsepower' (*L*, 254). The method requires Eden to stimulate the sow's erogenous zones while Olga Poljuchowa squirts in the boar's semen (*L*, 255).

Before the pig serum fails, however, Konarske decides to try it out on a human subject: he slips Krause and his wife nurse Angela the drug – it causes Angela to miscarry twice (*L*, 222). Worse still, Adele accidentally eats some chocolates spiked with the drug. Under the influence, she sleeps with one of the local youths.[71] Later, Konarske impregnates the soil with genetically modified mycelium in order to grow giant truffles to give to the pigs (*L*, 373) – at this point the text draws a parallel between the drugged truffles and the medicated chocolate truffles that Adele receives: 'Es ging den Tieren wie Adele' / 'What happened to the animals, happened to Adele' (*L*, 374). Konarske treats his wife, and nurse Angela, much as he would treat laboratory animals, thus dehumanising them.

The references to pig breeding in *Lärchenau* suggest associations with Nazi eugenics programmes designed to increase the fertility of preferred races.[72] However, the fertility programmes in *Lärchenau* are not underpinned by racial ideology, but by a more covert ideology of scientific neutrality and efficiency. They look ahead to the nightmare eugenics potential of contemporary genetics research. Thanks to the latest human genome editing techniques, scientists now believe that 'the future *à la carte* medicine is within reach, providing the ability to modify cells, tissues, and organs with high precision.'[73] Modifying human embryos is already legal in China and in many US states. In one recent experiment, Chinese scientists used molecules called CRISPRs (Clustered Regularly Interspaced Short Palindromic Repeats) to cut DNA in human embryos and then 'repair' it by introducing new DNA. The team used non-viable embryos obtained from fertility clinics in an attempt to head off ethical concerns.[74] Even so, the study provoked considerable debate about the dangers of 'playing god'.[75] There were calls for a clinical moratorium on these applications, 'while the ethical and safety concerns of human-embryo editing are worked out'.[76] Jennifer Doudna, an expert in the field of 'gene hacking', confesses that she has dreamed about meeting Hitler:

> 'I had a dream recently, and in my dream' – she mentioned the name of a leading scientific researcher – 'had come to see me and said, "I have somebody very powerful with me who I want you to meet, and I want you to explain to him how this technology functions." So I said, Sure, who is it? It was Adolf Hitler. I was really horrified, but I went

> into a room and there was Hitler. He had a pig face and I could only see him from behind and he was taking notes and he said, "I want to understand the uses and implications of this amazing technology." I woke up in a cold sweat. And that dream has haunted me from that day. Because suppose somebody like Hitler had access to this – we can only imagine the kind of horrible uses he could put it to.'[77]

Genetics research of the twenty-first century has a destructive potential that is incalculable, and it remains haunted by the spectre of Nazi eugenics.

After Reunification: Genetic Experiments and Anti-Age Serum

In the last third of the novel, covering the post-reunification period from 1990 to 2007, Konarske's position of authority remains unchallenged, and he further extends his dominance over Adele. At this point he starts to present the characteristics associated with the legendary Bluebeard figure: he starts to keep her locked in a chamber of the house, and he has a private laboratory in the basement of his house that his wife and son are forbidden to enter. The reference to Bluebeard is an allusion to Bachmann's *Das Buch Franza*, but it also points towards a broader patriarchal discourse, as Mererid Puw Davies has shown.[78] Konarske now starts injecting Adele with an experimental youth serum in an attempt to win the Nobel Prize. The rejuvenation serum can be interpreted in a number of different ways. On one level, as Klocke suggests, it can be read as an allegory of Western consumerism with its cult of youth and its cosmetics industry, with its artificial attempts to preserve youthful appearances.[79] On another level, as Garbiñe Iztueta argues, Adele's artificial rejuvenation could suggest the post-*Wende* federal German government's treatment of East Germany. According to Iztueta, Adele's body symbolises 'the manipulated and unnatural "rebirth" of the weak, dying GDR into a new, renovated and polished Federal Republic, injected and revitalised with capitalism's "vitamin serum"'.[80] In this sense, the brutal power relationship implied by the reversal of Adele's aging process in *Lärchenau* alludes to the idea that the GDR was effectively 'colonised' by the FRG in 1990.[81] On yet another level, a gendered reading of the youth serum suggests that it is an allegory of the infantilisation of women under patriarchy, and particularly within bourgeois marriage. Hermann Glaser notes the German conservative preference for the figure of Gretchen in Goethe's *Faust I*, the adolescent country girl seduced by the older, more experienced man.

Glaser argues that, instead of Goethe's sovereign women, Helena and Iphigenie, German reactionaries always preferred Gretchen, depicted as 'ein sauberes Mädchen in einem sauberen Stübchen' / 'a clean little girl in a clean little room'.[82] This Gretchen cult inaugurated a reactionary ideology of chastity, which cast women as wayward girls who had to be brought to heel by marriage,[83] and in which the word 'Mädel' functions as a code word for the reversal of female emancipation.[84] This is what Konarske does to Adele: he takes a bold, ambitious woman and reduces her to a weak, vulnerable child. The Faustian hero creates his own Gretchen by artificial means.

By the end of the novel, Adele effectively resembles a 6-year-old girl. She escapes from her room and smashes up her husband's private laboratory. Then she runs away into the woods and is murdered by three men who speak Russian. The name of Adele's murderer is, ironically, Oleg, which is also the name of the Russian soldier who saved her after the Second World War. This recalls the Kleistian dichotomy in *Die Marquise von O. / The Marquise of O.*, in which the male figure, Graf F., also a Russian officer, alternates between two opposing faces: the angelic saviour and the demonic predator. As in Kleist's tale, the figures of Oleg and Gunter Konarske suggest the duality of the patriarchal male figure, who harbours the potential to save or to destroy the female character whom he is supposed to 'protect'.

Klocke has shown that the final section of Hensel's novel references a debate that occurred in the German media in 1999, when the philosopher Peter Sloterdijk gave a speech, 'Regeln für den Menschenpark' / 'Rules for the Human Zoo', in which he claimed that the humanist project of 'taming' humans by means of education had failed; instead he called for selective genetic breeding to take on the tasks that humanism has failed to fulfil.[85] Sloterdijk's call for the manipulation of human DNA reminded many of Nazi eugenics programmes, and his controversial remarks were debated in *Der Spiegel* and *Die Zeit*.[86] On 27 September 1999, the front cover of *Der Spiegel* bore the headline 'Gen-Projekt Übermensch' / 'Gene-Project Superman'. Inside was a long essay on human gene manipulation, including a warning from the US molecular biologist Liebe F. Cavalieri: genetic design will be 'more significant than splitting the atom, and no less dangerous'.[87] Page 312 of the same article featured the image of a mouse implanted with a human ear. *Lärchenau* alludes to this controversy when Konarske produces a mouse with a human eye on its back (*L*, 293). Subsequent comments in the letters page of *Der Spiegel* appeared under the title 'Gentechnik als Zaubermittel' / 'Gene Technology as a Magical Cure', making the same connection between genetics and magic that Hensel makes in *Lärchenau*.[88] The brave new world conjured up by Sloterdijk, in which geneticists engineer an improved version of humanity, is refuted in Hensel's novel, which shows the cruel, sadistic side of genetic research. *Lärchenau* suggests the dangers involved when privileged physicians are allowed to play God and experiment on human beings. Significantly, Konarske's experiments on his wife become more radical in the years after German reunification, suggesting that, since 1990, medical research has become deregulated as a result of privatisation and globalisation, and lends itself to abuse even more than under the previous socialist system. Konarske's West German colleague, Dickescheidt, later wins the Nobel Prize. In this way, the novel suggests that practices associated with Nazi racial science have persisted, even as the racial ideology that informed them has faded.

The dehumanisation of the female characters and the unethical human experimentation described in *Lärchenau* suggest the need for continuing debate about the ethics of medical research and the violence that occurs when some human beings are considered more valuable than others. In *Lärchenau*, the characters abuse their power. Konarske abuses his authority as a doctor; Hanswerner Giersch takes advantage of his position as a Stasi officer to abuse another character, Helge Hemlock, sexually; and 'Admiral' Kai uses his neo-Nazi followers as cannon fodder for a suicide mission. This situation underscores the dangers of patriarchal authority, as hierarchies are continually reproduced and members of the underclass are encouraged to abdicate responsibility for their own lives and to put their trust in scientific and political elites. This state of affairs resembles the situation of 'Bevormundung' / 'tutelage', which Immanuel Kant describes in 'Was ist Aufklärung?' / 'What is Enlightenment?' (1784). Kant's essay examines how people abdicate responsibility and allow their lives to be controlled by 'jene Vormünder, die die Oberaufsicht ... gütigst auf sich genommen haben'/ 'those guardians who have kindly taken supervision upon themselves.'[89] Hensel's *Lärchenau* gives readers a literal image of tutelage, as an adult woman is artificially reverted to childhood. Not only is Adele reduced to the moral status of a child, she is also reduced to the physical condition of a child. Her physical condition is the embodiment of her psychic absorption by her husband, her acquiescence in his authority. When she finally rebels at the end of the novel, she is murdered by male predators.

The engagement with German history in Hensel's *Lärchenau* offers lessons for the present. *Lärchenau* shows recurrent patterns of abusive relationships between victims and perpetrators. Only recently have historians such as Weindling conducted sustained research into the testimonies of the victims of Nazi medical atrocities. In this respect, fictions by Hensel (and Bachmann) are ahead of their time, not only because they sketch out investigative, hypothetical approaches to uncomfortable issues of perpetration and collaboration, but also because they explore the long-term effects of post-traumatic stress on the victims themselves.

Lärchenau invites its readers to reflect on the politics of the present day.[90] It reminds us that eugenics is firmly back on the agenda in contemporary Germany, as is evident from the racist bestsellers of Thilo Sarrazin and the racist policies of Alternative für Deutschland (AfD).[91] On 11 January 2017, André Wendt, an AfD delegate in the regional parliament in Saxony, enquired about the costs of sterilisation programmes for under-age migrants.[92] In the context of a shift towards the right in Germany and 'the West', *Lärchenau* is salutary reading. Although published five years before the AfD came into existence in 2013, the novel is a powerful antidote to the new far right in Germany. It even has a subplot in which Adele's son Timm joins a group of neo-Nazis, and dies in a botched military manoeuvre. This scenario echoes Grass's novella *Im Krebsgang / Crabwalk* (2002), which relates the story of Konny, the grandson of an East Prussian expellee who becomes a neo-Nazi, and Bachmann's notes for her planned *Todesarten / Ways of Dying* project, of which *Das Buch Franza* was to form part, which describe three neo-Nazi youths who murder each other in the forest.[93] Hensel's *Lärchenau* implies that these fascist behaviour patterns will be repeated by following generations, unless they are addressed. Those who do not learn from history will repeat it.[94] In this sense, Hensel's novel makes a vital contribution to the task of *Erinnerungsarbeit* / memory work. It excavates the moral minefield of German history precisely because it wants to defuse some of the unexploded bombs (and poisonous ideologies) still present today.

Let us conclude by returning to the point about literary genre. Literary critics often operate with genre categories, and, as we have seen, there is a tendency to pigeonhole Hensel as a grotesque satirist. Grotesque satire is certainly one element among others in her repertoire. However, such categorisation does Hensel a real disservice, because it consigns her to a genre that is considered inferior in status. This form of labelling is ultimately reductive. It prescribes a narrow interpretive horizon, and stands in the way of a serious consideration of her complex, challenging work. The same holds true for interpretations that foreground Hensel's use of fantasy elements. While Iztueta's analysis of *Lärchenau* unpacks many of the political implications of Hensel's text, it might be possible to question her appraisal of *Lärchenau* as belonging to the genre of the 'Gothic supernatural'.[95] The medical atrocities depicted in *Lärchenau* are outrageous and bizarre, but this does not mean that they are unrealistic. A glance at the historical record of Nazi medicine invites a different interpretation of *Lärchenau*, not as a satire or a gothic fantasy, but as a lucid reflection on the repercussions of the worst medical abuses in human history.

Notes

1. Hensel, *Lärchenau* (2008). Further references appear in the text, preceded by the abbreviation '*L*'. Unless otherwise specified, all translations in this chapter are mine.
2. Mitscherlich and Burmeister, *Wir haben ein Berührungstabu*.
3. Bachmann, *Das Buch Franza*, 124.
4. Bachmann, *The Book of Franza*, 128.
5. Mitscherlich and Mielke, *Das Diktat der Menschenverachtung*. Revised edition: *Medizin ohne Menschlichkeit*. English edition: *The Death Doctors*.
6. Nicosia and Huener, 'Introduction: Nazi Medicine in Historiographical Context', 1.
7. Schmidt, *Selektion in der Heilanstalt, 1939–1945*; Klee, *"Euthanasie" im NS–Staat*; Bock, *Zwangssterilisation*; Lifton, *The Nazi Doctors*; Müller-Hill, *Murderous Science*; Proctor, *Racial Hygiene*; Kater, *Doctors Under Hitler*; Gallagher, *By Trust Betrayed*.
8. Friedlander, *The Origins of the Nazi Genocide*.
9. Weindling, 'Nazi Human Experiments, 251.
10. Bachmann, *Das Buch Franza*, 187.
11. Bachmann, *The Book of Franza*, 85.
12. Bachmann, *Das Buch Franza*, 183.
13. Bachmann, *The Book of Franza*, 85.
14. Bachmann, *Das Buch Franza*, 65.
15. Bachmann, *Das Buch Franza*, 126.
16. Bird, *Women Writers*, 27.
17. Bird, *Women Writers*, 35.
18. Mitscherlich and Mitscherlich, *Die Unfähigkeit zu trauern*; *The Inability to Mourn*.
19. Haug, *Sexualisierung der Körper*, 11.
20. Koonz, *Mothers in the Fatherland*.
21. For a summary of the debate, see Leck, 'Theoretical Issues'.
22. Compare Stoehr, '"Organisierte Mütterlichkeit"'.
23. Kerstin Hensel, *Karzinom* (second version, 1981). Kerstin-Hensel-Archiv der Akademie der Künste, Berlin. Vorläufige Signatur 4, Ordner 'Dramatik'.
24. Mitscherlich, *Auf dem Weg zur vaterlosen Gesellschaft* / *Society Without A Father*.
25. Bachmann, *Malina*, 290 / *Malina*, 182.
26. Dahlke, 'Weibliche Männer, männliche Weiber', 68.
27. In *Das Buch Franza* there is also a character called Prohaska: he is one of Jordan's junior colleagues. Compare Bachmann, *Das Buch Franza*, 59–61.
28. Twark, 'Negotiating the Politics and Aesthetics of Satire', 139.
29. Compare Nicole Henneberg, 'Kerstin Hensel: Da hört die Jeschichte uff', *Der Tagesspiegel*, 28 May 2008 http://www.tagesspiegel.de/kultur/literatur/kerstin-hensel-da-hoert-die-jeschichte-uff/1243246.html (accessed 14 July 2019).
30. Marven, *Body and Narrative*, 10.
31. Twark, *Humor, Satire, and Identity*, 247.
32. On the connection with Grass, see Stephan, 'Laudatio Kerstin Hensel', 156.
33. On the link with Morgner, see Marven, 'The Trobadora's Legacy'.
34. Twark, *Humor, Satire, and Identity*, 198.
35. Twark, 'Negotiating the Politics and Aesthetics of Satire', 139.
36. On the connections between *Übermensch* and *Neuer Mensch*, see Twark, *Humor, Satire, and Identity*, 247 (footnote 78).

37. Compare Ulrich Rüdenauer, 'Untertan, Untertänchen. Kerstin Hensel erzählt in ihrem Roman *Falscher Hase* deutsche Lebensläufe', *Der Tagesspiegel*, 2 March 2005. http://www.tagesspiegel.de/kultur/untertan-untertaenchen-kerstin-hensel-erzaehlt-in-ihrem-roman/589110.html (accessed 14 July 2019).
38. Schröter, *Heinrich Mann*, 9–16.
39. Tucholsky, 'Mit Rute und Peitsche durch Preußen-Deutschland'.
40. Compare Dyck and Stewart, *The Uses of Humans in Experiment*.
41. Compare Homedes and Ugalde, *Clinical Trials in Latin America*.
42. Weindling, 'German Eugenics', 314.
43. Weindling, 'German Eugenics', 320–1.
44. Weindling, 'German Eugenics', 321–2.
45. Weindling, 'German Eugenics', 325.
46. Hensel's novel may contain an allusion to this history in the description of the notorious collection of preserved foetuses in the Charité hospital in Berlin.
47. Lifton, *The Nazi Doctors*, 43.
48. Bock, *Zwangssterilisation*, 376, 453.
49. Lifton, *The Nazi Doctors*, 274.
50. Lifton, *The Nazi Doctors*, 274.
51. Lifton, *The Nazi Doctors*, 271–2.
52. Lifton, *The Nazi Doctors*, 277. For testimonies of the victims of this procedure, see Bock, *Zwangssterilisation*, 455.
53. Lifton, *The Nazi Doctors*, 277.
54. Lifton, *The Nazi Doctors*, 43.
55. Lifton, *The Nazi Doctors*, 277.
56. Weindling, 'German Eugenics', 327.
57. The name 'Beate' derives from the Latin name 'Beatrix', meaning 'she who makes happy'. This is appropriate, given that she serves to gratify Konarske's sadistic tendencies.
58. Above his office desk, Rochus Lingott has a botanical print of *Wasserschierling* (*cicuta virosa*, northern water hemlock). The hemlock confirms his association with paganism, witchcraft and wizardry.
59. The children's home is named 'Anton Semjonowitsch Makarenko' after the pioneering Soviet educator of the 1920s.
60. Mitscherlich and Mitscherlich, *Die Unfähigkeit zu trauern*, 72.
61. Mitscherlich and Mitscherlich, *The Inability to Mourn*, 57.
62. Freud, 'Massenpsychologie und Ich-Analyse', 145. Compare Mitscherlich and Mitscherlich, *Die Unfähigkeit zu trauern*, 73.
63. Mitscherlich and Mitscherlich, *Die Unfähigkeit zu trauern*, 74.
64. Mitscherlich and Burmeister, *Wir haben ein Berührungstabu*, 10.
65. Compare Reichardt, *Authentizität und Gemeinschaft*; Barrett and McIntosh, *The Anti-Social Family*.
66. Klocke, *Inscription and Rebellion*, 161.
67. Bachmann, *Das Buch Franza*, 187.
68. Marven, *Body and Narrative*, 10.
69. Klocke, *Inscription and Rebellion*, 160.
70. Wolf, *Nachdenken über Christa T.*, 141.
71. This part of the plot alludes to Adele's favourite opera, Strauss's *Der Rosenkavalier / The Knight of the Rose*.
72. The racial theories of the Nazis can be traced back to Social Darwinism and early eugenicists such as Francis Galton (1822–1911). Compare Turda, 'Race, Science, and Eugenics'.
73. Tobita et al., 'From Hacking the Human Genome', 174.
74. Cyranoski and Reardon, 'Embryo Editing', 593.
75. Tobita et al., 'From Hacking the Human Genome', 179.
76. Cyranoski and Reardon, 'Embryo Editing', 594.
77. Specter, 'The Gene Hackers'.
78. Davies, *The Tale of Bluebeard in German Literature*.
79. Klocke, *Inscription and Rebellion*, 163.
80. Iztueta, 'Body and Grotesque', 157.
81. Iztueta, 'Body and Grotesque', 159.
82. Glaser, *Spießer-Ideologie*, 171.

83. Glaser, *Spießer-Ideologie*, 172: 'Ein Jahrhundert der "sorgsamen Gattinnen, treuen Mütter, frommen und keuschen Töchter" brach an, ein Jahrhundert der Keuschheitsideologie.' / 'A century of "caring spouses, faithful mothers and pious and chaste daughters" had begun, ... a century of chastity worship.' (Translation: Glaser, *The Cultural Roots of National Socialism*, 179.)
84. Glaser, *Spießer-Ideologie*, 171: 'Die ... Emanzipation der Frau wird rückgängig gemacht, ihre Entwertung und Entpersönlichung zu einem Element der deutschen Ideologie. "Mädel" ist ein Stichwort für diesen Vorgang'. / 'The process of female emancipation ... was reversed, her degradation and depersonalization became an element of German ideology. "Mädel" (maiden) is a key word in this process.' (Translation: Glaser, *The Cultural Roots of National Socialism*, 178.)
85. Klocke, *Inscription and Rebellion*, 158. Sloterdijk's claim that humanism tries to 'tame' human beings arguably shows that he wilfully misunderstands humanism.
86. Klocke, *Inscription and Rebellion*, 158.
87. Marco Evers, Klaus Franke and Johann Grolle, 'Zucht und deutsche Ordnung', *Der Spiegel*, 39 (27 September 1999), 300–16 (303).
88. 'Briefe: Gentechnik als Zaubermittel' *Der Spiegel* 41 (11 October 1999), 8.
89. Kant, 'Beantwortung der Frage: Was ist Aufklärung?', in Kant, *Was ist Aufklärung?*, 55. English translation: http://www.columbia.edu/acis/ets/CCREAD/etscc/kant.html (accessed 14 July 2019). On Kant's essay in the context of this volume's concerns, see also Mererid Puw Davies's chapter.
90. For a reading of Hensel in terms of eco-criticism, see Probst, *Vakante Landschaft*.
91. On Thilo Sarrazin, see Stanicic, *Anti-Sarrazin*.
92. Danys, 'Sterilisation von Flüchtlingskindern?'.
93. Bachmann, *'Todesarten'-Projekt*, III.2, 713–6.
94. Mitscherlich and Burmeister, *Wir haben ein Berührungstabu*, 10.
95. Iztueta, 'Body and Grotesque', 145–6.

Bibliography

Bachmann, Ingeborg. *Malina: Roman*. Frankfurt am Main: Suhrkamp, 1980.

Bachmann, Ingeborg. *Malina: A Novel*, translated by Philip Boehm. New York: Holmes and Meier, 1990.

Bachmann, Ingeborg. *The Book of Franza and Requiem for Fanny Goldmann*, translated by Peter Filkins. Evanston, IL: Northwestern University Press, 1999.

Bachmann, Ingeborg. *Das Buch Franza; Requiem für Fanny Goldmann*, edited by Monika Albrecht and Dirk Göttsche. Munich: Piper, 2004.

Bachmann, Ingeborg. *'Todesarten'-Projekt: Kritische Ausgabe*, edited by Monika Albrecht and Dirk Göttsche, 4 vols. Munich: Piper, 2005.

Barrett, Michèle and Mary McIntosh. *The Anti-Social Family*. London: NLB, 1982.

Bird, Stephanie. *Women Writers and National Identity: Bachmann, Duden, Özdamar*. Cambridge: Cambridge University Press, 2003.

Bock, Gisela. *Zwangssterilisation im Nationalsozialismus: Studien zur Rassenpolitik und Frauenpolitik*. Opladen: Westdeutscher Verlag, 1986.

Cyranoski, David and Sara Reardon. 'Embryo Editing Sparks Epic Debate', *Nature* 520, no. 7549 (2015): 593–94.

Dahlke, Birgit. 'Weibliche Männer, männliche Weiber: Gender in Transit'. In *Kerstin Hensel* (Contemporary German Writers), edited by Beth Linklater and Birgit Dahlke, 67–77. Cardiff: University of Wales Press, 2002.

Danys, David. 'Sterilisation von Flüchtlingskindern?', *Der Freitag*, 14 February 2017. Accessed 29 September 2019. https://www.freitag.de/autoren/david-danys/sterilisation-von-fluechtlingskindern.

Davies, Mererid Puw. *The Tale of Bluebeard in German Literature: From the Eighteenth Century to the Present*. Oxford: Oxford University Press, 2001.

Dyck, Erika and Larry Stewart, ed. *The Uses of Humans in Experiment: Perspectives from the 17th to the 20th Century*. Leiden: Brill, 2016.

Freud, Sigmund. 'Massenpsychologie und Ich-Analyse'. In *Gesammelte Werke, Band XIII*, by Sigmund Freud, 71–161. Frankfurt am Main: Fischer, 1987.

Friedlander, Henry. *The Origins of the Nazi Genocide: From Euthanasia to the Final Solution*. Chapel Hill: University of North Carolina Press, 1995.

Gallagher, Hugh Gregory. *By Trust Betrayed: Patients, Physicians, and the License to Kill in the Third Reich*. New York: H. Holt, 1990.

Glaser, Hermann. *Spießer-Ideologie: Von der Zerstörung des deutschen Geistes im 19. und 20. Jahrhundert und dem Aufstieg des Nationalsozialismus*. Frankfurt am Main: Fischer, 1986.

Glaser, Hermann. *The Cultural Roots of National Socialism*, translated by Ernest A. Menze. London: Croom Helm, 1978.

Haug, Frigga, ed. *Sexualisierung der Körper* (Frauenformen). Berlin: Argument-Verlag, 1983.

Hensel, Kerstin. *Lärchenau: Roman*. Munich: btb, 2010.

Homedes, Nuria and Antonio Ugalde, eds. *Clinical Trials in Latin America: Where Ethics and Business Clash*. Cham: Springer, 2014.

Iztueta, Garbiñe. 'Body and Grotesque as Self-Disruption in Kerstin Hensel's Gothic East(ern) German Novel *Lärchenau* (2008)'. In *Strategies of Humor in Post-Unification German Literature, Film, and Other Media*, edited by Jill E. Twark, 143–64. Newcastle upon Tyne: Cambridge Scholars Publishing, 2011.

Kant, Immanuel. *Was ist Aufklärung? Aufsätze zur Geschichte und Philosophie*. 4th ed. Göttingen: Vandenhoeck und Ruprecht, 1994.

Kater, Michael H. *Doctors under Hitler*. Chapel Hill: University of North Carolina Press, 1989.

Klee, Ernst. *"Euthanasie" im NS–Staat: Die "Vernichtung lebensunwerten Lebens"*. Frankfurt am Main: Fischer, 1983.

Klocke, Sonja E. *Inscription and Rebellion: Illness and the Symptomatic Body in East German Literature*. Rochester, NY: Camden House, 2015.

Koonz, Claudia. *Mothers in the Fatherland: Women, the Family, and Nazi Politics*. New York: St Martin's Press, 1986.

Leck, Ralph M. 'Theoretical Issues: Conservative Empowerment and the Gender of Nazism: Paradigms of Power and Complicity in German Women's History', *Journal of Women's History* 12, no. 2 (2000): 147–69.

Lifton, Robert Jay. *The Nazi Doctors: Medical Killing and the Psychology of Genocide*. London: Macmillan, 1986.

Marven, Lyn. *Body and Narrative in Contemporary Literatures in German: Herta Müller, Libuše Moníková, and Kerstin Hensel*. Oxford: Clarendon Press, 2005.

Marven, Lyn. 'The Trobadora's Legacy: Two Generations of GDR Women Writers'. In *Women's Writing in Western Europe: Gender, Generation and Legacy*, edited by Adalgisa Giorgio and Julia Waters, 54–68. Newcastle upon Tyne: Cambridge Scholars Publishing, 2007.

Mitscherlich, Alexander. *Society without the Father: A Contribution to Social Psychology*, translated by Eric Mosbacher. New York: Schocken Books, 1970.

Mitscherlich, Alexander. *Auf dem Weg zur vaterlosen Gesellschaft: Ideen zur Sozialpsychologie*. Munich: Piper, 1973.

Mitscherlich, Alexander and Fred Mielke. *Das Diktat der Menschenverachtung: Eine Dokumentation*. Heidelberg: Lambert Schneider, 1947.

Mitscherlich, Alexander and Fred Mielke. *Medizin ohne Menschlichkeit: Dokumente des Nürnberger Ärzteprozesses*. Frankfurt am Main: Fischer, 1960.

Mitscherlich, Alexander and Fred Mielke. *The Death Doctors*, translated by James Cleugh. London: Elek Books, 1962.

Mitscherlich, Alexander and Margarete Mitscherlich. *The Inability to Mourn: Principles of Collective Behavior*, translated by Beverley R. Placzek. New York: Grove Press, 1975.

Mitscherlich, Alexander and Margarete Mitscherlich. *Die Unfähigkeit zu trauern: Grundlagen kollektiven Verhaltens*. Munich: Piper, 2012.

Mitscherlich, Margarete and Brigitte Burmeister. *Wir haben ein Berührungstabu*. Hamburg: Klein Verlag, 1991.

Müller-Hill, Benno. *Murderous Science: Elimination by Scientific Selection of Jews, Gypsies, and Others, Germany, 1933–1945*, translated by George Fraser. Oxford: Oxford University Press, 1987.

Nicosia, Francis R. and Jonathan Huener. 'Introduction: Nazi Medicine in Historiographical Context'. In *Medicine and Medical Ethics in Nazi Germany: Origins, Practices, Legacies*, edited by Francis R. Nicosia and Jonathan Huener, 1–12. New York: Berghahn Books, 2008.

Probst, Inga. *Vakante Landschaft: Postindustrielle Geopoetik bei Kerstin Hensel, Wolfgang Hilbig und Volker Braun*. Würzburg: Königshausen & Neumann, 2016.

Proctor, Robert. *Racial Hygiene: Medicine under the Nazis*. Cambridge, MA: Harvard University Press, 1988.

Reichardt, Sven. *Authentizität und Gemeinschaft: Linksalternatives Leben in den siebziger und frühen achtziger Jahren*. Berlin: Suhrkamp, 2014.

Schmidt, Gerhard. *Selektion in der Heilanstalt, 1939–1945*. Stuttgart: Evangelisches Verlagswerk, 1965.

Schröter, Klaus. *Heinrich Mann: "Untertan" – "Zeitalter" – Wirkung: Drei Aufsätze*. Stuttgart: Metzler, 1971.

Specter, Michael. 'The Gene Hackers', *The New Yorker*, 16 November 2015. Accessed 27 September 2019. https://www.newyorker.com/magazine/2015/11/16/the-gene-hackers.

Stanicic, Sascha. *Anti-Sarrazin: Argumente gegen Rassismus, Islamfeindlichkeit und Sozialdarwinismus*. Cologne: PapyRossa, 2011.

Stephan, Inge. 'Laudatio Kerstin Hensel'. In *Kerstin Hensel* (Contemporary German Writers), edited by Beth Linklater and Birgit Dahlke, 153–61. Cardiff: University of Wales Press, 2002.

Stoehr, Irene. '"Organisierte Mütterlichkeit": Zur Politik der deutschen Frauenbewegung um 1900'. In *Frauen suchen ihre Geschichte: Historische Studien zum 19. und 20. Jahrhundert*, edited by Karin Hausen, 221–49. Munich: C.H. Beck, 1983.

Tobita, Takamasa, Jorge Guzman-Lepe and Alexandra Collin de l'Hortet. 'From Hacking the Human Genome to Editing Organs', *Organogenesis* 11, no. 4 (2015): 173–82.

Tucholsky, Kurt. 'Mit Rute und Peitsche durch Preußen-Deutschland'. In *Heinrich Mann: Texte zu seiner Wirkungsgeschichte in Deutschland*, edited by Renate Werner, 113. Munich: Deutscher Taschenbuch Verlag, 1977.

Turda, Marius. 'Race, Science, and Eugenics in the Twentieth Century'. In *The Oxford Handbook of the History of Eugenics*, edited by Alison Bashford and Philippa Levine, 62–79. Oxford: Oxford University Press, 2010.

Twark, Jill E. *Humor, Satire, and Identity: Eastern German Literature in the 1990s*. Berlin: Walter de Gruyter, 2007.

Twark, Jill E. 'Negotiating the Politics and Aesthetics of Satire: Satirical Novels in the GDR and Beyond'. In *Rereading East Germany: The Literature and Film of the GDR*, edited by Karen Leeder, 126–42. Cambridge: Cambridge University Press, 2015.

Weindling, Paul. 'German Eugenics and the Wider World: Beyond the Racial State'. In *The Oxford Handbook of the History of Eugenics*, edited by Alison Bashford and Philippa Levine, 315–31. Oxford: Oxford University Press, 2010.

Weindling, Paul. 'Nazi Human Experiments: The Victims' Perspective and the Post-Second World War Discourse'. In *The Uses of Humans in Experiment: Perspectives from the 17th to the 20th Century*, edited by Erika Dyck and Larry Stewart, 240–59. Leiden: Brill, 2016.

Wolf, Christa. *Nachdenken über Christa T*. Munich: Deutscher Taschenbuch Verlag, 1997.

9

Burnout Therapy, Cool Conduct and Cold Cinema

Annie Ring

Preface

This chapter makes the case for viewing therapies used in the treatment of work-related burnout as an inhuman medical apparatus, geared as they are toward exploiting recovered health for recovering profits. The global financial crisis of 2008 had major health effects on contemporary workforces, but governments and employers in the global North have dealt with these effects not via systemic change but by means of therapeutic treatment of individuals as if they were at fault for the structural insecurities besetting their workplaces and societies. To analyse the inhumanity underpinning burnout therapies used in work settings, this chapter offers close readings of Katharina Pethke's direct-cinema documentary of 2009, *In dir muss brennen / Burning Within*, which is treated here as a work of cold cinema.

This way of viewing the film is guided by leading cultural theories of burnout and self-optimisation, particularly from German-language and German studies contexts. It references in addition more long-standing analyses of psychic responses to crisis beginning with writing by Helmuth Plessner and Georg Simmel from the early twentieth century, when German-language philosophy contributed its most important insights into subjectivity in the modern age. This chapter draws also on Helmut Lethen's influential analysis of the stream of early twentieth-century German thought he terms *Cool Conduct* (1994). Against the background of these German philosophies of subjectivity in crisis, the chapter draws out the entrainment of cool, calm, temperate conduct in the recipients of contemporary burnout therapy, and argues for a rejection of the complicity of those therapies with new codes of cool conduct, which (among other things) restore the burnt-out worker's health for the sake of further exhausting work. The training of a cool, profitable subject is made starkly visible by the screen aesthetic employed by Pethke, whose work of cold cinema generates images that are abrupt, laconic, empty and chilling in service of a powerful critique of the self-optimising subjectivity elicited by neo-liberal economies after the global financial crisis.

To study burnout from the perspective of languages and cultural studies means considering the subjectivity it interacts with: who gets to be burnt-out, and who can access therapeutic treatment? It also means analysing the language that has been developing alongside the syndrome, a language that both shapes the experience and treatment of burnout *and* can provide ways into critiquing the invidious problem whereby treatment does not cure the syndrome but rather exploits the patient's recovery from it. The discussion that follows, therefore, is attentive to the underexplored metaphors through which current therapeutic practices handle burnout, namely the metaphors of temperature endemic to the syndrome's name. It approaches these metaphors by means of cultural theories not only of burnout and self-optimisation, but also of coolness and subjective sovereignty, theories that can help us to understand the experiences of individuality and often of isolation that the syndrome of burnout implies. Close reading demonstrates how Pethke's film offers a valuable aesthetic response to the burnout epidemic, and by looking closely at the film in relation to theories of subjectivity in crisis, the chapter propose a much-needed critical viewpoint on burnout, one capable of challenging the inhumanity underlying its causes and indeed much of its treatment in the present day.

Introduction

Burnout is the defining illness of contemporary capitalism. A cause of grave economic concern to global-North nations in recent years, the rise in burnout and related stress syndromes has led the UK government to instantiate a 'Mindful Nation' programme to improve the health of its citizens prophylactically, meanwhile Germany has seen the founding of a Federal association for the prevention of burnout, the Deutsche Bundesverband für Burnout-Prophylaxe und Prävention, and the problem of burnout occupies countless news articles in the contemporary

German-language press. Burnout is a relatively young medical condition, first diagnosed only in 1974, but in the intervening years it has become a matter of significant economic concern, with World Health Organization statements indicating a cost of billions of dollars each year. Indeed, burnout is anathema to economic models focused on growth because of the slowing down and halting of work that the syndrome implies – however beneficial such slowing down and stopping may be for the individual and the environment. Thus, burnout is a major concern for current governments precisely because of its place in the involved relationship between health, economic sustainability and the way we work in the present day. Moreover, burnout has been linked to technological changes since the turn of the millennium that mean workers in certain, often white-collar, industries are now able to take work home and even to bed with them.

There has been a boom in new therapies evolving in response to the burnout epidemic, to help burnt-out members of the workforce, especially white-collar or middle-class workers, return to productivity. Burnout treatments are different to the training or coaching that white-collar employees regularly receive to boost career success, and they include standard psychodynamic and cognitive-behavioural therapies delivered by therapists or coaches, often contracted by employers directly, or sought out by freelance workers, to improve the working subject's health, and thus recover profits.

A substantial ambivalence is therefore attached to the status of burnout therapies as medical or paramedical interventions, and in what follows I argue that they represent an inhuman medical apparatus, one that is cruel, barbaric and lacking in human compassion. Burnout therapies are complicit in governments' and businesses' attempts to boost productivity after the global financial crisis of 2008, and as such must be considered medical interventions that do not support the burnt-out patient to meaningful recovery but rather promote the retrieval of her ability to work profitably again through targeted behavioural techniques. As I show in the following pages, these structurally complicit therapies are also ideologically implicated in the suffering of their patients in that they encourage a set of temperate, sovereign behaviours through which the burnt-out employee or freelancer can cool down to the degree that she can return to work, and once back at work behave in a manner that makes her more effective in generating profits but not less vulnerable to the recurrence of burnout. It is to this specialised, structurally complicit and ideologically implicated medical apparatus of burnout therapy, and to the problematically cool conduct it encourages in burnout patients, that this chapter is devoted.

Burnout has risen as a mass syndrome in the global North in conjunction with the global financial crisis and the recessions that have followed it, as part of which we have seen the emergence of a capitalism defined by austerities and resulting inequalities in many areas, including access to health and healthcare. These conditions make burnout a rich but problematic object of study in this volume's approach to medical humanity and inhumanity. Moreover, the approach behind this volume implies analysing the aesthetic forms that have developed alongside the lived symptoms of ill health, in this case the forms that shape the experience of burnout as a syndrome and its treatment, but also provide ways into criticising the invidious problem whereby treatment does not cure syndrome.

In what follows, I therefore pay attention to the metaphors through which current therapeutic practices handle burnout, particularly the metaphors of temperature endemic to the syndrome's name, which have been neglected in scholarship to date on the syndrome. With these metaphors of temperature in mind, I analyse burnout as depicted in Katharina Pethke's direct-cinema documentary *In dir muss brennen / Burning Within* (Germany, 2009). Pethke's final degree film at the Kunsthochschule für Medien in Cologne, *In dir muss brennen* focuses on the culture of self-improvement and resulting burnout that affect the contemporary white-collar worker as she labours to keep unsustainable economies going.

Pethke's film is one of a small but important corpus of critical German-language documentaries made since the global financial crisis in the mode of direct cinema, a mode in which the film-maker records footage from historical actuality and presents it on screen without voice-over commentary. Other such works include Harun Farocki's late film *Ein neues Produkt / A New Product* (Germany, 2014) and Carmen Losmann's *Work Hard – Play Hard* (Germany, 2011). These documentaries are largely unknown outside of German-speaking Europe, but they excel in their critical engagement with capitalism's current core disciplining regimes of surveillance and economic precarity. The observations of these films are made possible by the decision of their directors to use the fly-on-the-wall, unnarrated technique of direct cinema, a decision indicating the film-makers' goal of empowering viewers to draw their own conclusions. *In dir muss brennen* is the only one of these films to focus on the health effects and therapeutic interventions accompanying the processes of surveillance and careful self-optimisation that together keep the contemporary white-collar worker functioning profitably.

Taking preponderant neo-liberal discourses and practices of self-optimisation at their word, I suggest here that we consider the therapies shown in Pethke's film as interacting with a disciplining regime I refer to as a *new code of conduct* concerning how subjects of late capitalism must comport themselves in order to live and work well after the global financial crisis. In doing so, I am adapting the work of Helmut Lethen, who wrote in the 1990s of the post-crisis era of Weimar Germany as a society in which the trauma of the First World War and modernity were processed by means of new 'Verhaltenslehren' / 'codes of conduct',[1] that advocated an overall cooling down of behaviour. Lethen found this code of cool conduct represented with special precision in the anthropological writing of Helmuth Plessner, but it can also be found reflected by thinkers stemming from surprisingly distant points on the political spectrum and vastly different intellectual fields, such as Bertolt Brecht and Ernst Jünger, as well as in the pre-Weimar writing of Georg Simmel.

Applying this key approach from within German cultural studies to the depiction of burnout and burnout therapy in Pethke's disturbing documentary has two key benefits. First, it offers a framework for analysing the frightening phenomenon by which contemporary white-collar workers are schooled in a new code of conduct, one communicated via surveillance, that includes the imperatives to work creatively and with enjoyment, to spend productive leisure time and, if necessary, submit to therapies and training that render an ailing subject fit to work again. Pethke's film depicts the new code of conduct for the contemporary white-collar worker in action: the demands of that code to self-optimise and be productive in service of a struggling economy are the source at once of her subjects' burnout and the goal of their, as it were, temperature-regulating therapies. Indeed, the second benefit of applying Lethen's theory of cool conduct to this film set in the contemporary era of capitalism in which, as the bestselling German–Korean philosopher of psychology, Byung-Chul Han argues, the subject has changed into a project of controlled self-improvement, helps us understand better the new crisis era into which capitalism's recent codes of conduct and their attendant illnesses, such as burnout, are emerging. Revisiting the crisis behaviours invoked in post-First World War German cultural theory offers a creative new way in to thinking about the relationship between the global financial crisis and the cultures of (self-)exploitation it has been used to justify.

I make the case below that there is a fruitful metaphorical link to be made between the temperature implied by a burnout diagnosis and the coolness of conduct that Plessner and others were advocating in response to crisis in Germany in the early twentieth century. The specific quality of burnout in diagnosis, and yet an element so far unexplored in scholarly approaches to the illness, is the element of a hot, indeed overheated passion. The burnout patient cannot produce any longer, and so she must be brought back to a cooler, more productive state. Subjectivity figures in this context as suffering an irregularity of temperature, and so a process of cooling down must begin. Furthermore, the metaphorical field of temperature guides the approach to burnout and burnout therapies within Pethke's film itself, such that – despite its titular promise of heat – the film develops a markedly cold aesthetic. It insists on harsh editing techniques that interrupt passionate moments in the diegesis, and returns again and again to chilling intermezzi filmed in empty office buildings, sequences overlaid with calm voice-overs exhorting the burnt-out subject to seek both blame and solution for the syndrome within herself. By viewing Pethke's film as a work of cold cinema, I demonstrate how she guides her audience to see and feel more critically about the ideal states of mind that are being promoted for the subject of contemporary capitalism. That subject must feel passionate enough about her work to ignite a fire of passion in others, but she must also be able to act coolly enough to set the right boundaries for herself, and so keep on working in just the right balance of sustainability for her own health while also producing profit – caring in this way for the health of the economy around her.

German-Language Accounts of Burnout

Comparative literature scholar Anna Katharina Schaffner looks back in her book *Exhaustion: A History* at the earliest understandings of burnout from the first diagnoses in the 1970s onwards. Thus she traces how the influential medical researcher Hans Selye, born in Vienna in 1907, analysed burnout as a result of excessive stress reactions that he claimed the body has to all stimuli and therefore cannot entirely avoid.[2] However, looking beyond Selye's work at the meaning of burnout today, Schaffner necessarily considers the role played by now ubiquitous personal communication devices, and she quotes the work of Jonathan Crary, who has adopted the term '24/7' for referring to the dominant mode of time as it is defined now by continuously awake technologies.[3] One effect of the continuous status as 'awake' or 'on' that pertains to personal devices is that sleep cycles are interrupted, leading to significant detriments to health. Burnout is, indeed, only one of the health conditions that arise due to such changes in sleep patterns and the broader experience of time.

Schaffner's account of burnout also examines the differing models according to which English- and German-speaking thinkers have explained the syndrome's causes. To exemplify English-language thinking about the syndrome, she quotes from a self-help book by Andrew and Elizabeth Proctor, who state encouragingly that burnout is a disease of the successful.[4] In that view, one must be goal-driven, a high achiever and an exception to some imagined rule of mediocrity, if one is to catch the syndrome of the successful worker – burnout. Far removed from the highly individualising tone of praise for the 'good' burnt-out worker in the Proctors' book, however, speculation about the causes of burnout is more system-critical in German-speaking thinking. Thus, Schaffner writes, in recent German-language analysis, burnout has been blamed on:

> radical changes in the organization and value of work. These include the transformation of an industrial into a service economy, the subjectivization of work as well as the adverse effects of globalization and resulting economic uncertainties, such as ever fiercer competition and more precarious work arrangements.[5]

One of the common factors connecting the radical changes to work in the past few decades is what Schaffner here terms 'subjectivisation'. By this, we can understand the contemporary demand to bring the self, with its thoughts, its body and emotions, into jobs that, in the white-collar context at least, are much more about people and service than about the production of goods, as was the case after the Industrial Revolution. Schaffner observes analysis of such systemic factors in the rise of burnout occurring much more regularly in German-language studies, suggesting a trend for more critical, economically informed approaches to the syndrome in the German-speaking context.

Such a critical economic approach as Schaffner finds in recent German-language thought about burnout is needed because burnout is not only the most defining but also one of the most socially divisive syndromes besetting contemporary capitalism. Despite the signs that burnout is being recognised as a widespread problem in governmental approaches in both English- and German-speaking countries, and although burnout is referred to in influential German news weekly *Der Spiegel* in several features as a 'Volksleiden',[6] the term for an epidemic whose etymology carries echoes of a malady *of*, or even *for*, the people, burnout must also be seen as an exclusive syndrome. Admittedly, burnout can affect people working in all kinds of settings, including settings that imply more physically intensive labour. However, the syndrome is diagnosed with most regularity in wealthy countries; furthermore, it tends to be diagnosed in privileged economic niches within those countries.

Not only does the diagnosis of burnout indicate wealth in particular kinds of capital, the syndrome also has a close relationship to a mode of self-optimising subjectivity that, as sociologist Ulrich Bröckling observes, is most often found among educated 'Wissensarbeiterinnen',[7] workers in white-collar milieux who are trained not only in profession-specific knowledge but also in more generalised techniques of self-optimisation. This mode of subjectivity, professionally knowledgeable but also making use of techniques from coaching, psychodynamic or behavioural therapies to strive for success, has proven of great interest to Han. Han has called the beginning of the twenty-first century a 'neuronal age',[8] claiming this era is dominated by discourses around depression, ADHD and burnout. Han sees these as the new epidemics, replacing bacterial diseases in privileged parts of the world as central medical concerns.[9] Han links the increase in 'neuronal' illnesses to the well-documented trend in which subjectivity in wealthier milieux has come to resemble a project.

For Bröckling, the self as project has become 'ein historisches Apriori unseres Selbstverhältnisses' / 'an historical *a priori* governing how we relate to ourselves',[10] and Han agrees, describing the contortions of logic underpinning this new historical self-understanding: 'Wir glauben heute, dass wir kein unterworfenes Subjekt, sondern ein freies sich immer neu entwerfendes, neu erfindendes Projekt sind.... Nun erweist sich dieses Projekt selbst als eine Zwangsfigur, sogar als eine effizientere Form der Subjektivierung und Unterwerfung.' / 'We believe today that we are not an oppressed subject, but rather a free, constantly self-refashioning and self-reinventing project.... Now this project is proving to be a form of oppression itself – even a more efficient form of subjection and oppression.'[11] Bröckling's and Han's assertions concerning the work the contemporary subject does on herself as a project are reflected in a wide range of current social sciences and humanities approaches to the entrepreneurial subject, but they also build on long-standing theories of subjectivation from within continental philosophy.

The change from a suppressed subject to an increasingly self-responsibilised subject was one that Michel Foucault already noted in his late work. The best-known model of modern surveillance is the panopticon, a prison design produced by Jeremy Bentham in 1785 and famously analysed by Foucault, in which the possibility of constant surveillance by a guard in a central watchtower efficiently polices the prisoner's behaviour. But in the five years before his death, Foucault reviewed the theory of power he had developed throughout his career, and in his last lectures set out the terms of a more dynamic model of power/knowledge,

Security, a system of open borders and more ambient surveillance. Such systems, Foucault believed, were replacing the strict structures of nineteenth-century discipline with the softer touch of liberalism.[12] The entrepreneurial subject analysed by Schaffner, Han and Bröckling closely resembles the subject of Foucault's later analysis of power in the more liberal, flexible model of Security. Whereas the disciplinary subject was compelled by architectural and legal conditions to obey, the entrepreneurial subject is incited by the burden of isolation and the ever-present threat of economic precarity – admittedly too by the more positive draw of creativity and flexible working – to perform.

Burnout Therapy as Inhuman Medical Apparatus in Pethke's *In dir muss brennen*

The exhausting effects of contemporary cultures of self-optimisation are represented with chilling clarity in Pethke's documentary, *In dir muss brennen*. In the film we see a montage of uncommented scenes from therapy and coaching sessions for employees in Germany who are suffering from burnout in the time immediately after the global financial crisis. All of these therapeutic interventions are based on medical or psychotherapeutic approaches, but they are delivered by companies offering tailored approaches in 'neurocoaching' and 'Persönlichkeitsentwicklung' / 'personal development',[13] approaches designed to improve employee performance for the benefit of profits. Despite the known high rate of burnout across the global North, and in apparent denial of its link to increasingly precarious working conditions even for the relatively wealthy, the discourse that unites all of the therapies shown in Pethke's film is that of a personal responsibility. Such responsibility is expressed in a regime of tireless self-optimisation that does not stop with a burnout diagnosis but must indeed continue if patients are to recover and return to work. The film shows how these therapies and therapeutic 'coaching' approaches make up the medicalised end of the countless strategies for self-optimisation in contemporary working cultures. In that sense, the film reveals contemporary burnout therapies as forming an inhuman medical apparatus, one that operates within a broader array of strategies currently being implemented for the all-round improvement of the self in service of economic recovery after the financial crisis.

Paradigmatically, in the film's opening lines, rhetoric coach Jörg Breuer states 'Die wichtigste Tätigkeit, die wir Menschen tagtäglich zu verrichten haben, das ist die Arbeit an uns selbst' / 'The most important task for us humans is the work we carry out on ourselves'. Pethke then goes on to depict this self-improvement work introduced by Breuer the coach in a slow montage characterised by abrupt cuts between sequences, such that the documentary depicts a long procession of thematically connected but distinct events in the recovery of its burnt-out subjects. What we learn from this montage is that the recovery of the burnt-out employee in middle-class Germany takes place via brutal, often medicalised processes of isolation in service of lonely self-improvement. Although the film succeeds in conveying the collective problems of burnout and its inhuman treatment, its greatest achievement is its joint thematic and aesthetic treatment of a host of isolated individuals all suffering from the same syndrome and similar therapies but without connection to one another.

The film uses effective distantiating techniques to emphasise the isolation of the burnt-out worker in therapy. Thus, in a *mise-en-abyme* depiction of a television show being filmed, the documentary records how a guest on business coach Ingo Vogels's television show describes his experience of burnout as: 'ein ungeheimer und unheimlicher Druck der auf mich lastet' / 'a striking, uncanny pressure that bears down upon me'. This figure is alone in coping with the pressure of burnout, as we see when the empathic response that might be expected to follow such a statement fails to emerge. Vogels, who is listening to his burnt-out guest describe the pain of his symptoms, is above all concerned with the effects on the guest's work as a salesman. He bemoans the negative effect of burnout here, that the guest's suffering will come across to consumers and stop them wanting to buy products from him.

Vogels's advice is to cultivate happiness by stepping into what he terms a 'Glücksquadrat' / 'square of happiness': a space of positive emotion into which the guest can imaginatively step, improve his posture, and so, apparently, recover from the negative experience of burnout. Vogels's concern is symptomatic of his status as a sales consultant specialising in emotional marketing. The tenor of his concern for his television guest, with its emphasis on a return to working productivity via the cultivation of pleasant emotions, bypasses a deeper therapeutic or indeed economic exploration of the burnout. Even more troublingly, such bypassing of a psychological or structural understanding of burnout also characterises the therapeutic sessions Pethke filmed for the documentary.

One such scene of individual therapy for burnt-out white-collar workers is so significant that Pethke breaks it up into short passages that unfold as a narrative throughout the film. In this unfolding narrative, we encounter a freelance writer, in therapy because she has lost confidence in her work and is unable to write. She is receiving one-to-one therapy with Sebastian Purps-Pardigol, an organisational consultant who uses contemporary neuroscience in business-oriented therapy. Purps-Pardigol works with the freelancer using a range of talking-therapy and practical, coaching approaches to help her let go of negative feelings about her capabilities. As seen in Figure 9.1, his therapeutic technique includes a shocking practice in which the woman has to push her body weight against an arrow pointing to the most vulnerable part of her throat and, by breaking the arrow with her body weight, break through her fears. This bizarre practice runs alongside talking therapy in which the writer gives voice to her self-doubts.

The scene of therapy in which the freelance writer must use her body weight to break the arrow is frightening. She flaps her arms dramatically, like wings, before trying to break the arrow by walking towards it, its point touching her throat. In the climactic sequence of the film, the writer unquestioningly goes along with this extreme act to try to produce a self who can work without so much fear.

Other therapies shown in the film are less physically risky, but still emotionally demanding. For instance, we see a patient with a stress-related gambling addiction undergoing a blend of therapies including hypnotism, affirmation practice and drama therapy, involving imaginative role-playing with his younger self. The patient here is being treated by Kurt-Georg Scheible, whose professional profile lists him as an 'Erfolgsverhandler' / 'negotiator of success'. As part of Scheible's

Figure 9.1 Extreme approaches to burnout in Katharina Pethke, *In dir muss brennen / Burning Within* (2009). © Bolbrinker/Doberenz/2Pilots

treatment, the patient chooses a Playmobil figure that gives his younger self advice on how to achieve a greater sense of security, as seen in Figure 9.2. The advice he gives his younger self is to let everything go, go out into nature, listen to himself and then follow the impulses that arise in that cool, undisturbed space.

The theme of self-improvement and cultivation of positive emotions in the isolated self, rather than critical, collective or deeper therapeutic insights is also present in sequences in which we watch Emotional Freedom Technique (EFT) therapist Christa Graves making videos for online distribution. These videos teach a balancing out of negative emotions through affirmative statements spoken by the patient while tapping key acupressure points on her own body. In the EFT videos, Graves offers a therapeutic practice that can be watched and mimicked at home, presumably again in isolation, and the sequences that show Graves making the videos furnish a further example of the film's success in using distantiation to isolate its figures. As seen in Figure 9.3, Graves records herself against a green screen, the *sine qua non* of projectability, reminding the viewer in one simple, bright colour of film's potential to create compelling images and thus invoke new realities. Soon afterwards, we see Graves picking the background to accompany her performance, and she chooses another green screen, one of grass photographed in close up with a blurry blue sky in the background.

Figure 9.2 Playing for success in Katharina Pethke, *In dir muss brennen/ Burning Within* (2009). © Bolbrinker/Doberenz/2Pilots

Figure 9.3 Distantiation techniques: the green screen as *sine qua non* of projectability, Katharina Pethke, *In dir muss brennen / Burning Within* (2009). © Bolbrinker/Doberenz/2Pilots

Against this backdrop of studied, cool calmness, Graves introduces her therapeutic approach, through which the patient may experience temporary relief but, we must assume, no genuine recovery. This is because the aim of the EFT therapy is to heal the patient without economic or psychotherapeutic analysis, analysis that might bring the patient to question the isolating project of self-optimisation in itself.

In Pethke's edit, these troubling scenes of individualising self-improvement therapy follow inexorably one on from the next, with the most shocking among them returning in key moments of the film's narrative. Another important recurring figure in the film, and a double figure in the regime of work on the self, is the motivational coach Jörg Breuer, who is first shown teaching coaches for the unemployed to use slogans such as 'Ich muss! Ich will! Ich kann!' / 'I must! I want to! I can!' in preparing the jobless to re-enter the working world with more self-confidence. In Figure 9.4, we see how Breuer, looking rather tired, exhorts participants in his training programme to be passionate about their work and inspire passion in others.

There is no verbal acknowledgement of tension by Breuer in that early scene, and yet at the close of the film Breuer seems to be struggling under the inherent contradictions of the ideology he propounds to his trainees. For the film's 10-minute-long epilogue, Pethke films him submitting to a session of outdoor coaching delivered by the neurocoaching therapist, Cla Mosca, as seen in Figure 9.5. Pethke organised this session for Breuer at his own request. In the film's long coda, the trainer-in-chief

Figure 9.4 'Ich muss! Ich will! Ich kann!', from Katharina Pethke, *In dir muss brennen / Burning Within* (2009). © Bolbrinker/Doberenz/2Pilots

Figure 9.5 Back to nature but not free of surveillance: an outdoor neurocoaching session in Katharina Pethke, *In dir muss brennen / Burning Within* (2009). © Bolbrinker/Doberenz/2Pilots

is shown dipping his hands into a stream, gathering sticks and stomping around disconsolately, as well as furiously describing to his therapist the long hours his work involves that have led to his burnout, and expressing anger about his feelings of disillusionment and difficulty enjoying his life.

We see in this frame another key feature of the therapies shown in the film, that of surveillance. There is always somebody watching the burnt-out workers in the film, ready to deliver feedback to them. In that sense, the burnt-out worker is not truly alone, but always subject to feedback, comment, and suggestions for further improvement. Moreover, the goal of the self-improvement being propounded in all the burnout therapies shown in the film is a positive contagion, not of the burnout symptoms themselves, but of the working subject's passion for her work.

The film's original German title, *In dir muss brennen,* is an abbreviation of a saying by St Augustine of Hippo, 'What you wish to ignite in others must first burn within yourself!' This maxim from a founding father of Western Christianity is redirected in the film to the behavioural culture of Western capitalism. Breuer cites it early in the film, introducing the first principle of self-entrepreneurial working, to burn with a passion that is hot enough to ignite a passion for your work in others, too: '"'In dir muss brennen, was du bei anderen entzünden willst!' Wenn Sie begeistern wollen, wenn Sie in Erinnerung bleiben wollen, dann müssen Sie das wirklich mit Begeisterung tun"'/ '"'What you wish to ignite in others must first burn within yourself!' If you want to fascinate, if you want to stay in people's memory, then you really have to do this with enthusiasm."' The kind of heat being advocated here is a positive one in the discourse of training and coaching: white-collar workers are incited to be passionate and so inspire one another.

Yet, as well as the passion needed to inspire others, here we also hear about the dangers that lie behind not burning passionately enough: being forgotten, which in a strained post-crisis employment market will mean not having a livelihood. The need to be inspiringly passionate about one's work is pitched here as an existential one. However, the film itself sets up a warning that there is a danger to this heated emotion, namely that of overheating and burning out – just as Breuer has himself. Thus the goal of burnout therapies, Pethke's film suggests, is to regulate the emotional temperature of the working subject and so keep her on the narrow path between the excess of heat implied by a burnout diagnosis and the lack of passion that would mean dropping out of the world of work altogether.

Cool Conduct: A Theory of Temperate Behaviour for Times of Crisis

Austrian-born researcher Hans Selye wrote in 1974 in his book *Stress without Distress* of a 'code of conduct' designed to counteract work-related burnout. He sets out guidelines such as 'don't waste your time ... Do not underestimate the delight of real simplicity in your life style', 'Try to forget everything that is irrevocably ugly or painful' and 'Admit that there is no perfection, but in each category of achievement something is tops; be satisfied to strive for that'.[14] Through this charming-yet-terrifying code of conduct for the constant optimisation of the self, Selye promised, readers should be able to find their way back to certain biological norms, which have been compromised by the fast-moving changes associated with modernity, and as a result recuperate their energy for achieving the best possible ('tops') results.

Selye's code was formulated in an era when burnout was beginning to be recognised as a risk for the individual and linked to technological and economic changes in the society around him or her. In this way, although its easy tone overlying an unquestionable, authoritative scientist's perspective clearly locate *Stress without Distress* in its intellectual era, Selye's code for the burnt-out individual has an uneasy resonance with Lethen's influential work on codes of conduct in an earlier era of modernity in *Verhaltenslehren der Kälte* (1994). Under the subtitle 'Lebensversuche zwischen den Kriegen' / 'Life-Experiments Between Two Wars', Lethen draws attention to a group of philosophical handbooks and self-help books, some satirical and others less so, published during the crisis period between the First and Second World Wars.

These varied texts by writers from surprisingly far-flung parts of the political spectrum – from controversial conservative philosopher Ernst Jünger via liberal anthropologist Helmuth Plessner, to Marxist dramatist Bertolt Brecht – offered advice on how their reader should behave in the confusing new world of modernity. A central tenet in all of these codes was a cooling down, with the less ironic texts encouraging their readers to adopt a distant attitude, tactful separation from others and emotional coolness necessary in an era that threatened to be overwhelming. Although the historical era was very different, the central recommendation of temperateness uniting these early twentieth-century handbooks has a quality of isolation and cool-headedness that arguably returns in the burnout therapies Pethke shows, and in the behaviours of balance and judiciousness ('don't waste your time …', 'try to forget …', 'be satisfied …') recommended in Selye's 1970s code for preventing the overheated symptoms of burnout.

As a handbook for preventing burnout, Selye's *Stress Without Distress* represents a much more user-friendly, self-help-oriented version of the philosophical and essayistic codes of conduct Lethen examines. And yet, a fruitful comparison can be made between Selye's work of self-help medical literature and a philosophical text central to

Lethen's study in *Cool Conduct*, anthropologist Helmuth Plessner's writing on the distant man. One of the most unironic texts Lethen refers to is Plessner's model of balanced, self-controlled behaviour propounded in his book *Grenzen der Gemeinschaft / The Limits of Community* (1924). Like Selye, Plessner based his theory on what he believed were certain laws of nature, in this case the belief that there is an element of artifice in all human life, artifice that can be mobilised to protect the self in an age of crisis.

In the Weimar Republic, Plessner, who was Jewish, looked with scepticism and concern at the rise of two communities or *Gemeinschaften*: fascism and communism. Plessner saw these radical communities as dangerous because of their purism of values, to which the individual must submit at risk of losing his or her own, separate selfhood. Against these common ideologies, in which he feared that the individual would be sacrificed to the whole, Plessner argues for his preferred social model of the 'Kühle der Gesellschaft' / 'coolness of society',[15] a shared, temperate space that he pitches against the excessive closeness of community. In a 'Gesellschaft' / 'society', according to Plessner, the individual is protected by techniques of distance that guarantee his (and in Plessner we only read of 'his') independence and allow him to move without risk of attack.

At the time when Plessner was writing, these risks were not only linked to individual attacks from hostile others, but also to the trauma of modernity more generally, with its indifferent war machines, rising fascist movements and – in the queer and feminist cultures not mentioned in Plessner's work but an important part of European modernity nonetheless – radical changes in the presumed fixity of identity. Of course, these concerns were as much collective as they were individual, and writing two decades earlier than Plessner, Georg Simmel analysed on a more structural level the distant, cool persona that was developing as a response to modernity in the form of a blasé attitude, part of a resistance modern individuals were developing against being 'nivelliert und verbraucht' / 'levelled out and exploited' by early twentieth-century capitalism.[16] Simmel presents the blasé attitude as an understandable consequence of 'jener rasch wechselnden und in ihren Gegensätzen eng zusammengedrängten Nervenreize' / 'those rapidly changing, contradictory and yet densely packed nerve stimuli' present in modernity.[17] Modern people need to act with reserve, Simmel writes, to protect themselves from the risks of overwhelm and, he writes, although a blasé attitude may seem like a worrying psychological dissociation, in fact it belongs to modernity as 'eine ihrer elementaren Sozialisierungsformen' / 'one of its most fundamental ways of relating'.[18] Much more so than Plessner, Simmel relates the need for a distant attitude to the risks of exploitation and the erasure of individual experience by new forms of capitalism emerging in conjunction with technological and sociological modernity.

Even though Plessner was less concerned with structural or economic factors, and much more worried about individual risks such as exposure and embarrassment, the quality of distance endemic to Simmel's notion of the blasé attitude also permeates Plessner's advice for the modern subject. To protect himself from the stresses of modernity and submergence into the group, Plessner's ideal man learned what he called a worldly 'Kühle' / 'coolness', adopting that coolness as part of what Plessner viewed as a growing trend of respectful distance and balance:

> die erzwungene Ferne von Mensch zu Mensch zur Distanz geadelt, die beleidigende Indifferenz, Kälte, Roheit des Aneinandervorbeilebens durch die Formen der Höflichkeit, Ehrerbietung und Aufmerksamkeit unwirksam gemacht und einer zu großen Nähe durch Reserviertheit entgegengewirkt.
>
> the forced distance between people is transformed into a noble distance, the insulting indifference, coldness and rawness of living in spite of each other are neutralised by forms of politesse, reverence and attentiveness, and excessive closeness is countered by means of reserve.[19]

Recovery from crisis comes, for Plessner, through the practising of balancing techniques that lead from excessive intimacy to a protective distance. Through these techniques, Plessner's distant man becomes safe from the raw, unboundaried space of the community, instead maintaining an act that takes some effort but ultimately comes as a relief both from the crisis of modernity and from the threat of loss of self in the communities Plessner feared.

Relevant to the high levels of individualisation exhibited in contemporary burnout cultures, the highest proof of balanced selfhood for Plessner's distant man is in the extremely refined balancing act of holding distance towards oneself: 'In Nichts kann der Mensch seine Freiheit reiner beweisen als in der Distant zu sich selbst' / 'There is no purer proof of man's freedom than in the distance he can take towards his own self'.[20] Thus the kind of subjectivity recommended in Plessner's anti-vulnerability model is extremely sovereign: in control of itself to the degree that it can even hold a critical distance toward its own personality, and thus maintain a sense of cool balance despite the crisis experiences of the post-First World War era.

Vulnerability to crisis is not completely overcome in Plessner's model for distant subjectivity, however. As a basis for the behaviours of balance and critical self-reflection, Plessner advocated for what he termed the 'agonistic' attitude, a protective stance, 'das bei einem Maximum an Ehrlichkeit und Aufrichtigkeit ein Maximum an Sicherheit vor dem ironischen Zerstörerblick … verbürgt' / 'which, along with the utmost honesty and uprightness, offers the utmost in security from the destructive irony of the other's gaze'.[21] The world around Plessner's 'agonistic man' is fraught with dangers of exposure and attendant embarrassment, and at the same time terrible indifference. Plessner's agonistic man appears in the midst of a threatening modernity as a vulnerable type who must take on protective practices, learning to hide his instincts and emotions behind what Plessner calls a 'Maske' / 'masque', and thus master his encounters with others with skilful, protective artifice. Yet the risk of basing a code of conduct on such a protective premise is that anxiety will remain the envisaged society's ruling affect.

Indeed, in his influential reading of Plessner, Lethen rightly points out the vexation of the distant man when he writes: 'Die Aufgabe der Bewachung der Grenzziehung, mit der das Ich sich seiner Identität vergewissert, versetzt es in einen chronischen Alarmzustand' / 'Constantly supervising its borders, the ego exists in a state of permanent alarm.'[22] Regardless of the freedom promised by the ideal, cool subjectivity, the *Alarmzustand* of anxiety indeed operates at the core of Plessner's ideal man's watchful self-work. He experiences an excessive need for protection from the fearsome events of exposure and embarrassment. With this in mind, the cool conduct Plessner was advocating looks less protective, and more vexed with anxiety about the code's potential failure and the resulting vulnerability of the subject in an increasingly hostile world. The subject in Plessner's model, indeed, appears like a vexed sovereign attempting to control his realm while suffering increasing paranoia. Moreover, a contemporary version of that cool but anxious persona appears to surface again in the burnout treatments shown in Pethke's film. In these therapies, techniques of coolness and self-distantiation are used as ambivalent cures for the burnout syndrome, as the film reveals them to be dubious techniques of personal sovereignty enacted through excessively self-controlling behaviour.

Cool Conduct as Ambivalent Cure in *In dir muss brennen*

There is an uncanny return of early twentieth-century German philosophies of distant, sovereign selfhood in the business-oriented burnout therapies that attempt to cool down their patients in the era after the global financial crisis. The burnout patients in Pethke's film are exhorted to develop techniques of the self through which they behave independently, with a cool head and so feel more secure, act more decisively, and distance themselves critically from their own behaviour in order to become more resilient in the face of burnout. Cool or resilient does not mean 'not passionate' in these new settings. It does, however, mean an encoding of resilience, the ability to keep working, and indeed to lead others in a continued functionality despite conditions of precarity.

Those new codes of conduct for the burnt-out worker in contemporary capitalism form the focus of Pethke's film, in which burnout therapies and training promote recovery from a hot, rebellious state of burnout, back to a cool resilience in which the subject is functional for more, profit-making work. In the film, the maxim 'Yes you can!' appears in both written text and motivational speeches by figures of coaching and training. As part of the capability promoted by this phrase, burnt-out workers are exhorted to feel responsible for their own experience.

Thus, the sequence immediately before the opening title image, showing empty corridors flooded with pools of water and strewn with abandoned furniture, is overlaid with a coaching voice-over blaming the listener for the losses and disappointments they are suffering: 'die Verantwortung liegt in dir für all das was dir geschieht oder auch nicht geschieht' / 'the responsibility for everything that happens to you, or doesn't happen to you, lies with you.' In this meditation, the burnout patient is guided to reflect on their own responsibility for their failures to be a successful, entrepreneurial subject. The voice on the track speaks slowly, leaving pauses and issuing instructions to breathe deeply and relax. The pauses are enhanced by a sound design that has the track echo along the flooded corridors, abandoned by the human users for whom the upended furniture was designed. The echoing presentation of the meditation track, signalling as it does an absence of any other people nearby, emphasises the logic of the therapies in which the burnt-out subject is meant to cultivate more feelings of security within themselves through their sole, sovereign agency.

Indeed, the exhortation to the subject, to take responsibility for his or her own freedom, is emphasised by conscious sound and image design throughout the film, for instance when the patient with a gambling addiction is encouraged to repeat the mantra 'Ich bin frei' / 'I am free'. The patient's repetition of the mantra begins with a clean sound, contained by the therapeutic consulting room, but the soundtrack lingers on the end of the word 'frei' / 'free' as the image changes, and the harsh 'ei' sound continues echoing into silence following a sharp cut to another eerie office building, as the camera begins to track slowly down an empty corridor. The camera then enters a room and settles on a static shot of a black leather armchair facing outwards at a floor-to-ceiling window showing the world outside the office.

The editing decisions here create a feeling of lingering horror as viewers are guided to hear and stay with the echo from a phrase that for some viewers will carry uncomfortable echoes of the promise of freedom carried on the doors of the Auschwitz concentration camp, that the prisoners' work there would make them free ('Arbeit macht frei'). Viewers are haunted by the echo and by the following sequence of empty corridors separated from the world seen far below through the window. Moreover, these cinematic techniques render ironic the positive message structuring the man's therapy – that is, the message that the man's feelings of freedom can improve if he only takes responsibility and acknowledges his freedom.

Corporeal gestures of a self-governing subjectivity are also shown as necessary for performing into being the feelings of security these patients are being taught. For example, if the freelance author is going to break the arrow successfully in her burnout therapy, her therapist says she must have a 'körperliche Haltung, die sehr stabil ist' / 'very stable posture' which will help generate 'eine klare innere Ausrichtung, worum geht's' / 'a clear inner sense of what it is all about'. She must keep looking straight forward, breathing and flapping her arms/wings to gather strength in her body. These symbolic gestures are important because they help the patient overcome the contradiction wherein, at the same time as knowing she is vulnerable to injury by the arrow, she is supposed to know deep down 'dass ich mein Ziel erreiche, und dass es gut wird' / 'that I will reach my goal, and that everything will be ok'. This patient later goes on to work with the symbolism of colour, which appears at several points in the film to indicate how burnout patients are being trained in generating a feeling of coolness in themselves. Thus, the freelance author chooses a red slip of paper to represent her current period of difficulty and green one to represent the state of mind she wants to attain, prioritising her work as an author above everything else in her life and feeling 'ruhiger' / 'calmer'.

Immediately after this sequence with the coloured paper, seen in Figure 9.6, Pethke's edit takes viewers back to the gambling addiction therapy. This patient chooses a green Playmobil figure to represent himself in the future, at a time when he will have overcome his difficulties, and a red-clothed figure to represent his struggling past self. In this therapeutic play, green is the calmer colour chosen to represent a cooled-down subject recovered from burnout, whereas the stress of the present is represented by red.

Plessner writes that the distant man can decide on and must enforce the boundaries around his private self, necessary for his self-protection. The drawing of personal boundaries also figures as an important gesture for securing the emotional states that burnout therapies promote in Pethke's film. In the long epilogue, Breuer tells his therapist as he undergoes the outdoor coaching that he is angry because he has not set clear boundaries for himself in his work, to which he is passionately attached, and has therefore burnt out. Breuer seems to believe that *he* is to blame for his symptoms of burnout, not the system in which he is embroiled. On that logic, if Breuer improves his own behaviour, he should be able to overcome his problems. This logic in turn recalls the ultimate gesture of freedom Plessner described, that of self-distantiation. Breuer's hope echoes the hope Plessner offered for the distant man, that he could protect

Figure 9.6 Cool colours such as green symbolise desirable (because disciplined) states of mind, Katharina Pethke, *In dir muss brennen / Burning Within* (2009). © Bolbrinker/Doberenz/2Pilots

himself from his own era of crisis through the ability to show distance in relation to himself. More than simply receiving feedback from others, the subjects of Pethke's documentary are called upon again and again to perform self-evaluation as a means of recovery. Self-evaluation is the complicated arabesque through which business-oriented therapy aims to train its patients to be effective and independent in their work and life more generally, and so less susceptible to burnout.

Thus, the film shows specialised burnout therapies attempting to control the hotness of the burnout syndrome by cooling down their patients and training them in techniques of self-distantiation and surveillance. The often-playful exercises and encouraging tone of the coaching and therapy sessions in the film reveal new behavioural rituals that promise resilience, even independence for the subject, all the while securing her ongoing participation in profitable work. However, along with these encodings of the ability to recover and work productively again, an anarchic and apparently unconscious counter-conduct emerges in the film as the expression of resistance to overwork and to the demand for constant self-surveillance. Pethke's subjects are often depicted resisting the encoding of overwork and self-as-project, through their corporeal and psychological expressions of burnout, and indeed the persistence of their disillusionment, compulsions and inability to work. The gambling addict has undergone a lot of therapy by the end of the film, and yet he is still gambling, as he admits to his therapist who looks on with an empathic but unsurprised gaze. The freelance author does not succeed in breaking the arrow, the technique that is meant to free her from fears.

Even Breuer, who coaches motivational trainers in his own work, does not respond to the therapy he requested the film-maker to organise. After Breuer has confessed his rage at his unhappiness and lack of boundaries, therapist Mosca asks how great his anger is in on a scale of 1 to 10, where 10 is 'heftig: Vulkan' / 'massive: volcano'. Mosca then has Breuer recite the following penance: 'Ich nehm' all meine Energie, die in dieser Wut gebunden ist.... an den richtigen Ort in mir selber zurück.' / 'I take all the energy that is bound up in this rage ... back to the correct place in myself.' Even after Breuer has recited this disciplinary prayer for the overheated subject, he states that his anger is still at 10 on the scale. We then see him sawing away at a thick tree root with gusto. After a further, strained conversation about Breuer's unhappiness, Mosca leaves Breuer to ponder his predicament. Breuer walks forward and contemplates the cool water passing over a rocky riverbed but there is no sign that his anger has abated, rather he remains standing in the same, tense posture until the screen turns black and the film ends.

Any sign of resistance to the inhuman medical apparatus may seem salutary, and it certainly lightens the dystopian tone of the film. Christoph Büttner interprets the freelance author's failure to break the arrow in terms of a queer art of failure,[23] one that can interrupt the norm of entrepreneurial self-making, and even queer that norm through gestural or rhetorical practices of rebellion. However, any hope viewers feel when they see the burnout patients exhibiting symptoms that persist and so seem to resist their therapies is complicated by how painful the symptoms of such an unconscious, psychosomatic resistance are. Moreover, such resistance is not effective in the long term because the least painful and most economically survivable option for the burnout patient will be to recover from her symptoms and, once recovered, return to work profitably within the same system of self-improvement that has exhausted her.

Techniques of Cold Cinema

A less painful resistance to the inhuman cooling techniques of burnout therapy exists in the resistant aesthetic of Pethke's film itself. Its title suggests heat, passion and warm imagery may be at the heart of its aesthetic, and indeed the film contains repeated discursive descriptions of heated emotions such as passion and anger. However, its core imagery is cold: empty corridors, a grey colour palette, blank whiteboards and a preponderance of pools and drips of water are the troubling backdrop to this film in which anything hot always rapidly cools down. As such, the film forecloses any sustained experience of the warm emotions described in the diegesis, such as anger or passion. This forbidding of warmth is technically achieved in the film's cold-cinema aesthetic, as Pethke employs sharp cuts rather than fades or pans, recurrent symbols for the extinguishing of fire such as water and even fire extinguishers, repeated sequences of empty corporate interiors and lingering close-ups of the faces of members of this corporate culture looking bored, discouraged and exhausted.

The term 'cold cinema' has been applied to the works of Italian film artist Gianfranco Baruchello,[24] and of Mexican feature-film director Carlos Reygadas. The moving-image oeuvres of these two otherwise very different film-makers are united by experimental approaches free from the strong identificatory affect of the Hollywood genre film. They instead engage viewers in contemplative gazing through, in Reygadas's case, long takes that break with the techniques of what Deborah Shaw calls 'hot cinema, American film, which relies on audience identification, and fabricated emotional moments'.[25] Baruchello's cold cinematography, meanwhile, is achieved by putting together found footage in service of a critical anthropology of economic conditions, in montages focused on critically analysing consumer society. Pethke's critical documentary also achieves its critique of complicit burnout therapies via techniques that cut through warmth and emotional engagement in the viewer, in her film that aims to produce a critical analysis of economic conditions surrounding the burnout syndrome. Like other cold-cinema directors, she makes ample use of defamiliarisation techniques, such as demonstrative gestures that make visible the rehearsal of seemingly naturalistic performances, and of the apparatus of film-making itself, two components of a classic Brechtian *Gestus des Zeigens*, the gestural logic of showing.

Thus, in the very first scene, the speaker Gerhard Huhn rehearses and receives feedback on his performance of a speech about the experience of happiness analysed in business terminology as 'flow', in a sequence that turns out to be a film being filmed within a film. Later, during the filming of Ingo Vogels's coaching show, Pethke's camera takes on a tertiary position, from which it observes the show's performers involved in an interview and the television camera capturing that performance. Yet Pethke adds to these common techniques of defamiliarisation a conscious aesthetic of coldness to counterbalance the heat invoked in her title and indeed the burnout diagnosis. This is the logic behind her presentation of sequences of filming connected only by the inhumanity of the techniques shown in them, rather than by any kind of voice-over or intertitles. Such an absence of narrative explanation is standard in direct-cinema film-making, but Pethke emphasises the disconnection of passages in the film further by means of a relentless episodicity, wherein the viewer is bombarded with countless scenes of therapy, training and coaching, to the point of being overwhelmed.

The film's relentlessness, issuing from the absence of discursive narration and episodic overload, is however tempered by a tendency towards abrupt cuts with no visual links made, such as match cuts or visual rhymes. Pethke's cuts are always brutal, but they offer a kind of narratological relief to the viewer. Thus she cuts with icy abruptness from Breuer telling his trainees they have no need to worry, to a long static close-up of the process of a tooth guard being made for the film-maker to wear to stop her grinding her teeth at night, presumably due to her own stress.[26] Later in the film, the atmosphere between therapist and patient in the arrow training is that of a warm engagement and narrative tension rising in intensity as the writer flaps her arms and prepares to push her weight against the arrow angled towards her throat. But the film does not permit the warm affect of the scene to be sustained, instead it suddenly cuts to a blank white pinboard. From here, viewers begin to process a new, unrelated sequence, which will again build in narrative tension only to be cut off again.

The abruptness of Pethke's editing prevents the feeling of relentlessness in the episodic narrative from becoming some kind of 'hot' affect such as excitement or annoyance in the experience of the viewer. If such abruptness makes the film easier to watch, this is not because the processes it shows are humane or meaningful, but because it enables the film to do something other than mimic the affective arc structuring the therapies and feedback sessions it shows, instead always forcing the viewer to experience the hard work *and the welcome relief* of constant, conscious disconnection.

The film also displays a preponderance of cold imagery, with a recurrent object of its camera being pools of water. In one office corridor sequence, a chair lies on its side in a pool of water that has dripped down from a broken pipe. Pools of pale purplish water later gather on the machine used to make the tooth guard. As recurrent passages set between scenes of therapy and coaching, the office buildings themselves provide an important space in which Pethke's camera slowly pans in order to cool down the diegesis. This technique thus breaks up the montage of therapy sessions, and so interrupts the (potentially inspiring) speeches about passion and success as viewers are taken again and again back to unpeopled and sparsely furnished corporate interiors. The camera glides through corridors looking laterally out of windows on to grey buildings opposite. A black wall dividing the rooms from the corridor slides in front of windows like a black screen sliding over a view to outside, giving an impression of entrapment in a climate of punishing self-improvement, which could induce panic in the viewer. Yet the mood in these unpeopled sequences is laconic, invoking a treadmill or a conveyor belt but keeping the tone of the image cool and uninvolved by forcing a constant interruption of the images that the viewer's eyes would otherwise be able to rest upon. A droning soundtrack of industrial white noise completes the chilling effect of the office buildings, which convey extreme pessimism about current approaches to burnout, in marked contrast to the encouraging slogans spoken by coaches and therapists in the remainder of the montage. These droning interludes then give way, again and again, to shocking sequences depicting the inhumanity taking place between burnout patients and their therapists.

In contrast to the unpeopled office sets, the sequences depicting therapy sessions make plentiful use of close-up head shots, in which human

Figure 9.7 Subject to feedback, Katharina Pethke, *In dir muss brennen / Burning Within* (2009). © Bolbrinker/Doberenz/2Pilots

figures appear downcast amid the passionate therapeutic rhetoric. Despite the presence of the human face here, that ultimate site of identification, these are perhaps the coldest images in the film. With extraordinarily effective simplicity, Pethke leaves her camera rolling on faces that look despairing, such as the woman in Figure 9.7, whose gaze becomes darker and more disengaged as she receives lengthy feedback on her performance.

When they are not shown alone, the burnout sufferers appear caught in agonistic duos between therapists and patients, often facing the same way as each other, or looking at an angle not quite toward the other. Pethke makes their unconscious conflict known through careful camera angles and her rejection of suturing, shot-reverse-shot editing, so refusing to unite the figures in any dialogical images. Through these cold-cinema techniques, Pethke succeeds in depicting the terrible isolation of the burnt-out worker and, furthermore, the inhumanity of the therapies that advocate self-surveillance as an ambivalent, system-sustaining cure.

Conclusion

In cultural theories from the German context and in Pethke's film, we see that burnout needs to be understood as a syndrome both produced and treated, but not meaningfully cured, by techniques of the self as an individualised project. In this sense, there is a basic inhumanity defining the therapies that treat burnout through further self-optimisation, the very cause of the syndrome. I intend that the term I use to encapsulate that shocking complicity underpinning burnout therapies, 'inhuman medical apparatus', should give rise to a productive tension as we read these therapies as both neglecting the human element of burnout – they seek to return the patient to work as soon as possible – and at the same time isolating the patient as human individual, because they neglect the syndrome's social causality. Instead, the therapies place responsibility on the individual to work better in future.

The metaphor of temperature has been crucial to my reading of these therapies, as they set to work cooling down the burnt-out patient, helping her only partially, while binding her very securely to cultures of passionate overwork and self-improvement. Patients might feel themselves to a certain degree recovered when they assert their decision-making power at work and try to develop through coaching or therapy an individuality that can coolly persist in the precarious economies of today. But the suggestion of the film with its repetitive, doom-filled passages of empty, depressing office corridors unpeopled by anybody at all, healthy or otherwise, is that those feelings of recovery are likely to loop around to more ill health in the future.

The idea of the self as project is revealed in the film as being at the heart of the therapies employed in current treatments of the burnout epidemic. Moreover, that notion of the self as self-regulating project has an intellectual history reaching further back into early twentieth-century German philosophy. I have suggested above that Plessner's 'distant man', with his code of conduct including distance in relation to others and, most crucially, sovereign distance in relation to himself, can be read as a precursor to the burnout patients who learn in Pethke's film to stand apart from negative experiences and instead cultivate feelings of freedom, security, decisiveness, and the ability to set their own boundaries. These qualities even share certain metaphorical gestures, of decisiveness and the drawing of lines, with the political theory of Carl Schmitt, the father of sovereignty theory.[27] Schmitt's concept of totalitarian sovereignty could find horrifying echoes in the contemporary ideal of the sovereign individual as a self-governing project, if one were willing to read the self-as-project so pessimistically. Certainly, German-language philosophies of sovereign *selfhood* from the early twentieth century make an uncanny return in Pethke's film, in which burnout patients retrieve their productivity through tactics of resilience, decisiveness and self-distantiation. The talking cures, role plays, mantras and meditations they undertake contribute to the construction of a defended, sovereign subjectivity that becomes more and more productive in relation to working conditions that are actually exhausting. Therapy or coaching of this kind, which promotes a selfhood capable of working on productively despite the persistence of a catastrophic health problem, is ethically untenable, but it is also, admittedly very technically refined.

The film critiques the current, intricate and frightening treatment of burnout with great clarity, and in doing so it provokes thinking about the connection between neo-liberalism's codes of conduct and the cool conduct Lethen discovered dominating German philosophies in the crisis era of the early twentieth century. The links between the two codes include attitudes of coolness, isolation of the subject, and a vexation of the codes themselves by the potential for their failure, or by the risk of resistance of those who are meant to be enacting them.

There are certain crucial instances of failure in therapy drawn out in the film. The man with a gambling addiction does not attain liberation within the narrative time frame, but rather confesses his compulsive symptoms have continued to trouble him. Breuer, although he undergoes the outdoor coaching, carries on feeling the anger tainting his work training the motivational coaches of the future. Yet the film's interest in the anarchic persistence of burnout symptoms is complicated by the problem that any counter-conduct resistant to self-improvement and therapy will necessarily be painful, and will necessarily take the form of an expression of ill health in the subject. While ill health may resist the expectations of neo-liberalism that the subject work well, it is still an ambivalent resistance for those whose bodies or minds are resisting control in that way.

There is a risk, moreover, in Pethke's depiction of these ongoing resistant symptoms, of the exposure of her documentary's subjects. Pethke reports that the participants in her film were not system-critical and did not feel embarrassed at seeing their treatment on screen once the documentary was complete.[28] Yet, even if the documentary's participants did not feel embarrassed, there remains an ethical problem with exposing people, even if they are willingly enmired in such exploitative processes, to the analysis that film makes possible.

More effectively critical, because less painful for the individuals in question, is the film's mobilisation of a cold-cinema aesthetic. The cool colours and sparse decoration of the training and therapy environments Pethke depicts are remarkable, considering that these are spaces for the inspiration of renewed passion, which should be a hot phenomenon. Oddly, in these spaces of training for the passionate working subject, not human warmth but a studied passion is cultivated, one meant to be contagious to others, certainly, a fire that is catching, but crucially a fire that can also be kept under control within the boundaries of the sovereign, entrepreneurial self. We watch these spaces through Pethke's cold cinema, its brutality and creepiness forcing us to witness the shocking processes of therapy whereby a subject hot with rage – an understandable rage at the demands of contemporary capitalism – is brought back to a cooler state. That state is more manageable for the current economic system and useful for its recovery, but ultimately destructive because it produces interminable compliancy, not health, in the subject under treatment.

Notes

1. Lethen, *Verhaltenslehren der Kälte*, 7.
2. Schaffner, *Exhaustion*, 204.
3. See Crary, *24/7*.
4. See Schaffner, *Exhaustion,* 217–8, and Proctor and Proctor, *The Essential Guide to Burnout*.
5. Schaffner, *Exhaustion*, 9.
6. The term 'Volksleiden' has been used regularly in *Der Spiegel* to define the status of burnout as a shared illness of the German people, as in a short article by prominent career coach Martin Wehrle in 2013, author of the popular book *Bin ich hier der Depp?* (Original article titled 'Bleibst du auf der Strecke, liegt es nur an dir!', *Der Spiegel*, 10 October 2013).
7. Bröckling, *Das unternehmerische Selbst*, 49.
8. See Han, *Müdigkeitsgesellschaft*.
9. See also Dernbach, 'The Uncanny of Surveillance', 50–1.
10. Bröckling, *Das unternehmerische Selbst,* 282.
11. Han, *Müdigkeitsgesellschaft*, 6.
12. Foucault, *Security, Territory, Population*, 1–53.
13. Therapeutic terminology here is taken from the company websites of Flowmanagement http://www.clamosca.ch/wir_clamosca_ausbildungen.php and Gartner-Steffen Coaching und Konfliktberatung http://www.gartner-steffen.de/de/team_engelhardt-rafi_de.html. Both accessed 17 September 2018.
14. Selye, *Stress without Distress*, 105–6.
15. Plessner, *Grenzen*, 30.
16. Simmel, 'Die Großstädte', 116.
17. Simmel, 'Die Großstädte', 121.
18. Simmel, 'Die Großstädte', 121.
19. Plessner, *Grenzen*, 80.
20. Plessner, *Grenzen*, 94.
21. Plessner, *Grenzen*, 79.
22. Lethen, *Verhaltenslehren der Kälte*, 84; Lethem, *Cool Conduct*, 59.
23. Büttner, '"In Dir Muss Brennen!"', 211.
24. See, for instance, the title of the exhibition *Gianfranco Baruchello: Cold Cinema. Film, video e opere 1960–1999*, held at La Triennale di Milano in 2014 and 2015.
25. Shaw, '(Trans)national Images and Cinematic Spaces', 127.
26. Compare the inclusion of this clue to the film-maker's own burnout to the comment by Carmen Losmann, director of *Work Hard – Play Hard*, concerning the extremes of creative work that go into making a film, even one critical of its own complicity in cultures of exploitation. See Ring, 'System Error', 488n.
27. Schmitt, *Politische Theologie*. Schmitt's sovereign is known by the ability to define 'das öffentliche oder staatliche Interesse, die öffentliche Sicherheit und Ordnung, … besteht' / 'what constitutes the public or state interests, public security and order' (Schmitt, *Politische Theologie*, 13). In times of crisis, the sovereign can declare a state of exception, which calls a halt to the political order in order to protect the security of the realm. Such a decision involves the demarcation of the limits of a national territory, and the identification of the subjects who may reside within those limits. In contemporary German, the adjective *souverän* has a more everyday usage than it did in the political theory of the early twentieth century. It denotes a state of mind in which the individual can feel that they are independently self-defined, and therefore

that they hold a power of decision-making over their time and activities, that they are their own boss, and that they can feel capable and set their own boundaries in their lives.

28. Email conversation with the film-maker, March 2017.

Bibliography

Bröckling, Ulrich. *Das unternehmerische Selbst: Soziologie einer Subjektivierungsform*. 5th ed. Frankfurt am Main: Suhrkamp, 2013.

Büttner, Christoph. '"In dir muss brennen!": Self/Change-Management in Arbeitswelt und Dokumentarfilm'. In *Opus und labor: Arbeit in autobiographischen und biographischen Erzählungen* (Schriften des Fritz-Hüser-Instituts für Literatur und Kultur der Arbeitswelt 31), edited by Iuditha Balint, Katharina Lammers, Kerstin Wilhelms and Thomas Wortmann, 191–212. Essen: Klartext, 2018.

Chen, Mel Y. and Dana Luciano, eds. *Queer Inhumanisms* (Special issue of *GLQ: A Journal of Lesbian and Gay Studies* 21, no. 2/3). Durham, NC: Duke University Press, 2015.

Crary, Jonathan. *24/7: Late Capitalism and the Ends of Sleep*. London: Verso, 2013.

Dernbach, Rafael. 'The Uncanny of Surveillance: Architectures of Hyperactive Incapacity in Nikolaus Geyrhalter's *Abendland* and Falk Richter's *Unter Eis*'. In *Architecture and Control*, edited by Annie Ring, Henriette Steiner and Kristin Veel, 46–64. Leiden: Brill, 2018.

Farocki, Harun. (dir., 2012) *Ein neues Produkt* (documentary, Germany).

Flowmanagement, webpage. Accessed 17 September 2018. http://www.clamosca.ch.

Foucault, Michel. *Security, Territory, Population: Lectures at the Collège de France, 1977–78*, edited by Michel Senellart; translated by Graham Burchell. Basingstoke: Palgrave Macmillan, 2007.

Gartner-Steffen Coaching und Konfliktberatung, webpage. Accessed 17 September 2018. http://www.gartner-steffen.de.

Gianfranco Baruchello: Cold Cinema. Film, video e opere 1960–1999. Exhibition held at La Triennale di Milano, 9 December 2014–22 February 2015.

Han, Byung-Chul. *Müdigkeitsgesellschaft*. Berlin: Matthes und Seitz, 2010.

Lethen, Helmut. *Verhaltenslehren der Kälte: Lebensversuche zwischen den Kriegen*. Frankfurt am Main: Suhrkamp, 1994.

Lethen, Helmut. *Cool Conduct: The Culture of Distance in Weimar Germany*, translated by Don Reneau. Berkeley: University of California Press, 2002.

Losmann, Carmen. (dir., 2012) *Work Hard – Play Hard* (documentary, Germany).

Pethke, Katharina (dir., 2009) *In dir muss brennen* (documentary, Germany).

Plessner, Helmuth. *Grenzen der Gemeinschaft: Eine Kritik des sozialen Radikalismus*. Frankfurt am Main: Suhrkamp, 2002.

Proctor, Andrew and Elizabeth Proctor. *The Essential Guide to Burnout: Overcoming Excess Stress*. Oxford: Lion, 2013.

Ring, Annie. 'System Error: Complicity with Surveillance in Contemporary Workplace Documentaries', *Seminar: A Journal of Germanic Studies* 52, no. 4 (2016): 465–89.

Schaffner, Anna Katharina. *Exhaustion: A History*. New York: Columbia University Press, 2016.

Schmitt, Carl. *Politische Theologie: Vier Kapitel zur Lehre von der Souveränität*. 6th ed. Berlin: Duncker und Humblot, 1993.

Selye, Hans. *Stress without Distress*. Philadelphia: Lippincott, 1974.

Shaw, Deborah. '(Trans)national Images and Cinematic Spaces: The Cases of Alfonso Cuarón's *Y tu mamá también* (2001) and Carlos Reygadas' *Japón* (2002)', *Iberoamericana* 11, no. 44 (2011): 117–31.

Simmel, Georg. 'Die Großstädte und das Geistesleben'. In *Aufsätze und Abhandlungen 1901–1908, Band I*, edited by Rüdiger Kramme, Angela Rammstedt and Otthein Rammstedt, 116–31. Frankfurt am Main: Suhrkamp, 1995.

Wehrle, Martin. '"Bleibst du auf der Strecke, liegt es nur an dir!"', *Der Spiegel*, 10 October 2013. Accessed 18 June 2018. http://www.spiegel.de/karriere/martin-wehrle-ueber-die-arbeitswelt-der-globalisierung-a-926817.html.

Wehrle, Martin. *Bin ich hier der Depp? Wie Sie dem Arbeitswahn nicht länger zur Verfügung stehen*. Munich: Goldmann, 2016.

Index

Page numbers in *italics* are figures.

CPSIA information can be obtained
at www.ICGtesting.com
Printed in the USA
BVHW021309200920
589199BV00022B/511

9 781787 357723